# Building Powerful Community Organizations

## A Personal Guide to Creating Groups that Can Solve Problems and Change the World

# MICHAEL JACOBY BROWN

LONG HAUL PRESS
ARLINGTON, MASSACHUSETTS

Long Haul Press
10 Brattle Terrace
Arlington, MA 02474
U.S.A.
781-648-1508

**Publisher's Cataloging-in-Publication Data**

Brown, Michael Jacoby.
Building powerful community organizations:
a personal guide to creating groups that can solve problems
and change the world / Michael Jacoby Brown.
p. cm.
Includes bibliographical references and index.
ISBN 13:  978-0-9771518-0-6
ISBN 10:  0-9771518-0-8
1. Community organization—Handbooks, manuals, etc.
2. Social action—Handbooks, manuals, etc.
3. Citizens' associations—Handbooks, manuals, etc.
4. Community development—Handbooks, manuals, etc.
5. Community power—Handbooks, manuals, etc.
6. Organizational effectiveness—Handbooks, manuals, etc.
I. Title

HM766 .B76 2006
361.8—dc22                                        2005907712


Cover and book design by Arrow Graphics, Inc., info@arrow1.com
Printed in the United States of America

### Acknowledgments

Grateful acknowledgment is made for permission to reprint quotations from the following:

Bai, Matt, *The Multilevel Marketing of the President*, reprinted by permission, The *New York Times*.
Bellah, Robert, et. al., *Habits of the Heart*, reprinted by permission, University of California Press.
Frankl, Victor, *Man's Search for Meaning*, reprinted by permission, Simon and Schuster.
Gladwell, Malcolm, *The Tipping Point*, reprinted by permission, Little, Brown, and Co.
Hoerr, John, *We Can't Eat Prestige*, reprinted by permission, Temple University Press.
Kotter, John P., *The Heart of Change*, reprinted by permission, Harvard Business School Press.
Lewis, John, *Walking With the Wind*, reprinted by permission, Simon and Schuster.
Osterman, Paul, *Gathering Power*, reprinted by permission, Beacon Press.
Weisbord, Marvin, *Productive Workplaces*, reprinted by permission, John Wiley & Sons.

## For Minnie Jacoby

*An inconsequential contestant in her day*
*Her day was made of plans and pleasures*
*But if I had my way*
*I'd be a sculptor and plant*
*Her statue in the park*

# CONTENTS

# EXERCISES

# CASE STUDIES

# QUICK TIPS

# STORIES

## SECTION III: MAKING CHANGE

### Chapter Ten / Organizing: Pathway to Change

### Chapter Eleven / Taking Action, Solving Problems, Getting Results

### Chapter Twelve / Building Community

## SECTION IV: OUR FUTURE

### Chapter Thirteen / Where Do We Go From Here?

### Afterword / Your Turn

### Appendix / How to Get Tax-Exempt Status

### FEEDBACK FORMS

# ACKNOWLEDGMENTS

Many people helped to improve this book by reading drafts along the way and offering helpful comments. They include: Alec Dubro, Arinne Edelman, Lew Finfer, Bob Van Meter, Jim Wessler, Bob Lamm, Heather Booth, Mike Gecan, Hilary Goodridge, Barbara Beckwith, Lois Gibbs, Carl Offner, Daniel Hunter, Tia Zlotnikoff, David Trietsch, Ellen David Friedman, Wally Roberts, Ruth Fein, Bruno Tardieu, Sue Marsh, Peter Shapiro, Chris Argyris, Marc Miller, Desmond Bailey, Tom Levinson, Shel Trapp, Ashley Adams, Ken Galdston, Janet Strassman Perlmutter, Corita Brown, Lee Staples, and Robert Houseman. Thanks to Sam Mendales for his photographic expertise.

I am indebted to my parents, Bob and Frieda Brown, who taught me right from wrong, were my role models for how to change the world, and brought me to my first picket lines as a child.

I am indebted to the many organizers and leaders who taught me and showed me the ropes along the way. There are so many. Israel Jacoby, Arnold Langberg, Dick Powell, Gregory H.C. Knox, Bob Jones, Sandy Turner, Anthony Thigpenn, Len Calabrese, Mark Toney, Heather Booth, Si Kahn, Kim Fellner, Mary Ochs, Ellen David Friedman, Wally Roberts, Horace Small, Ron Bell, Steve Edelstein, Warren Heyman, Elizabeth Meier, Jim Mehigan, Veronica Harding, Peg Swartz, Tom and Sally May, Alan Biederman, Tom Wylie, Jake Sherman, Merrill Kaitz, Kelly Gloger, Debbie Katz, Susan Carter, Jimmy Landau, Chris Argyris, Don Schon, Ronnie Heifetz, Sue Williamson, Jon Pratt, Mike Frieze, Michael Sales, Mark Horowitz, Simon Klarfeld, Janice Fine, Jeanne DuBois, Johnny O'Connor, Paulette Ford, Dan Violi, Gladys Vega, Dick Moskowitz, Larry Kushner, Lorel Zar-Kessler, Marie Manna, Lew Finfer, Sam Mendales,

Charlie Garguilo, Rich Gatto, Cathy Clement Saleh, and Cheri Andes. Many have contributed their stories to this book, making it stronger.

Words cannot adequately thank my wife, Jessica Goldhirsch, who teaches me and challenges me to be real about building community where it needs to start—in our own family. Special thanks to my daughters, Corita, who has become my coach and consultant, and Nessa, who continues to amaze and inspire me.

I am most indebted to Nechama Katz, the editor and co-creator of this book. Nechama took a haphazard, loosey-goosey bunch of writings and beat it into some semblance of order. She constantly challenged me to figure out what I meant and then to say it—clearly. She not only put this book in order, but also re-wrote parts so they made sense and added some parts herself so it would come out more clearly. She kept my spirits up when I wanted to just get it done (enough already!). She challenged me to go deeper, define terms, and fill in the gaps so readers could follow the message. If this book communicates, thank Nechama Katz. Where it falls down, it is my failing.

This book is dedicated to my grandmother, Minnie Jacoby, who showed me how to ride the subway, made me laugh with all her stories, and amazed me with her resilience. Her memory—her spirit, her sense of humor no matter what—inspires me daily.

# ABOUT THE EXERCISES

A note about the exercises in this book: One of my favorite books is *What Color is Your Parachute? A Handbook for Choosing and Changing Careers* by Richard Nelson Bolles and Mark Emery Bolles. That book, like this one, is a personal guide that includes exercises to help you reflect on your path. I used the book twice. One time I just read it. I failed to write down my responses to the exercises as the author suggested. This was a big mistake. The next time, I wrote down my answers to the questions in the exercises. Writing forced me to slow down, think harder, and get better answers. When I only read the exercise, I thought I knew the answers—but I did not. Don't make the mistake I made. Don't just *read* the exercises. *Do* them with pencil and paper.

*—M.J.B.*

# INTRODUCTION

## For Anyone Who Wants to Make a Difference

This book is for people who want to change the world and know that they cannot do it alone.

It is a practical, step-by-step guide to starting or strengthening a community organization. It is for those who care about the world around them and know that improving it requires the active involvement of the people closest to the problem. It is for people who know that they need the power, perspective, and sense of community that come from being part of a group.

You might be thinking of starting a new organization. Maybe you've never joined a group, but you see a problem brewing in the world around you that just won't go away. It could be in your neighborhood, at the local school, in your congregation, at your workplace.

You might be a volunteer or a staff person in a group that wants to be more effective. Perhaps your group has been around for years. No new members are joining and the old members are getting tired. You need new blood but are not sure where or how to get it.

You might be a government official, serious about public service. You could be involved in community development, public health or safety, transportation . . . or any area that makes a difference in people's lives.

Whoever you are, you are someone who sees that the world around you is not as you think it should be and you want to do something about it. Whatever the idea, whatever the problem, you have decided to start a new group or fix an old one.

## Finding the Problem is Not Usually the Problem

Sometimes you choose a problem.

Maybe it is the slow decline in the schools in your town. The classes seem to be getting bigger each year. The good teachers are leaving.

Maybe the drugs in your community are getting out of hand and you just can't close your eyes to it anymore.

Sometimes an existing organization identifies a new threat. It seems like all the cards are stacked against you, but still, you have to act.

Maybe you are fed up with your elected officials. It's been the same people for years and none seem able to listen or to get anything done. You think it's time that someone new, maybe you, ran for public office. You know you can't do that by yourself.

## Sometimes a Problem Chooses You

And sometimes, the problem comes right to your door.

### Story: Keeping Their Homes

*The residents of Camfield Gardens, a housing development in the Lower Roxbury-South End of Boston owned by the U.S. Department of Housing and Urban Development (HUD), woke up one morning in 1992 to find a note tacked to the front doors of their buildings: HUD was selling their development.*

*The residents were worried: Would they lose their homes? They were mad: Their development was close to the rapidly gentrifying South End section of Boston. This looked like another chapter in Boston's long history of displacing minority residents.*

*They had no organization. One resident, a mother of five who worked as a school secretary, knew someone at the local HUD office who had once helped her get reimbursed when a broken hot water heater ruined her rug. She called the HUD employee. He told her about the HOPE Program, a new resident-ownership initiative. She got together with a neighbor and they organized the Camfield Tenants Association.*

*Over the next ten years, through enormous effort and perseverance and hundreds of meetings with tenants and government officials, they built an organization with the power to negotiate for what they wanted with federal, state, and city officials. They stuck together. They managed to demolish Camfield Gardens and then rebuild it from the ground up. It took years of organizing, but the residents now own the development.*

## So What's Next?

How do you start? What do you do first? What do you do after that? And what do you do after that? How do you keep it going? How do you avoid doing it all yourself and burning out?

If any of these thoughts have ever crossed your mind—if you are serious about actually building a group and seeing it succeed—then this book is for you.

This book shows how to bring people together for effective action. You will find here stories and lessons that describe models and methods that organizers and individuals from across the U.S. have used successfully to build powerful organizations.

Building effective organizations requires knowledge of practical steps and procedures. This book will lay out that knowledge for you. Building effective organizations also requires that we know ourselves and know why we are doing what we are doing. The work is public and political; it also is intensely personal. You need to understand the economic, social, and political forces that are constantly changing the world around you, and you also need to understand your own experience and your own community.

If you looked at the Table of Contents or peeked ahead, you saw outlines of the steps for building an organization. But don't be fooled. No two groups—or situations—are alike. Organizations are not widgets. There is nothing mechanical about building a community organization. Effective organizations are built with passion, persistence, and personal understanding of why you are doing this work.

This book will guide you through the process of forging your own way. It can be your own personal paperback mentor—a reference point and a sounding board. The step-by-step instructions are designed to ground and guide you. The stories illustrate the complexity of the work; they are intended to inspire, motivate, and instruct you.

Be warned: This is a workbook, not an instruction manual. Expect to *work* your way through this book. The exercises will help you to figure out how to respond creatively and effectively to the challenges before you. They offer you a place to think through your personal path to building or improving a community organization.

# THE INSIDE STORY

## ▶ Towards a Definition of a Community Organization

Community is one of those things that is hard to define, but you know it when you are in it. It is a feeling that you are not alone, that you are part of something greater than yourself—but yet, even when you are in it, you are still yourself. It does not swallow you up; rather, it builds you up. It is not all for you and you are not all for it. In a community there are people around you whom you like, although you probably do not like all of them equally. The people of the community are there for you when you need them and you will be there for them when they need you.

Community organizations come in all shapes, sizes, and varieties. Every community organization holds all the complexities and all the hopes, dreams, and visions of the people who join it. Community organizations may look different but they all have at least two things in common:

1. Community organizations strive to develop a sense of community among their members.
2. Community organizations organize people to do what they cannot do by themselves.

In the world of real problems and real power (or lack of power), a community organization is a method for getting results and solving problems that affect you. Community groups organize people to change the conditions that affect their lives. Alone, most people are powerless to wrest change from big institutions. Community organizations re-align the balance of power, creating "power for the people" by bringing people together in large blocs around shared concerns. They help you to accomplish what you cannot do by yourself, to make your life and the lives of those around you better.

## A Passion for Justice

The theories and skills that I lay out in this book can be (and have been) used effectively by groups across the political spectrum. My emphasis is on harnessing these techniques and strategies to increase equal opportunity and justice in our society. A passion for democracy, for caring for one another, and for making our society more equitable—these are the core values that drive my work and the path to creating powerful community organizations that I lay out in the chapters ahead.

The exact alchemy that transforms a group of individuals into a community organization is elusive, but it is clear that the process requires intuition, a good sense of timing, a gift for strategy and for relationships, and healthy doses of boldness, leadership, persistence, perseverance, passion, commitment, and courage. One person usually does not have all those qualities; that is why it takes a group. Add to the list: *mistakes.* You will make mistakes along the way, and that is to be expected. You can learn from them.

In addition, there are concrete steps and strategies you can employ that will help you to create a powerful community organization. Read the next few chapters to immerse your-self in the process of creating strong and effective commu-nity organizations. These chapters will guide you to become not only a community _organizer_, but a community _builder_.

# CHAPTER 1

# What Is Community Organizing, Anyway?

*(If you already know what community organizing is, you could skip this chapter. But if you read it anyway, you still might learn something.)*

## ▶ Community Organizing: Power, Self-Interest, and Relationships

Community organizing, building the power of a group to change the world, is both an art and a science. It requires understanding your self-interest in the deepest sense, building relationships with others, and a desire to change the world.

### Story: Me and My Dad

*When I was a little boy, I went with my father, a commercial artist, to collect the pay for some work he had done. We went to the home of the man who had hired him.*

*I remember the big house. My dad and I stood there on the porch, dwarfed by the tall white pillars, waiting. Finally, the door opened. The owner came out and stood in the doorway. He told my dad he couldn't pay him. I looked at the grand house and thought about how rich this man must be. He had such a big house! I remember riding back home, in silence, feeling powerless, unable to make that rich man pay. By himself, there didn't seem to be any-*

*thing my dad could do. I wanted to do something about that. My dad had already done the work for that man. I wanted the power to make the man pay my father.*

Like developing successful intimate relationships or raising children (and you can find hundreds of books on these subjects!), bringing groups of people into effective community organizations takes skill and attention to many details and dynamics at the same time. It takes knowledge of yourself and your community. It takes understanding how groups work, why people join them, how to structure them, how to lead them, how to pay for them, how to set dues, goals, and rules, how to develop values, and how to move people to action. Successful groups need solid internal management, good group process, secure funding, effective communication, and a sense of trust and community among their members.

Like intimate personal or family relationships, groups can be disturbed, and even destroyed, by internal dynamics. With more people than the usual family, the opportunities for imbalance, disunity, and self-destruction are magnified.

There are plenty of horror stories about poorly run nonprofit community organizations—just as there are such stories about government and business. There are sloppy finances, poor communication, and backbiting among staff and members. There are authoritarian directors, inadequate resources, overworked staff, and under-appreciated volunteers. Some organizations pressure everyone to work 80 hours a week. Meetings run on too long. There are corrupt and incompetent leaders, financial mismanagement, and worse—all the ills to which humans and groups of humans are susceptible.

Yet, we need organizations—for justice, for democracy, for a sense of community, and for effective problem-solving. Humans have always lived in groups. Groups have accomplished almost all important contributions to human welfare. Leaders play key roles, but so do groups. We learn that Washington crossed the Delaware to defeat the British, but we know he didn't do it by himself. Lincoln may have freed the slaves, but he had a lot of help.

Groups have won improvements in civil rights, women's rights, working conditions, the environment, and health care, to name just a few examples. Organizations have improved the treatment of groups of people, including veterans, children, and people with disabilities. People have come together in alliances that have improved schools, neighborhoods, playgrounds, arts education, business ethics, and many other areas of public (and private) life.

Part of the genius of America has always been our ability to form grassroots groups to solve problems. As Alexis de Tocqueville noted in his travels here in the early 1800s, Americans, unlike Europeans, build community organizations to deal with our problems. De Tocqueville must have been on to something. His book, *Democracy in America*, is still in print almost 200 years after it was written.

## Horatio Alger at the Barn Raising

Americans have long held on to two dissonant beliefs about individualism and community. On the one hand, we glorify the "self-made man." On the other hand, we idealize the sense of community in small towns and neighborhoods. We long for a place where neighbors help each other out: the quilting bee, the barn raising, the old neighborhood bar or diner. These two themes have run throughout American history and continue to influence our thinking, culture, and politics today.

Although groups have won improvements in many areas, the number and magnitude of the challenges don't seem to diminish. Toxic chemicals and global warming threaten our environment. Many of our schools are not succeeding. Health care is more costly and unavailable for many. Basic services for our more vulnerable citizens are disappearing. Our roads are clogged with cars. Jobs are evaporating, or if they're still available, they're too stressful. Higher education is too costly for most people. Sexism, racism, violence, anti-Semitism, homophobia, and many other ills continue to plague us.

Government and business cannot solve all these problems. Businesses must compete on a daily basis for customers. They must cut costs and improve efficiency to make a profit and stay in business. Corporations are not going to provide national or neighborhood security, environmental protection, public education, roads, water supply, safe food and drugs, or other things we need. Nor can government solve all our problems. Government officials often are too distant from the details to be effective. Sometimes those in authority do not care about or understand the problems people face.

## ▶ The Theory Behind Community Organizing

### Group Dynamics and Group Theory: Why We Need the Involvement of People at the Grassroots

Solving peoples' problems and improving their lives requires the active participation of those most affected by the problems.

Kurt Lewin, the first theoretician of group dynamics, figured this out in the 1930s. Lewin discovered that *those closest to any change must be involved in the change in order for the change to be effective.* Lewin's discovery about human behavior points to one reason why we need to build community organizations to drive change: If we did not need the active involvement of those closest to the problem, then good policies or the dissemination of good ideas alone would achieve the improvements we seek. They do not. The right information alone is not sufficient when it comes to making social improvements or changes in people's behavior.

Lewin developed this theory over 60 years ago. Working with anthropologist Margaret Mead in Iowa during World War II, Lewin designed an experiment to discover how best to reduce the consumption of rationed meats. Lewin first located the "gatekeepers" (Lewin's term) who controlled the selection of meats. It was the housewives, who were responsible for acquiring food and preparing meals for their families. Their reluctance to buy and prepare non-rationed meats had to be reduced. Lewin designed an experiment with two groups of homemakers. He had a nutritionist lecture one group, explaining the benefits of eating the non-rationed meats. In another group, he facilitated a group discussion among the women about how they could prepare the non-rationed meats so that they would be good to eat. The members of the facilitated discussion group changed their consumption behaviors much more than those in the group that received the nutrition lecture. The conclusion was clear. *Changing people's behavior requires the active involvement of those whose behavior you are trying to change.*

This theory has been corroborated over many years by experience in the workplace. Marvin Weisbord, an organizational consultant, has observed:

*From 100 years of experience repeating the same patterns over and over again, we can predict social consequences of any improvement project: the less involvement of those affected, the less likely will be the implementable solution.*

—Marvin Weisbord, *Productive Workplaces*

If we need the active involvement of those most affected for an improvement project to succeed, then what does it take to involve those affected?

It takes a powerful group.

And what does it take to get a powerful group? Developing a group powerful enough to represent people's opinions and interests takes skill. Even in Lewin and Mead's simple experiment, the housewives needed a skilled group facilitator to get them to come to agreement. It took skill to recruit the participants and to explain the goals of the group. It took skill to facilitate the meeting so that the women felt that their voices were heard as they devised strategies for changing their behavior.

Lewin first recognized that groups behave differently than individuals. Groups are more than the sum of their individual members. He was the first person to use the term *group dynamics*—in an article he wrote in 1939. He saw that groups had lives of their own, so he explored how they worked. This theory is central to the methods, theories, and art of building community organizations. Those who build organizations must understand and work with groups as special entities, with distinct developmental processes and their own rules for growth, maintenance, and health.

Alfred Marrow, Kurt Lewin's biographer, summed up Lewin's early theory of group dynamics:

*The gist of his theory might be stated as follows: A man who joins a group is significantly changed thereby. His relations with his fellow members alter both him and them. A highly attractive group can bring great pressure to bear upon its members; a weak group will not have as much molding power. . . .[Lewin's] formulation was simple: "The whole is different from the sum of its parts; it has definite properties of its own."*

—Alfred J. Marrow, *The Practical Theorist*

One of my first lessons in group dynamics came when I was in high school. I learned something about how "a highly attractive group can bring great pressure to bear upon its members":

## Story: How Quickly a Group Can Achieve (and Lose) Power

*Riding the bus, I saw a boy who was beaten black and blue after pledging with a high school fraternity. I wanted to be in a fraternity, but I didn't want to get beaten up. So I got together with a few friends and we formed our own fraternity. We called it "Sigma Tau." We got some "Sigma Tau" sweatshirts printed at a sports store and soon had underclassmen pledging for us. I learned about the power of a group when the captain of the junior varsity football team, only a year younger than me, did pushups in the dirt on my command.*

*We soon gave up giving orders. We wanted friends more than we wanted power over younger kids. But it struck me how powerful a group can be and how quickly it can exercise authority.*

*I also learned how fragile a group can be. Soon after we graduated, the fraternity faded—even before our sweatshirts wore out.*

## Active Participation Requires Organization

Given the power differentials in our society, most people cannot be heard without the amplified voice a group provides. Those without money cannot buy ads to get their message out. Most people without fame, wealth, or power do not appear on TV talk shows. They have a tougher time getting elected to public office. For many, it's a stretch to go to an evening meeting. Given the pressing demands of everyday life, they rarely have the time even to write a letter to the editor, let alone to negotiate with government decision-makers about the conditions that affect their lives. Sometimes, with long hours at work and long commutes, they can't even find the time to vote on Election Day, even though voting is one of the most streamlined methods our democracy offers for taking action about conditions that affect our lives.

The voices of those who are the real experts, those closest to and most affected by the various social problems, are rarely heard—because no organization represents them. People who want to help themselves often have nowhere to go to make a difference. It often takes the creation of a new community organization—or, sometimes, attention to strengthening an old one—to combine individual voices into an organized group that can force those with power or authority (such as government officials or owners of large businesses) to do the right thing.

## It Takes an Ongoing Organization to Solve Problems

Community groups can provide the intelligence we need to solve the problems we face. No one individual, no matter how smart or experienced, can solve difficult social problems by herself or himself. No one person can see all perspectives and imagine all possible consequences of any action. It takes an ongoing organization—one that focuses the energies and intelligence of many people who are close to the problem, one with the power and resources to exist for the long haul—to solve problems.

### Story: The Person Closest to the Problem Sees the Solution

*At the time when the Camfield Gardens housing development was being demolished and rebuilt, it was owned by the federal government's Department of Housing and Urban Development. HUD and the tenants were in part-*

nership with the State Housing Finance Agency in the redevelopment. All but three families had relocated to allow for reconstruction of the entire development. The three remaining families had leases with the City Housing Authority. The federal and state agencies could not figure out how to break the leases with the three families so that they could relocate them. The Camfield Tenants Association called a meeting with all the parties to resolve this. Representatives from the entire congressional delegation came, as did representatives from HUD, the State Housing Finance Agency, the City, the Mayor's office, and the Housing Authority, as well as the tenants and their advisors, including me.

None of the government officials could figure it out. At one point, the HUD official (I am not making this up) said we would need an Act of Congress to move the three families.

The Tenants Association President was annoyed. She had already been moved off-site and every day the three families stayed in the development was another day her family had to wait to move back. She knew a lot about the leases because she had lived there for a long time. So she came up with a simple solution: Have another agency take over the leases. No Act of Congress needed.

Someone close to the problem came up with a solution while others, not so close to the problem, could not.

I call this the $10,000 meeting, based on an estimate of the cost of all the staff at the meeting, including me. The irony, of course, is that the one person not being paid to attend the meeting had the answer.

The problem was solved because the Tenants Association had the power to bring all the government officials together into one room, so none of them could pass the buck. Getting that power took years of work. Without that organization, who knows how long it might have taken to relocate the three families.

## ▶ The Group Provides a Sense of Community

Aside from the social, economic, health, educational, and other improvements that groups have brought us, these same groups have given many of us a sense of community and meaning in our lives. Congregations, veterans' groups, Granges, PTAs, civic associations, and many other community organizations have provided many of us with a sense of belonging, friendship, and community in an often isolating and difficult world.

Many of us are looking for a greater sense of meaning and community in our lives. Government, corporations, and other authorities do not provide this sense of belonging, caring, and purpose. It is in community groups that we find people to pray with us and people to stand with us as we mark the passages of our lives—birthdays, graduations, confirmations, weddings, housewarmings, and deaths in our families. Community groups can provide a place where, like the *Cheers* bar, "Everybody knows your name"—where we find people to drive us to the doctor or deliver meals when we are sick, watch our children while we go to the market or out to dinner, and do all the other little things in life that we can't do by ourselves and that make the world a friendlier, more human, more enriching and nurturing place.

Whether the organization is a congregation, a neighborhood civic association, a community group working to improve schools, or a statewide or national association to change national policy, many of the group dynamics and skills needed to build the organization are the same. Groups both small and large require attention to group development.

## Community as Organizational Life Insurance

Community is important not only because it feels good. It also is the organization's best safeguard for the future. An overarching sense of community that supersedes any individual decision or relationship protects the organization when arguments over tactics or issues arise.

Disagreements can lead to lost membership and a smaller, weaker, and less effective organization. And there are certain to be arguments. You can count on it. Most of us are taught to value our own opinions. People who feel passionately about an issue or problem tend to have strong feelings and opinions about how to go about addressing the problem. This is one reason that organizers spend so much time building relationships at the beginning and fostering bonds and community throughout the development of the organization. I have seen more organizations fall apart from internal disagreement than from damage inflicted by those who oppose their goals.

When people are connected only by a shared interest or concern about the problems they face, the organization can easily fall apart once the particular issue is resolved. It won't be around to help its members address the next issue that comes up. A group that is also a community offers members something larger and more enduring than any particular issue. Community can function as the glue that holds the members together in an ongoing organization.

## ▶ Who Does It?

Specific people organize community groups. We may call them organizers, leaders, coordinators, directors, or facilitators, but it's their work that counts. Community groups succeed on the skills and understanding of those who build and lead them.

## Organizers: NOT as Seen on TV!

The role of the organizer is not widely understood or recognized. There are no TV shows about organizers, as there are about lawyers, doctors, and cops. But lawyers, doctors, and cops can't solve all our problems. They may be able to solve crimes, save us when we are bleeding, and put away the bad guys, but they can't develop community or solve all our civic or workplace problems.

The work of organizing groups is often overlooked. Some people assume it to be so easy that they think it happens by itself. Others see it as so complex that it defies description. It does not defy description—but it does not happen by itself.

## Every Organizer Has Two Jobs

Organizers build organizations *and* develop other leaders.

Organizers get people to come together and do the work of the group. They think about the group as an entity in and of itself—and they think of all the things the group needs in order to function well: money, staff, structure, rules, office space, bylaws, strategy, action, plans, training, and more. For some of this work, they may need to draw upon technical skills (their own or somebody else's), such as accounting, computer networking, writing grant proposals or press releases, or designing flyers. But organizing does not focus primarily on such skills.

Organizers also develop the skills and the leadership of other people in order to strengthen the organization. Leaders are people who influence others. Leaders are people to whom other people turn. Other people listen to them and follow their lead. Leaders also do the *work* of the organization. They take responsibility for the organization. Leaders can bring people to meetings and get others to complete tasks.

Building an organization takes a group of leaders with varied skills and perspectives who can work as a team. The organizer's job sounds simple. The goals are clear:

**1. To develop leaders**
and
**2. To build the organization.**

Sticking to the goals is not so simple. Doing the job well is even tougher. It takes a wide range of skills. No one person has them all.

## ▶ The Organizing Alchemy: A Look At How It All Works

### One Definition of Organizing

**Organizing = Getting something done that you can't do by yourself by working together with others.**

### What an Organizer Does

**An organizer builds community with a purpose.
An organizer provides a means (an ongoing group) by which people solve their own problems.**

An organizer is always looking for ways to build community, ways for people to get to know each other better, ways for people to come together in face-to-face contact. It may be a celebration, a block party out in the street, or a meeting in someone's living room or in a church basement. The organizer knows that when people get together, they have a chance to solve their own problems. I can almost guarantee that when you put a group of people who share a common concern into a room together, even if it is just four or five people, they can come up with an action plan to improve their situation.

# Starting an Organization that Makes a Difference

## Start With What People Care About

There are many ways to start an organization. Some start with the specific problems that concern people in the community. The problems can affect a particular group, neighborhood, or workplace. It could be the speeding traffic on a street, a school closing in a neighborhood, the threat of a toxic waste dump coming in up the street, the pollution from a local factory, the threatened sale of a local business. Those most affected by the issue are most likely to be involved. Those looking for the immediate relief are most likely to take the lead and do the work. This is often a quick way to attract interest from potential members. The response will show you which people have the passion that will help drive the organization.

## Start By Getting To Know Each Other

Don't forget: Some really good people also want to get to know their neighbors better. Sometimes the job of the organizer is just to get people who have something in common into the same room with each other. People who have been in a community organization often say that they liked getting to know their neighbors or other members, in addition to addressing the actual issue or problem.

It is possible to start building an organization by providing the means for people to get to know each other. This is likely to draw people who are most interested in getting to know and relate to others, people interested in "affiliation," in being part of something bigger than themselves or their immediate family.

## Story: Traffic and the Block Party

### A Common Neighborhood Problem

*Years ago, I was an organizer for a statewide community organization that was trying to build small "neighborhood groups" into a statewide coalition. When I went knocking on doors on one street, many mothers and fathers with small children spoke of their concerns about the traffic that sped by on their street. This street was commonly used as a bypass off the main highway to get from one side of town to the other.*

### The First Action: A Block Party

*Many new people had moved onto the street and most people did not know their neighbors. I thought that the first thing we needed to do was introduce the neighbors to each other. So I suggested that we ask the Board of Aldermen (the city government) to close off the street for one afternoon for a neighborhood block party. This would include a potluck dinner, a chance to play games in the street, some time to get to know one another, and time to talk informally about how to deal with the traffic problems. Several neighbors were enthusiastic about the idea.*

*Our initial focus was simple: To provide some means for people to get to know each other better. I recognized that once they got to know each other, they would be likely to start talking about common problems. If they got to know each other in a social group setting, they would have more to talk about than the speeding traffic alone. They would get to know each other in more ways. These bonds would be important "glue" for keeping the organization together.*

### Public Action

*I went with one couple from the street to a regularly scheduled City Council meeting. We waited for our turn. When it came, we respectfully asked to have the street closed off for one afternoon. I expected that we would get a quick approval. Instead, the Council said, "No way." The police chief said he'd never close off such a busy street. Never! This was a busy street! Closing it off would create problems all over town.*

*We were back to square one. What to do now? We went back home to think about our next step. Closing off the street, which we had thought would be a minor matter, had turned into a big deal.*

*So we went again to City Hall, this time with more people. Other neighbors talked to the police chief in person. Weeks dragged in to months. It was early summer and we thought the snow would fall before this would be resolved.*

## It Took a Big Turnout to Get the Council's Attention and Agreement

*A couple of neighbors met with the City Councilor who represented the street. There was lots of talking back and forth. The neighbors explained to the Councilor why they wanted to have the street closed off. The Councilor explained how things worked at the full City Council meetings. Finally, the neighbors went back to City Hall, to the next Council meeting, with a much larger contingent in tow. This time the neighbors brought many families, all with their children. The Council chambers had never been so full. The Councilors had never seen anything like it. They were used to one or two people coming to the meetings, at most. Generally they were all alone, talking to themselves. It took families getting out and showing up at the Council meeting to show the Councilors how many people cared deeply about this matter. The Council agreed to close off the street.*

## Block Party!

*When the police car showed up and the officer pulled the blue sawhorses out of the cruiser's trunk and set them up to close off the street, I couldn't quite believe it. What I had thought would be an easy thing to do had taken months of meetings. But when the people started spilling out of their homes with covered dishes, tables, drinks, and games, it all seemed more than worth it. There was music. A volleyball net was strung up across the street.*

*The street that the city had said was too busy to close off was closed off. Nothing terrible happened. No major traffic jams were reported, but a lot of neighbors got to know each other.*

## A Vision of a More Perfect World

How do you overcome that "You can't fight City Hall" feeling? Overcoming that feeling is a big part of the organizer's job.

The block party did this—and more. With the block party, we accomplished three valuable objectives:

People got to know their neighbors.

People began to develop a sense of their own power. Before we organized, they felt powerless to stop or slow the traffic.

We also stopped the traffic, at least temporarily. The block party showed us all what life on the street might be like without all the traffic.

Holding the block party was one simple event that provided some opportunities for neighbors to begin to build community on their street. We probably could have gotten new traffic signs with fewer neighbors participating and certainly without the block party. But the block party provided the opportunity for people to meet each other— in many cases, for the first time; to participate in the process of making improvements in their community; to share their food, their games, and their ideas.

## It Took a Group

"Organizing"—people doing with others what they could not have done by themselves—closed off the street. When just one or two people showed up at the City Council meeting to ask to close off the street, nothing much happened. But because we kept at it, week after week, because we came out in numbers, the Council listened and agreed to close off the street. Later, several more speeding signs were put up and the police started paying more attention to speeders on the street.

## It Took an Organizer

I will never forget my feelings as I watched the police officer pull those sawhorses out of the trunk of the cruiser, after we had heard so many times how it could not be done. And although I knew it took many people working together to make that happen, I also knew that it took an organizer to prod them along, to suggest that they could do it, to encourage them to keep at it. And when I saw all the people coming out of their homes with their potluck dishes, many of whom I did not even know, I got a glimpse of what organizing could achieve. Bringing people together to talk and meet each other, to see each others' children, to hear each others' stories, to find out who their neighbors are, was a powerful start.

To achieve this, somebody had to be the organizer. In this case, I was on staff of a statewide community organization, but it also could have been a volunteer. Many good organizers are volunteers. It can be anyone who thinks that what "they" say "can't be done" really can be done. It can be anyone who is willing to keep at it to make sure it happens. It doesn't have to be a big deal. This street closing and potluck dinner and block party certainly were not world-changing events. But they were a start: the start of building a powerful ongoing organization.

The method is not mysterious or difficult to learn. Persistence is probably the main ingredient, along with skill at overcoming peoples' defeated feeling that "nothing can be done."

## Where Are You Going With the Group?

If the organization had rested with the block party, it would not be much of an organization. An organizer's job is to think ahead. How can we build this block party into an ongoing organization? What structure, specific membership, rules, money, leadership, decision-making processes, mission, and plans will it take to build an ongoing organization? Who are these people? What can these people do next week and next year? What other problems do they face that they could solve by working together? How can they stay in touch to make sure that they keep thinking of how they could solve those problems as well?

Who will do the work of keeping in touch with all the newly found acquaintances? (Remember Rule Number One of block parties, meetings, etc.: **The organizer gets the sign-in list.** Always have a sign-in list, with enough space for names, addresses, organizational affiliation, work and home phone numbers, and e-mail addresses.)

How will subsequent communication happen? Will there be a phone tree? Will there be other regular meetings? An annual block party? What other issues should they think of addressing as an organization?

## The Organizer (or Organizers) Think About the Group as a Whole

The organizer is thinking about all these things while the party is going on. She or he is watching to see who knows whom. To whom do people listen? Who seems to be respected by the other neighbors? Who works hard? Who stays behind to pick up the trash? Who makes sure that things get done? Those people are likely to be the leaders. They might not be the people most likely to be thought of as leaders.

The people who take responsibility are the ones the organizer(s) watch and will re-visit later to ask to do more, gradually to take some responsibility for the organization. That might mean asking them to bring the cookies next time, or host the meeting in their home, or chair the meeting, or come along to City Hall to look up some records, or call up a few of the others to ask them to come to the next meeting. The organizer will think of specific tasks for people to do.

# CHAPTER 2

# Step by Step—Building a Community Organization

*Step by step, the longest march*
*Can be won, can be won*
*Many stones will form an arch*
*Singly none, singly none*
*And by union what we will*
*Can be accomplished still*
*Drops of water turn a mill*
*Singly none, singly none.*

—An old union song

## ▶ The Basic Steps of Building a Community Organization

Building an organization is like building a house. Home-builders know that if you start with a square and level foundation you will have fewer problems when you put the roof on. If the walls are plumb and square you have an easier time sheetrocking. You *can* fix mistakes later on, but it saves you time, money, and aggravation to do it right the first time. Building a successful organization is a little like that.

This chapter lays out one way to think about building a community organization. It is not the only way, but it works. The chapter includes steps, tips, ideas, stories, case studies, and exercises. Together with what you know about yourself and your community, they should help you to build an effective organization. This chapter covers many of the elements you need to build a community organization. The steps are presented in a certain order. You may find that a different order makes more sense for your organization. The steps are a general guide, not a rigid hierarchy. Use them flexibly, with knowledge of your own community and issues. Most important, as someone once said, "It takes a lot longer if you don't get started."

## The Basic Steps: An Overview

These basic steps can be used to start a new organization or to strengthen one that already exists.

**1. The idea arrives:** You think something needs fixing. Sometimes a problem or new situation in your world confronts you and you have to do something about it. You have an idea of what needs doing and know you cannot do it alone.

**2. Develop a vision:** This means painting a picture of where you eventually want to go, how you would like the world to be.

**3. Find your motivation—Tell your story:** Understand why *you* are doing this. What about your history, family background, or experience moves you to take this on?

**4. Listen to others:** Sometimes known as "the long march through the kitchens or coffee shops." To whom do you need to listen in order to develop your idea? This is about taking the time to hear what others think of your idea or issue. Do others share the problem or your ideas? Can you get their help?

**5. Put your idea in writing:** What is the problem? What is your solution? A written vision can be broadcast widely and clearly. It also adds legitimacy to your idea.

**6. Develop a sponsoring committee:** Get the written support and commitment of others.

**7. Bring together a core group:** You will need ten to fifteen people who share your vision and will do the work to get the organization off the ground.

**8. Draft a mission, identify goals and objectives:** Now you need to clarify what you want to accomplish.

**9. Develop a structure:** It is critical that you build your organization with the right foundation and framework, so that it stands over time.

**10. Build power:** What will it take to accomplish what you want? Power comes from organized money, organized people who have strong relationships with one another, good information about the details of what your group wants to accomplish, and, most important, the ability to move people to action and to ask for what you want. Power requires that you **mobilize resources:** Recruit people, develop leaders, gather information, and raise the money you need to accomplish what you want.

**11. Understand strategy:** Strategy is your overall path. It helps to understand the general plan you are following and the assumptions behind it.

**12. Move to action, evaluate, and reflect:** Good things come to those who act, negotiate, evaluate, reflect, learn from their actions, and keep acting.

## ▶ Getting Started

### Step One: The Idea Arrives

*When I die and I come to stand before my Maker, God will not ask me, "Why were you not Moses?" Rather, I shall be asked, "Why were you not Zusya?"*

—Rabbi Zusya of Anipol (18th century)

*The first step is the idea.* It may come to you on its own. You may have an idea of how to make the world better. Maybe something has changed in the world around you that you cannot ignore. Sometimes an idea takes hold of you. Now what?

Maybe your child is not doing well in school. The books are old and the paint on the classroom walls is peeling.

Maybe you are just tired of not knowing your neighbors. People lock themselves in their houses. You are tired of driving by and wondering, "Who *are* these people?" Maybe one of them could be a babysitter for your five-year-old or a new friend for you. It wasn't like this when you grew up. People knew their neighbors.

Maybe you think your congregation could be more of a caring community for you and for others. You think other people might want this, too.

You may face budget cuts in your town or city that are slowly destroying the schools and public safety. There could be illness spreading among those you love.

Maybe you have adopted a child and you think the adoption system needs fixing. There might be pollution from a factory or the buses near you, layoffs at a workplace, a hospital closing, or toxic waste about to be buried near you.

Maybe you are tired of sitting in traffic day after day and think that there should be a better way of moving people from point A to point B.

You may be talking to a co-worker or neighbor, or with a small group, and you discover that you all have the same problem. You may decide to work with each other to do something about it.

Maybe you have a small group of volunteers and realize that with staff or more members you could do so much more.

Or maybe there is just this feeling inside you that life could be better, brighter, different—that there is more to life than getting up in the morning, going to work, driving home, watching TV, doing the shopping on the weekend, and then starting it all over again on Monday.

The idea has come into your head. You cannot get rid of it. It may be hard to say it out loud. Many of us have been told to keep these thoughts to ourselves. Don't advertise your idea. Don't try to make it come true. Yet if we don't contribute that gift, we give up a piece of ourselves, and our community also suffers the loss.

The idea has walked in your door. What do you do now?

## Step Two: Develop the Vision

*If you don't know where you are going, how will you know when you get there?*

—Old saying

### What Is Your Vision?

Once you have the idea, you need a vision describing where you want to go. A vision inspires and motivates. To build or rebuild a powerful organization you need volunteers to take on responsibility so all of the work does not fall on your shoulders. A compelling vision can inspire and motivate others.

To achieve a shared vision, you also need to be clear about where you are going and why. People hold out hope for a better future. To provide that hope you need to paint a picture of what that better future looks like. It is a funny thing about people. Even with all the bad things that happen, many people do not lose hope for a better life. Sometimes it is something better for their children, stemming from the love parents feel for their children and the hope that children represent. Sometimes that hope comes from family stories or personal experience. The vision taps into that hope. The vision inspires people to work for the organization when they might otherwise get tired or discouraged.

Put the vision into words. You also may want to draw or paint it. If you envision a better school, a picture of a new playground in the parking lot might do a better job than words. If your vision is a neighborhood where people know their neighbors, a picture of a street fair might express it better than words.

**Personal Reflection: Vision Exercise**

# Putting Your Vision Into Words

What is your vision? A vision is a picture of where you want to go. Try one of the following as a guide. Just fill in the blanks:

"I see a congregation that ... _____

_____."

"I see a school (or school system) in which ... _____

_____."

"I see a neighborhood where ... _____

_____."

"I see a group of *[describe who or what you see]* _____

where ... *[describe what is happening that concerns you]*

_____."

"I see a street where ... _____

_____."

"I see a _____ *[fill in the blank with what-*

*ever it is you are trying to change]* where ... _____

_____."

## Don't Hide the Long-Term Vision

If you have a long-term vision, if you intend to build a bigger organization (and there is nothing wrong with that), let those in the core founding group know this from the start—even if you start small, which you probably will. Be honest about the long-term vision, but recognize that this can also scare some people away. Along with the hope people have (and you *are* peddling hope) often comes its twin: resignation that things can't change. It is a tricky balancing act, where you have to be both honest and realistic. There is no simple formula that always works. Manipulation does not work.

### Story: People Won't Come Along If You Don't Tell Them the Whole Story

*In the late 1970s, when I was working as one of the staff organizers for the Vermont Alliance, a statewide grassroots community organization, the staff had a long-term vision of where the organization should go. We thought it could be a statewide group of low-income residents who would work for lower utility rates, fairer taxes, and other statewide issues that concerned many low-income Vermonters.*

*Our method was to visit people in their homes and ask them about their immediate concerns, which often included traffic safety and other neighborhood problems. We would then work with them to win improvements around those concerns, such as helping people to negotiate with the town for crosswalks and "Watch Out for Children" signs. The people we visited thought they were part of a neighborhood group. That was what they saw. We thought we could get them interested in addressing the traffic issue (or whatever their immediate concern was) and then move on to bigger and tougher issues without missing a beat.*

*We were wrong. When we started talking about a statewide group and working on utility or tax reform, they were sometimes confused but mostly uninterested. We could not entice them to come to the statewide meetings. They explained that their interest was the traffic on their street. They had thought that was what we were about, too.*

We, the staff, had not been honest about our long-term vision for the group. They thought the group was about solving traffic problems. And no wonder. That was all we talked about when we met them.

Winning those small improvements—the crosswalks and the traffic signs—helps in building the group, by showing that the group can be effective in making change. At the same time, you cannot hide where you hope to go over the long haul. You have to be honest and willing to let people deal with the problems they see as their problems and also be willing to push them to do more. The trick is to keep one eye on the ultimate vision while slowly building hope by winning the smaller day-to-day improvements that can make life better. This is where the process you went through of articulating your vision can help. Although the long-term vision alone won't motivate most people, your group needs to know the big picture.

## Story: Dignity, Democracy, and a Dental Plan

*The Harvard Union of Clerical and Technical Workers once demanded, "Dignity, Democracy, and a dental plan." Harvard University, a wealthy institution, gave the employees a dental plan. If the union had only wanted the dental plan, their problem or "issue" would have been solved. They would have had no more purpose. But, since their goals also included "dignity and democracy"— things that Harvard University would not or could not "give" as easily—the union still had a purpose and stayed in business, working for "dignity and democracy."*

I learned how long-term vision worked when I observed the pattern of neighborhood crime watch groups. Groups that started out as neighborhood crime watches wanted to remain crime watches. The crime watch vision of a safe neighborhood involved keeping a look-out for criminal activity on one block—what people could see out their windows. When I worked with neighborhood crime watch groups, that is all those who joined wanted and expected when they joined. Attempts to bring in other concerns did not work. Those who established the organizations, in one case the organizer from the police department, wanted to keep the groups the way they started. When the crime problem that had sparked a group dissipated, so did the group.

This may be fine if your entire vision is to rid the neighborhood of the immediate crime problem. But if you are looking for more, if you are looking beyond the immediate issues, if you think you want to tackle other problems that might arise or already exist, you are going to have to think about how to build a longer-lasting organization. How can you get the resources you need to accomplish that goal? You will have to do some thinking about what it will take to get what you want. You will have to think about power— the ability to do something bigger.

## Step Three: Start with Yourself— What Makes You Tick?

### Telling Your Story

*Who somebody is or was we can only know by knowing the story of which he is himself the hero.*

—Hannah Arendt, *The Human Condition*

The next step in building an organization is about *you*. Why are *you* doing this?

You need to understand your motivation. You will meet frustration and opposition. If you, at a deep level, are not clear and connected to the reason for this organization, you are going to have trouble keeping at it. Whether you have started a new organization or are strengthening an old one, you need to know, inside yourself, the connection between you and the mission of this organization.

Those whom you want to lead will also want to know who you are and why you are involved in this cause or this organization. They need a personal connection they can believe in. Others need to invest themselves in the group. They want to know your *story*, the personal experiences and memories that motivated you to start this organization.

Your story can be a model for others. For others to invest in the group, they need to know each other's stories. We remember stories that tell us who people are. Stories show what people do. Stories connect us to actions, not abstractions. Stories connect people directly with one another with a power that generalities miss. They strengthen our relationships, human to human, heart to heart, eyeball to eyeball. Sharing and weaving together the members' stories—these personal experiences, memories, and motivations—solidifies the group.

Start with yourself. What is your story? How does it connect to the organization?

The following is part of my story—how I understand what I do and why I do it. It includes stories I heard about my family as I grew up, combined with my own experiences and how I interpret them. Often family stories connect to a theme or central idea. It may not always be quick or easy to see the themes, but it is valuable to think about your stories and take the time to make the connections.

## My Story: Let Me Start with Minnie

*I could start in many places, but let me start with Minnie, my grandmother. When I was ten, her husband died and she moved into our house. We lived in a house in suburban New York in the 1950s and '60s. Minnie came from another world. She told me lots of stories. She was very funny and dramatic. I learned a lot about her life.*

*Minnie was born in 1893 on the Lower East Side of New York. Her mother died when she was eight. Her father was so poor that he could not support her and her younger brother. Her brother went into the Hebrew Orphan Asylum. The Orphan Asylum said a single father should be able to support one child. But her father was often without work, living as a boarder in someone else's home. He couldn't support his daughter. So Minnie went to live with the janitor in an apartment building while her father went to Pittsburgh to work in a coal mine, the only job he could find. She worked cleaning out the chamber pots in the building's bathrooms.*

*Life was like that for many people in those days. Minnie later worked as an errand girl in the Garment District, in stores, and then as a sewing machine operator in various clothing factories—which she always described to me by what they made and where they made it, such as, "In petticoats on Spring Street."*

*When she was a young woman, Minnie was vivacious, pretty, and popular. She would regale me with stories of all her dates, of all the men who wanted to marry her.*

*She told me about the tragedies that were part of her daily life: a ferry sinking with hundreds on board, the Triangle Shirtwaist fire of 1911, where hundreds of young factory workers like her died. How the coffins of the dead girls were lined up on the street. And the little indignities: her schoolteacher making fun of her for wanting to be a bookkeeper (instead of a factory worker), of not having the money to buy the cloth to make an apron in school, of not having a nickel to ride the subway, and how "a penny meant everything."*

*She wanted to be a schoolteacher. But she never got far in school, so that was not possible. Still, she had these dreams. Here was someone I loved. Poverty and circumstances prevented her from using her gifts.*

Part of my story is Minnie's story. I knew her first as a little boy who loved his grandmother. She was fun and kept me laughing. Later, I wanted to protect her—and by extension, all little children like her—from all the bad things that happened to her as a little girl. I could not go back to 1900 and do that, but I could do something today and that made me feel better.

## Anger and Practicality

Mixed in with what I do is my anger at the world that did not do better by that little girl. Anger that her father could not find a job that paid enough to support his children. Anger at the people who had money but would not share it with Minnie or her brother or father. Anger at the factory owners who timed my grandmother when she went to the bathroom, anger at the teacher who made fun of her for wanting to be anything but a factory worker, for crushing out any hope of being a teacher or even a bookkeeper.

Mixed in with that anger is admiration for my grandmother for coming through all that with her sense of humor intact and with a continued ability to tell stories, to memorize Shakespeare, and to find love.

*Communities . . . have a history—in an important sense they are constituted by their past—and for this reason we can speak of a real community as a "community of memory," one that does not forget its past.*

—Robert Bellah, et al., *Habits of the Heart*

# *The Strong Pull of Community*

*My grandmother told me a lot about her husband, my grandfather. He worked as a garment worker and went to school nights at Cooper Union, studying engineering. She told me he wanted to be a doctor but it was very hard for a Jew to get into medical school. So he tried engineering. When he graduated in 1920, the only job in engineering he could get was on a railroad in Oklahoma. My grand-mother did not want to move there.*

## Microeconomics Meets My Grandmother

When I went to school, I took microeconomics. Microeconomics assumes that all people maximize their economic self-interest. If a person can make more money in Oklahoma than in New York, he or she moves to Oklahoma. People are all rational actors in a free market. Everyone pursues his or her own economic self-interest. The free market creates the best goods and services at the lowest possible prices. That is the theory.

There is another story. My grandmother valued the life and community she had always known more than a better job for my grandfather in Oklahoma. She didn't want to leave New York. For her, going to New Jersey was a big trip.

## Maximizing Self-Interest

Microeconomic theory ignores the benefits of community, even when an individual considers community to be a personal benefit. Part of the story of building community organizations involves people's search for meaning in community, for personal benefit from community. For many people, like my grandmother, a part of individual self-interest is connection to community. In this case, self-interest moves beyond the self. Our motivations are broader than making more money in Oklahoma than in New York.

If we examine self-interest, we uncover complexities about self-interest and motivation. This is why people's stories are important. Telling our stories helps unravel what motivates us. Underneath the story lie the complexity and reality of our lives.

## Childhood Lessons

Whenever I've asked myself why I was doing whatever I was doing, I remembered what I had learned as a child, what I had been told and taught by my parents and grandparents.

## Story: My Father—The Artist's Gift

*My father had the artist's gift. At three, he made beautiful drawings. As a teenager he illustrated a book. He spent most of his life doing commercial art, working to support his wife and four children.*

*When I was growing up, I saw him working long hours, often seven days a week, to make enough money to support us. Watching him work, I wished he could be the creative fine artist he really was, instead of just doing commercial work in order to pay the bills. Like my grandparents and so many others, my father never seemed to be able to use his gifts. (Although, in his case, he retired early and then was able to do the kind of art he had the gift to do. Now he makes beautiful pottery, paintings, and drawings that adorn the homes of his family and friends.)*

Part of my story was: Here are all these members of my family who have not been able to use their gifts. It made me angry. This was my own family. I am sure it was more complicated than how I saw it as a child, or even than how I see it as an adult, but the loss stuck in my mind. I saw this happening and did not want it to happen to me—or to others.

## Story: Discrimination

*Another piece of my story was the recurring theme that my family was discriminated against—or worse— because we were Jews. I was born in 1947, just after World War II. When I was growing up, my mother would show me the family photo album of my relatives, including little cousins, who had lived in Poland or the Ukraine. "Hitler killed him," my mother said, pointing to the little boy in the photo album who looked so much like me. "Hitler killed her," she told me, pointing to another child. It seemed to me that I had barely escaped the same fate.*

*Even though my mother was born in New York, her father had been born in Poland. He had left relatives behind whom Hitler had killed. So it was clear to me: Some people were out to get us and we had to defend ourselves.*

*My father was born in Hungary and came to America as a baby. Many relatives stayed behind in Hungary. One jumped off the truck taking her to Auschwitz. Her friend jumped to one side, and she to the other. Her friend was shot. My cousin survived, eventually finding us. Other relatives survived by leaving Budapest to fight with Tito in Yugoslavia. Still others survived, hidden by Catholics in Budapest. Some did not survive. My mother's aunt survived the Warsaw ghetto, but when she and her son returned to their village after the war, they were killed by people who lived there.*

If I was going to survive I had to defend myself and other Jews. I also should do what I could to make the world the kind of place that would not tolerate Nazis, hatred, or discrimination. It seemed to me that any kind of racism or discrimination was directed at me, or could be.

The combination of the desire to see people use their gifts, whatever they are, and the need to stop any kind of racism or discrimination burns like a slow flame inside me. It has forged a compass that has guided much of what I do. If I am going to understand why I do what I do and stay focused, I need to know this story.

The discrimination against my family made me angry. It made me want to defend my family and people. That anger has simmered and spread, so I get angry when I see others discriminated against. I take it personally. It is a slow pissed-off-ness that stays lit, like the red-hot coals from an evening campfire that you find still burning in the morning. Just add tinder, blow a little, and the fire is going again. It does not take much to get me going.

There are many other parts of this story, including my own experiences and the satisfaction I feel from being part of a group that is doing something worthwhile to make things a little better. This gives me a sense of meaning in my life and a sense of community. I like that sense of not being alone—of being with others who share some of what I feel and think.

## Life Lessons Stick

My mother always said, "There is a right and a wrong. In some things there are no areas of gray." This message underlies the values I embrace. This message made it easier to keep on course. Unless life experience strongly contradicts what our parents tell us, those messages stick.

These stories and messages form the foundation that has guided my work as an organizer. When I think about what helped my family over the years, I come up with the following list: unions, public housing, unemployment insurance, Medicaid, Medicare, free quality public education, health and safety regulations at work, Social Security, affordable housing, good public transportation, public parks, and permanent changes in laws, policies, and norms. Reflecting on what helped my family, I realize that these social changes were the result of groups organizing and working hard to demand these changes. They were not the result of charity.

I have drawn some important lessons from thinking long and hard about my family's story, about what helped us, and why. These lessons have become the backbone of my own work:

- Poor people don't need or want sympathy or handouts.
- We all suffer when there are too few opportunities for as many people as possible to use their gifts.
- We all need all the help we can get.
- People are smart enough to figure out what they need. They just need the time and space to get together to figure it out.

- Don't do for people what they can do for themselves.
- Ask those in authority for what you want. If you don't ask, you don't get.
- People need organizations to get our voices heard and our needs met.

## Your Story

Each of us has a story. There is not a right or wrong story. There is only an honest story, *your* story. You can start off rich or poor or anywhere in between. Some move far from their families of origin. For some, life experience and reflection play the strongest role. For others, memory plays a powerful role. Whatever your story, if you are going to build a strong organization, enlist the help of others, motivate them, and maintain focus and direction, you need to know and be able to articulate your story. Unraveling your story may take remembering and reflecting over many years. You can start now.

**EXERCISE**

## Finding the Stories that Guide You

*"Stories tell us of what we already knew and forgot, and remind us of what we haven't yet imagined."*

—Anne L. Watson

This exercise is one way to start to learn and tell your story.

1. What is something you feel passionately about? What bothers you so much that you think someone should do something about it? Change that to: "I should do something about that!"

_____

_____

_____

2. Why does this subject matter to you? _____

_____

---

---

3. Write down a story from your life that relates to your answers to Questions 1 and 2. Don't worry if it does not seem clear to you why you chose this particular story. It does not have to be the most important thing in your life. Just start with something you care about. (Use a separate piece of paper.)

4. What does this story mean to you? Think about why you chose this story.

---

---

---

---

---

---

---

## Your Own Leadership Plan

If you intend to start or strengthen an organization, it helps to examine how your own attitudes and motivations will affect the organization. When you decide to be responsible for the success of the organization you are going to encounter obstacles. Sometimes the strongest opposition comes from your own mind. Many of us harbor beliefs about ourselves that stop us from fulfilling our dreams or pursuing what we really want. This exercise is designed to help you examine your attitudes about yourself.

## Looking Into Yourself Is the First Step of a Good Leader

We all come into organizations (and relationships of all kinds) with baggage. What do we keep? What do we get rid of?

1. What is an attitude about yourself that you have to let go of?

_____

2. What is the benefit for you in keeping this attitude?

_____

_____

3. What is the cost to you—and to your organization— of keeping this attitude?

_____

_____

4. What specific behavior(s) can you practice to change this attitude?

_____

_____

The commitment to *practice* some other behavior is based on the idea that you must consciously and intentionally change specific behaviors to develop new habits.

For example, I may have the attitude that I know best how to do everything. Therefore, I feel that I have to speak up and show others how to do it right—whatever the task. The benefit to me might be ego gratification and the satisfaction of hearing my own voice. But it might cost the organization others' ideas and energy. This leads to big losses. I may need to let go of that attitude.

One specific behavior I might practice is to hold my tongue when I think I have a great solution and listen more intently. I may want to do this at a specific meeting or on a specific day. I do not assume that I can change a long-standing habit overnight, but changing my behavior in one meeting and then maintaining this behavior can change my attitude and behavior over the long run.

5. When, specifically, will I commit myself to practicing this behavior or these behaviors?

_____

Make a commitment to practice this. It is helpful to find someone to hold you accountable.

6. Get someone to hold you accountable. Who will this be? Write that person's name here: _____

It also helps to monitor your behavior on a daily basis. This may only take five minutes at 5:00 p.m. each day. Ask yourself: How did I do today with changing that behavior? Don't kick yourself too much if you did not do it perfectly. The goal is not to be perfect, but to be aware of your behavior, to practice the behavior you want, and to monitor how you did in various situations during the day. The goal is eventually to make the new behavior your norm.

7. Make a commitment to reviewing your behavior daily:

Each day at _____ [write in the time] I will spend a few minutes reviewing how I am doing at changing this behavior.

## Know Thyself

Just as it is important to examine personal beliefs about yourself that might hold you back or affect your leadership, it is also important to examine beliefs about the world that might hold your group back. Many of us have core beliefs and values that will have a critical effect on how our group operates.

There is nothing wrong with having core beliefs and values. In fact, they are essential. But we need to reflect upon those core beliefs or personal theories in order to know when they might get in the way of being effective or successful in our work. Some examples are listed below. They are put in stark language not because you are likely to have such black-and-white thinking, but to demonstrate how beliefs can affect your group's work.

For example, one might think: *"Corporations are out only to make money and therefore we will not work with them to improve product safety."* This stops us from working effectively with a company that might actually be interested in improving product safety.

An individual might believe: *"All people in public housing are lazy, sponging off the government."* We might miss an opportunity to work with public housing residents to improve conditions in our city or town.

We might believe: *"Our church is in the business of helping people live in the Spirit. We are not in the real estate business."* We miss an opportunity when land in the neighborhood goes up for sale and we don't buy it, even though we could have used it to build needed affordable housing for our members.

Or you might believe that *"all pro-life people are fanatics."* We miss an opportunity to work with them to cut down on the number of unwanted pregnancies.

We might believe that *"picketing a company whose policies we want to change is the best way to achieve our goals"*—even though we have picketed ten times already and have failed every time to achieve our goals.

One might believe that *"the teachers' union is only out to protect the teachers' jobs"* and therefore would fail to work with the teachers' union to improve our children's education.

Other beliefs that might affect your group include:

*"The free market is the best way to solve our community's problems."*

*"Government is the best way to solve those problems."*

*"Our church should solve our community's problems."*

All of us have beliefs about how the world works and about other people, including other groups. Many of these are based on experience and hold some truth. But some may be outdated or untested. In forming any organization, it helps to list those beliefs and to re-examine them. Are they still accurate? Do they still work? Are we missing something? Are they helping us to reach our goals—or are they hurting us?

**EXERCISE**

## Finding Your Core Beliefs

1. What are some of the core beliefs I hold that apply to this group?

_____

_____

_____

2. Where did I learn these beliefs?

_____

3. Have I tested or reflected on the accuracy of these beliefs?

❏ Yes    ❏ No

4. Can I test these beliefs now?    ❏ Yes    ❏ No

5. How can I test them? _____

_____

_____

6. Am I willing to do that? (Or do I want to hold on to these beliefs no matter what?)   ❏ Yes   ❏ No

Comments: _____

_____

_____

_____

7. How will these beliefs affect the group? _____

_____

_____

8. Do other members of the group also share these beliefs?

❏ Yes   ❏ No

After you've done this exercise alone, it might be interesting to do it again, with your group, to see what values the group shares and also to find out if there are any deeply held "group-think" attitudes that might be getting in the way of your group's work.

## Step Four: Listen to Others

*Now if you want higher wages, here's what you got to do, you got to talk to the workers in the shop with you ...*

—Woody Guthrie, "Talking Union"

After you have written your story and taken a hard look at yourself, the next step is to listen to other people. The point is *to really listen* to them. Listen to what they think about your idea and vision. They might have good or better ideas of their own. Are they interested? Listen to at least ten people. If you hope to have broader impact, listen to at least fifty people.

You need to listen in order to hear if they are going to help or take responsibility. If the people you approach say, "Great idea, you go do it," they are not likely to help and your idea is in trouble. You want to listen for specific offers of help and support, especially for offers of time and/or money. You want to listen for passion. You also want to listen for who these people are. What motivates them? How does the problem or concern that is the group's focus affect them? You listen for a personal connection between them and what your group intends to do or already does.

The listening has to be real. You have to be willing and able to meet people on their terms, on their turf. John Lewis, the former Chairman of the Student Non-Violent Coordinating Committee, describes the listening he and others did during the Civil Rights Movement:

*"[W]e were meeting people on their terms, not ours. If they were out in the field picking cotton, we would go out in that field and pick with them. If they were planting squash, we planted too. Whatever the people were doing, we were with them, really there. We lived with them in their homes, held hands and prayed with them, shared their food, shared their beds, shared their worries and their hopes. We listened to them. Before we ever got around to sharing what we had to say, we listened. And in the process, we built up both their trust and their confidence in themselves. Essentially we were out to spread faith and courage, and naturally we had to find those things in ourselves first."*

—John Lewis, *Walking With the Wind*

## Take Your Time

All this listening takes a lot of time. Making appointments; having some of them cancel at the last minute; travel time to meet people—all these elements can make this step seem endless. Some want fast results. We think we know what has to be done and only need a little help along the way. The work of listening to others is not just a matter of getting your ticket punched at the gate, not just another step on a road you have already decided upon. This kind of listening takes a commitment and willingness to be open to changes in your plans and an ability to go way beyond simply delegating jobs to others. It requires the openness to shape the enterprise into something that others care about as deeply as you.

There are a number of ways to listen. Your methods will depend on your style, the size of the group you want to build, your culture, the culture of those you want to engage, and what you think works best in your own situation.

## To Whom Do You Need To Listen?

That depends on what your idea is and what you want to accomplish. But you always start with those closest to the problem or situation you want to address. If you want to reform the adoption system, start with those it affects: adoptive parents, adopted children, birth parents, adoption agencies. If it is a problem affecting your school or neighborhood, you need to listen to all those in the school or neighborhood.

One common mistake you can make at this stage is to talk to only a few people and then swing into action. Don't come up with an idea, write a grant to fund it (not that getting a grant is so easy!), or come up with the money yourself to make it happen. Test your idea among many people. Building an organization that can be sustained over time is going to take broad support. Without that support, or if there is broad opposition, or if some other group is already doing what you have proposed to do, your organization is not likely to succeed. If your organization is not sustained over time, its effect will be severely limited.

## Keep In Touch With People You Talk To— Especially Those With Influence

You might have a good idea to improve your neighborhood or want to stop some new hazard from moving in. Not everyone you talk to will agree with your approach. They may have a different point of view. Listen to them, especially if they are gatekeepers to others or have positions of authority. Try to understand their point of view. (This can be tough, especially when you feel passionately about something, but try, even if it means biting your tongue.) You want to know where they stand even if they are in opposition to this particular idea. Later, even years later, they might be in agreement on another issue. And even if that does not happen, at least try to maintain a respectful relationship.

## "No Permanent Friends, No Permanent Enemies"

Working with people to build a grassroots organization is different from making friends. You are in the public arena. (Although you can make wonderful friends in this work. I certainly have, and there is nothing wrong with that.) But when you are listening to someone who might have some influence on the success of your idea or issue, remember this guideline: You are in a public relationship now, not a private or personal relationship. If the person disagrees with you and you disagree with him or her on this issue, *this disagreement is not with the person, but on the issue.*

## Distinguish Public and Private Relationships

This distinction between the public and private arenas is often hard to understand because there is little understanding in our media or educational system about public life. People in public life, including most elected officials, often act as if they want to be your friend. They kiss your babies, eat your food, and describe all the ways they are just like you, whoever you are. They want you to like them as people. That is because many people vote for the person they like, not necessarily for the person whose public policies meet their own needs.

Don't confuse or combine the person and the issue. Someone who disagrees with you on an issue is not an enemy. The disagreement is not personal. Don't hold grudges. Someone who disagrees with you on one issue may be helpful on another. Don't assume that people's economic self-interest will automatically put them on one side of an issue. Follow what they do—not who you guess they are.

### Start with All the People You Eventually Want in Your Organization

Listen *now* to people from all the constituencies that you *eventually* want to be part of your organization. One mistake people sometimes make in starting a group is to listen only to those with whom they already feel comfortable and assume that others will join later on. The others will *not*, at least not without tremendous extra effort on your part.

If you are building a community group and want people from all the neighborhoods in the city to be part of it, listen to people from all neighborhoods *at the beginning*. If you want people of all religions to be part of your group eventually, listen to a representative sample *now*, to hear what *they* think. Trying to "diversify" later is much harder. People like to be part of organizations where they are involved in the planning and decision-making from the beginning.

## Listening to Others, Method One: Informal Chats, With Nothing in Writing

Tell the person ahead of time that you want to discuss an idea you have and that you are looking for his or her ideas and opinions. Ask for a specific amount of time, say 30 minutes. After 30 minutes, say: "I know I said 30 minutes. I would be happy to go now." If they say, "Yes, I have to go," then thank them and leave. If they indicate that they have more time, take the time—but only if you need it.

Present your idea orally. Ask, "What do you think of this?" It is important to ask an open-ended question, rather than, "Do you think this is a good idea?" You are looking for feedback, not a *yes* or *no* vote. This is not an opinion survey or an election. The person will have questions. These help focus your idea and vision. You are seeking their advice and help.

## Other Questions:

Is anyone else doing anything like this?

>(Is anyone trying to do something about the budget cuts in the schools?)
>(Is anyone trying to set up a different way to adopt children?)
>(Is anyone else trying to get better bus service?)

If so, who?

What do you think of them?

Are there any meetings about this?

Who do you think really knows about the budget cuts?

Is that organization really doing anything worthwhile about the cuts?

Who else should I talk to?

Can I use your name when I contact them?

*Can I use your name?*

(I make it a policy to *ask people twice* if I can use their name in saying that so-and-so referred me to them. This avoids potential misunderstandings and embarrassment.)

Would you like to help?

What would you like to do?

Do you have any advice?

After the meeting, keep notes of what people say. I use a notebook, or you might use a computer. When I started doing this I used 3 x 5 index cards. Your memory may be great, but taking notes reminds you what each person said and what help they offered. I take notes *immediately after, but not during*, the meeting. I want to focus my attention on the person I am talking to. This is a conversation, not a survey.

Then write a thank-you note. I prefer handwritten notes. Most people do.

## Listening to Others, Method Two: Put Your Idea in Writing and Then Listen

On one or two pages, include:

1. The problem you see and want to solve.
2. Your solution.
3. Why this new group is needed now. If you hear that another group is doing what you propose, make it clear that other groups exist, but are not really doing the job the way it needs to be done.
4. Your contact information: name, address, phone numbers, e-mail.
5. The date. You might write several drafts. The dates identify them.

Send this concept paper to the people whose advice you want, with a note saying that you will contact them to hear what they think of your idea.

Then conduct the interview as you would with the more informal method. Bring several copies of your concept paper with you in case the person lost it or wants to show it to others.

### Got Help?

Are they interested and also willing to offer *real help*? If some people do not offer you something tangible and useful to help make your idea happen, reconsider your idea. Without the time, money, and assistance of others, you are unlikely to succeed at getting a group together to fulfill your vision. If people offer real help, then you know that you are on to something. If only one or two out of fifty people offer their time, money, or anything else beyond kind words, your idea is in trouble.

## Listening to Others, Method Three: Focus Groups

In addition to the individual meetings, you might also hold focus groups—small groups of interested people who brainstorm about specific aspects of your idea. Invite a group of five to fifteen people to come to a session for an hour or an hour-and-a-half. Provide food or other incentives. Use a sign-in list to collect the names, addresses, phone numbers, and e-mail addresses of all who come. Look over the sign-in list before people leave to make sure you can read their writing, especially for phone numbers and e-mails. One misread letter or number makes for problems.

Focus groups are useful, but don't let these be your *only* means of gathering information. There is no alternative to the one-on-one meetings to build relationships and get people's real in-depth opinions and offers of help.

**QUICK TIPS**

### How to Run a Focus Group

1. Bring someone with you to take notes (not a focus group member).

2. Introduce yourself. Be brief (one minute).

3. Ask those invited to introduce themselves, including something about their background and why they have come, so people get to know each other a little. The focus group is often one of the first meetings of your potential new organization. For introductions, ask specific questions, like: "Please tell us your name, where you live, and in one sentence why you are here." You might ask someone you know to model a brief introduction. If you can't ask someone, model it yourself. The time the first person takes will likely

be the time those who follow take. If the first introduction is brief, those that follow will be. You can be
flexible here, depending on the culture, number of
people in the group, amount of time you have, etc.

4. Provide a brief history of the idea and the potential
group.

5. Explain the vision. Three minutes: Practice so that
you get the words right. I practice with a tape or
video recorder, to get the exact words and emphasis right and not take too much time.

6. State that the goal of the meeting is to gather their
opinions. You value their opinions. That is why you
asked them here.

7. Ask their opinions about the proposed group or
idea.

8. Ask questions along the lines of the following:

What is it that draws you to this group?
How did you hear about this meeting?
What might this group do that would be helpful or
meaningful to you?

Depending on how much support you already have
for your idea and group, you might want to get
down to more specifics about how to organize the
group. You might ask:

When should it meet?
For how long?
How much should the dues be?
Is anyone else doing anything like this?
Who else do you know who might be interested in this?
Ask participants to write down the names of other
people who might be interested next to their names
on your roster or sign-in sheet.

9. Thank those who came. End on time.

## Step Five: Put Your Organization In Writing

Assuming that your organization still seems viable after listening to at least 50 people, it is time to write down your idea for others to read. If you already have put your idea into writing, have listened to all those people, and have gotten their feedback, now is the time to make any necessary changes to your written document.

Putting your idea into writing commits you more powerfully to the idea. Now there is a document with your name and contact information on it. Writing forces you to be more specific and allows for broader feedback. Many Americans learn the story of the Declaration of Independence. Before it was written there was a lot of talk in the colonies about independence from England. The written document solidified resolve, codified reasons for the solution, and allowed signers to commit their "sacred honor" to abide by the document. Your written statement need not have the eloquence and historical impact of the Declaration of Independence, but the written statement is an important step to advance your idea.

### Writing Gives the Idea Staying Power and Wider Reach

Many ideas need time to take root and gain the necessary support. Putting the idea on paper allows people to see it when you are not present and reflect upon it at their own pace. The written statement gives your potential organization added staying power.

## Story: A Written Description Helps to Spread the Idea

*A couple of years after I got the idea for the Jewish Orga-nizing Initiative, after speaking to many people, I put the idea into writing. I gave the paper to a friend. Later that year, he interrupted the normal order of a Passover Seder at his home, handed out copies of the paper, and suggested that the guests read it. One man who knew he would be a guest at the Seder the following year figured he ought to read it. He did, liked the idea, and later became one of the organization's leaders. Having the idea in writing made a big difference. It gave the idea staying power from one year to the next. It also allowed someone else to share the idea with people he knew, giving it broader reach and greater potential support.*

## Words Matter . . . What's In a Name?

This is a good time to name the organization. Putting your idea into writing means you have to call it something. What you call it matters—a lot. The name affects membership and the scope of your work. If your school improvement association is called a "parents' organization," supporters who are not parents will not feel welcome. The "Spalding-Anson Street Crime Watch" will attract only residents on those streets, and only those concerned about crime. "The Spalding-Anson Street *Improvement* Association" would attract residents on those streets concerned about a wider range of issues.

An organization dedicated to increasing income equality began as "Share the Wealth." It later changed its name to "United for a Fair Economy." "Share the Wealth" is an imperative statement suggesting a program that takes wealth from those with more, to share it with those with less. This might have seemed threatening or too direct. "United for a Fair Economy" connotes a group of people who share a common goal of a fair economy. How it reaches that goal is not specifically mentioned.

An organization that calls itself "ecumenical" is indicating that it includes various Christian denominations. An "interfaith" organization indicates that Jews, Muslims, Hindus, and other non-Christian religions are also welcome. These distinctions matter.

In fact, you might want to wait to name your group until all those you want in the group are present, to make sure that all agree about the name.

When the Vermont Public Interest Research Group wanted to pass state legislation for funding for children's dental services, Vermont PIRG called it "The Tooth Fairy Bill." Who can vote against the tooth fairy? The first attempt at a racially integrated bus ride was called a "Journey of Reconciliation," sponsored by the Fellowship of Reconciliation. James Farmer changed the name to "Freedom Rides." "Freedom," a well-known, respected two-syllable word representing an American value, beats a nine-syllable phrase that most people can't understand. When housing organizers found out that some low-income home owners were being charged high rates for loans secured by their property, the organizers called this "predatory lending." Nobody likes a "predator." Several foundations that spent millions of dollars trying to defeat the federal estate tax renamed it the "death tax," even though it did not tax death. (It taxed the heirs of estates that were worth more than several million dollars.) A rose by any other name may smell as sweet, but in a campaign, words matter. They help you win or lose.

# Step Six: Develop a Sponsoring Committee

Now that you have listened to at least 50 people and have decided that your organization is needed and have crafted a written document outlining your vision and have selected a name (or at least a temporary one), you are ready for the next step: Developing a public list of people who support your idea and organization. For this list, you want people with credibility in the community where you are working. This list provides your fledgling organization with credibility among those whose help, support, and money you need.

The sponsoring committee is a fairly standard tool in the community organizing business. As the name implies, this is a list of people who agree to have their names publicly listed in support of your idea. Depending on the size and scope of the organization you intend to build, the sponsoring committee may have five or five hundred names, or anything in between.

## How Do You Use the Sponsoring Committee List?

Generally, the sponsoring committee list is attached to your written statement and used with publicity, to get the word out. People who are checking out your organization are likely to read a few lines and then scan the names on the sponsoring committee list to see who they know. They are asking themselves, since they have never heard of the organization, "Is this a club I would want to be part of? Who else is on board?" If they see people they know, they will think, "This group is okay." If they see people they do not like, it has the opposite effect.

## Using People's Organizational Affiliation

The standard way affiliations are handled is to print the person's name, followed by his or her organizational affiliation and an asterisk (*). A note under the list states, "* For identification purposes only." This tells the reader that only the *individuals*, not their organizations or employers, have endorsed your idea or organization. Don't forget to do this. There may be many Susan Smiths. Yours is the one from the PTA at the Fessenden School, not the Susan Smith who is the President of the Retail Grocers Association. Identifying the affiliation makes that clear. But you want to clearly state that it is Susan Smith (the individual), not the PTA (the organization), who has joined the sponsoring committee.

## Story: Get It In Writing

*When I was asking people to be on the sponsoring committee for an organization, I had lunch with a potential supporter. Over lunch, I asked him to join our sponsoring committee. He said, "Yes." Or so I thought.*

*Months later, after I had circulated the list of the sponsoring committee, I got an e-mail from him, telling me that he had not agreed to be on the sponsoring committee. He sent copies of this e-mail to the person who had originally given me his name and to all the people on the list. Obviously we had different recollections of the meeting.*

It taught me a lesson: Don't rely on verbal *okay*s when it comes to willingness to be on a sponsoring committee. Get the agreement in writing. This mistake did not destroy the fledgling organization, but it certainly was no help.

## Sample Sponsoring Committee Agreement Letter

*This letter need not be long. It might look like this.*

[Date]

Dear Michael [replace my name with your name]:

My signature below indicates that I agree to be on the sponsoring committee of the Any Town Improvement Association. I agree with the Association's basic principles and goals. I give you permission to include my name, listed as follows, on the Sponsoring Committee roster:

Susan K. Smith, Fessenden School PTA*

*Organization listed for identification purposes only

I understand that this list will be public and will be circulated with information about the proposed organization.

Thank you.

Signed:
Susan K. Smith

Note:
Susan,
Please sign above if you agree with these terms and then return this letter to me. If you want to make any changes in how you will be listed, please mark the changes clearly. Call me if you have questions. A list of the sponsoring committee (in formation) is attached, for your information. Thank you again,

Michael Brown
Temporary Chair
Any Town Improvement Association
Address
Phone number
E-mail address

You can also find members of the sponsoring committee at the same time that you do your one-on-one interviews to get opinions and ideas about the organization. The steps often overlap as you build interest in your idea and commitment to your organization.

Carry copies of the blank sponsoring committee letter when you go to one-on-one meetings so that the people you meet can sign the letter right on the spot, if that seems appropriate. But do not pressure anyone who expresses reservations to sign on. You don't want people saying that they were pressured into sponsorship. You also want to make sure that all your sponsors know that their names will be publicly circulated, as the agreement letter indicates.

## Step Seven: Bring Together a Core Group

Up until this point *you* have been the organization. Now that you have your sponsoring committee, bring together a core group to launch your organization and start doing its work. This is a tricky step. Your task is to shift some of the responsibility to others and to get the intelligence of a group to guide and build the organization.

### Who Chooses the Members of the Core Group?

You do!

When inviting someone into the core group, make the expectations clear—and stick to whatever you promise. If you say the meetings are on the third Tuesday night of the month for an hour-and-a-half, don't make them more frequent or longer. If someone wants to be in this core group but you do not think that she or he should be, do not allow the person in just to be nice. People who do not agree on the basic principles do not belong in the core group, even if they beg or bully or even if someone else suggests that you invite them. At this point, you need control. *Boundaries* are essential. The boundaries include the criteria for core group membership and for general organizational membership.

## Who Are You Looking For?

What kind of people should be in the core group?

### 1. People who agree with the basic principles of your group.

If there is an essential element that underlies the group, this is the time to be clear about it. Include only people who agree with the essential issues or perspective. Do not expect or hope that people who do not share your core concerns will come around later by virtue of your charisma, logic, or group pressure. They will not. They will only cause you grief.

What might those essential deal-breaking issues be? That is up to you. Let me illustrate.

## Story: Know Where Your Group Draws the Line

*When Kim Fellner and several colleagues started the National Organizers Alliance (NOA) as a national professional association of community and labor organizers, one of the important issues they wanted the organization to address was **how paid staff organizers are treated within their own organizations**. For some of the founders, treatment of staff organizers was the one critical issue that they wanted NOA to address. No other organization was addressing this issue. So they established openness on that particular issue as a central criterion for recruiting the core group members.*

*Had they not been clear about this principle from the outset, NOA might have been derailed from this aspect of its mission as it grew from a circle of colleagues into an organization with hundreds of members across the country. Because the founders established this boundary at the very beginning of their internal leadership recruitment, they succeeded in embedding the issue into NOA's core business. The issue was controversial among some community and labor organizers, and NOA also lost some potential members because of this choice. This underscores the importance to a group of starting with a core circle of leaders who agree about where to draw the line. In the face of opposition, it is particularly important to have a clearly established vision and shared sense of purpose that can guide the core group.*

## Story: Stop Division at the Start

Effective groups require clear boundaries, including a common perspective on core issues. Openness to other perspectives may seem nice, but in actuality, this approach can destroy the group before it is launched.

*The founders of a group working on state budget issues felt that involvement in federal or international issues would be divisive and would dilute the organization's effectiveness. They agreed to restrict their work to state issues and they made it clear to all who expressed interest in getting involved that this was the boundary.*

Vigilance and clear boundaries were necessary at the beginning, to keep the seedling organization from getting washed away in a flood of extraneous issues.

If you think that your organization will be torn apart by issues that are not related to the core business, then make it clear from the start that the organization won't address other issues. Other organizations focus on those issues. If someone wants to work on those other issues, they should join one of the other organizations.

## 2. People with other talents, inclinations, and backgrounds.

In developing your core group, you want people who can bring talents, insights, skills, and backgrounds *that are different than your own*. I may be high on enthusiasm. Therefore I look for people who are good at planning and analysis. I often fail to recognize the details needed to carry out a program. In developing a core group, I intentionally search for people who are good at the details, scheduling, and putting things in writing—all weaknesses of mine. I look for a mix of backgrounds.

I ask myself:

*What are all the constituencies the group needs?* I search for people who represent them.

*What are the backgrounds I eventually want in the group?* I look for people representative of those backgrounds.

*Does the organization need legal help?* I look for a lawyer.

*Does it need accounting help?* Yes. All organizations need to keep good track of their money.

## How Many People for the Core Group?

You want a core group of ten to fifteen people. Once a planning group moves beyond fifteen (some social scientists say twelve), it is much harder to manage, make decisions, or work together.

## Story: Small Is Beautiful

*I've heard that former Mayor Koch of New York knew this. Whenever a group came to him asking the city to do something that was not his priority, he would appoint a "task force" of fifty people. Fifty people with little history of working together cannot make a decision or get anything done. These "task forces" never accomplished much, but they created the appearance that the mayor was doing something about the issue.*

## The First Order of Business for the Core Group

The core group will work, or not work, largely based on its spirit and sense of purpose. Groups that work well tend to have people who like each other. For people to like each other, they need to get to know each other. Spend time in the beginning learning about each other's histories, families, motivations, interests, and personal needs. Aside from supporting the business of the group, help the group to support the individuals in the group.

I generally start meetings with, "What's new with everyone?" and then give each person a chance to answer, even if each of us just speaks for a minute. Putting this first guarantees that it happens. This way, people have the opportunity to report some good or bad news, rather than sitting on the information and being distracted by it throughout the meeting. By starting this way, there is an ongoing vehicle for members to get to hear what the others care about, are thinking about, and are concerned about.

## Building Your Core Group

This exercise is designed to clarify your essential principles and identify the kind of people you need in your core group.

As you look for members of the core group, consider:

### Section I. What are your talents?

1. I am good at _____

_____

_____

_____.

2. My default mode of operation is _____

_____

_____

3. I am detail-oriented.　❑ Yes　❑ No

4. I tend to see the big picture and miss the details.

❑ Yes　❑ No

5. I am good at planning.　❑ Yes　❑ No

6. I tend to think first and plan carefully.　❑ Yes　❑ No

7. I tend to want to act first and plan later.　❑ Yes　❑ No

8. I tend to weigh decisions carefully and act slowly.

❑ Yes　❑ No

9. I tend to be intuitive.　❑ Yes　❑ No

10. When I volunteer, I like to _____ .
    *(My day job may be grant-writing, but I may not want to do any grant-writing when I volunteer. I may be a carpenter, but the last thing I want to do as a volunteer is install the church's cabinets. That's okay.)*

## Section II. What else do you need?

Understanding how you behave helps to show what skills and styles of working and learning are missing.

1. Knowing your personality, what other kinds of personalities would be most useful in the core group? _____

_____

_____

_____

2. What special knowledge do you have? _____

_____

_____

_____

3. What special knowledge or skills do you lack that the core group needs? _____

_____

_____

_____

4. Who has this knowledge or these skills? _____

_____

_____

_____

5. What other skills or areas of knowledge are needed in the core group? _____

_____

_____

_____

6. Who has these? _____

_____

_____

_____

### Section III. What does the organization need?

Answering these questions can help you clarify what the core group membership criteria should be.

1. What are the organization's essential principles? (What are the deal-breaker agreements you require for any member of the core group?) _____

   _____

   _____

   _____

2. What skills does the organization need?

   ❑ Accounting

   ❑ Legal help

   ❑ Fundraising

   ❑ Community support

   ❑ Special knowledge of _____

   ❑ People who can recruit

   ❑ Other _____

   ❑ And more "Other" _____

3. What are the groups or communities (old people, young people, tenants, home owners, Blacks, Italians, Catholics, Latinos, business owners, labor unions, etc.) you eventually want in your organization? _____

   _____

   _____

4. Who is representative of these groups? _____

   _____

   _____

5. Do you have someone from all of these groups in your core group?   ❑ Yes   ❑ No

6. Who are they? _____

_____

_____

7. Who is missing? _____

_____

_____

8. Who might represent this missing group?

_____

9. If you don't know, how can you find someone who might?

_____

Remember: If you don't start out with all the groups whom you eventually want represented, it will be much harder to "diversify" later on.

## Congratulations!

If you've accomplished these first seven steps, one thing is sure: You're no longer building the organization alone. You have company. Now you are a group. The remaining chapters walk you through the rest of the process of growing a community organization—whether you've just started one or you're strengthening an existing one—in order to solve problems and change the world.

# Developing a Mission, Goals, and Objectives

Mission, goals, and objectives perform different functions in building an organization. The mission should inspire people and unify them around a shared purpose. The goals should clarify your direction and your destination. The objectives should be specific enough to allow you to measure whether you got where you wanted to go.

## ▶ Mission Statements

The mission is a short written statement of the organization's overall purpose. The mission statement provides a guide and compass for the organization. All the organization's work and efforts should fit under the umbrella of its mission statement.

### Why Write a Mission Statement?

Once you have a core group, it is time to write your mission statement. If your organization has been around for ten, twenty, fifty, or one hundred years, it may be time to revisit the organization's mission.

Does what you intend to do make sense? Does what you have been doing for years still make sense? Why do you have this organization anyway? What business is it in? What is its reason for being? If you are going to take the time to build an organization or strengthen one that already exists, be clear about why the organization is necessary and what it is supposed to do. To clarify your purpose and make sure your members agree with that purpose, and to inspire people to work toward this purpose, you need a concise statement that describes what the organization does—*and does not*—do. Groups with clear missions function better. If you want a group to be a team and to work together, everyone on the team needs to agree where the group is going and why. This is the reason for a mission statement.

## Clarify Your Purpose

Writing the mission statement provides an opportunity for your group to reflect upon and possibly revise its basic purpose. Even with the best intentions there can be disagreement or misunderstanding about the mission.

Putting your purpose into words, especially into a concise statement, forces debate to clarify your reason for being. You may *think* everyone agrees upon the mission, but until you craft the actual words you do not really know what the group thinks. Without this exercise, differences of opinion and emphasis can grow.

## Keep It Simple

You want to keep the statement short enough for everyone to be able to remember it.

## How Do You Develop a Mission Statement?

Carefully. You need to think clearly: What is the real long-range purpose of your group? What are you really trying to accomplish?

## Stories

The following stories illustrate how a few organizations crafted their mission statements.

### Looking Beyond the Wolf at the Door

*A college students' association owned a building to house low-income students. It was a cooperative. Everyone pitched in to maintain the building. The association was 50 years old and had a long list of dedicated alumni. One year, the college decided that it wanted to take over the building for its own purposes. No more home for low-income college students. When the group members (students and alumni) asked themselves what their organization's mission was, they said, "To stop Old University from taking over our building."*

*That was their immediate task. They would not exist if Old U. bought their home. But that was not their mission. When they reflected, they recognized that their group's mission was* **to provide low-cost cooperative housing to low-income students who otherwise could not attend Old U.** *That was a mission they could rally behind. The mission lasts beyond immediate threats or tasks. It is the basic reason for being.*

### What Are You Really About?

*The residents of Camfield Gardens, as represented by the Camfield Tenants Association, were extremely dissatisfied with the management's poor maintenance record and the overall shoddy upkeep of the development. The tenants wanted to buy the apartment complex; as resident owners, they believed, they would do a better job of taking care of the property and maintaining a quality living environment.*

*They first wrote their mission as "to provide safe, affordable housing." Upon reflection they realized that they wanted to create a caring community. They talked about what kind of future they wanted for their families. They wanted the young to help the elderly. They wanted a playground. They wanted a space to gather and to house activities on-site. They wanted to help young people with their homework. They wanted people to help each other carry their groceries up the stairs. They wanted a place where people would know each other, check up on each other, and care about each other. Later, they decided they wanted a computer center where residents and their children could link with the Internet and improve computer skills.*

*Clearly, they wanted more than "safe, affordable housing." They probably could have gotten that with a different landlord or management company. So they changed their mission statement. After much discussion, it read: "To create a community of residents who will maintain Camfield Gardens as safe, decent, affordable housing, a place to live, work, learn, and help each other."*

*Their new mission statement made a difference in what they accomplished. Their goal became not only to achieve resident ownership, but also to demolish the substandard housing and rebuild the apartment complex from the ground up. Over the nine years it took, the mission statement helped them to remember that they wanted a community center. This was a major additional expense in the re-development, but they stuck with their desire. At times the center was a source of conflict with the federal and state agencies with whom they had to negotiate for the re-development. If their mission had only been "safe, affordable housing," they might have given up on the community center.*

*Now, the community center has been built and is in use. Children do their homework there and adults surf the Internet there to look for jobs and other information. Those hours spent to develop the mission statement, years before they knew that they would rebuild the entire devel-*

*opment, guided the re-development to include construc-*
*tion of a community center. It was time well spent.*

## Say Where You Are Going and How You Will Get There

*A group concerned about drug and alcohol problems wrote this mission statement:*

*"The Neighborhood Initiatives Task Force is an organizing committee representing all Worcester neighborhoods that advocates for effective alcohol, tobacco, and other drug abuse prevention policies. It will develop self-sustaining representative neighborhood action teams that address the needs of their respective neighborhoods and send representatives to the task force. The task force will work with other community groups and create a permanent citywide organization."*

*Then they started to realize that they wanted to do more than be an "organizing committee . . . that advocates." They realized that key descriptive words in that statement— "develop self-sustaining . . . action teams that address . . . needs"—did not really spell out their purpose. They started to realize that their mission was "to build a democratic organization of people from all the neighborhoods of Worcester to end alcohol and drug abuse." They realized that they had been using the language of drug prevention professionals, not their words. They came to realize that they did not want to "advocate" for anything. They wanted to end the abuse. That was their mission. They did not want to be an "organizing committee representing. . . ." They wanted to "build a democratic organization." The words are different, had a different meaning, and represented a different mission.*

## Words, Words, Words . . .

Verbs are key in mission statements. They say what you are going to do. That was a strength of the Neighborhood Initiatives Task Force's first statement: It used active verbs to state what its activities would be ("advocates for") and how they would be structured ("develop . . . action teams . . . and send representatives to the task force").

But the verbs were not enough. That first statement did not say *why* they were doing these activities. Where was the mission? The purpose has to be clear.

Guiding principles are also important. In this case, it was important that the organization be "democratic" and include "all the neighborhoods." It also was important that the group would "build a[n] . . . organization" to reach members' goals. Building the organization was itself an important part of the group's mission.

## Story: The Power of a Word

*I was once part of a group of people who provided training for community organizations. When we came together to develop a mission statement, one woman did not want to use the word "training." Her mother had been forced to go to a "training school" in the South, which was common for Black women at the time. The word "training" had negative connotations for her. To include her, our mission statement had to use another word.*

## Group Exercise:
## Crafting a Mission Statement

1. Come up with a sentence that describes the overall purpose of the organization.

2. Get your core group together.

3. Write down that sentence in large block letters on a piece of flip chart paper. Read it aloud to the group. Ask for feedback.

4. Take some quiet time for everyone to think about that sentence. Then have each person write his or her own statement about the organization's mission. Write these on other pieces of flip chart paper and post them around the walls of the room.

5. In *silence*, have all the core group members walk around the room and look at the new statements.

6. Then sit down and discuss as a group the various statements—what you liked about this or that word, what each word communicates. You might want to break down a group of fifteen into three groups of five, to make sure that everyone gets a chance to speak.

7. Then see what the three groups came up with.

8. Slowly see if you can craft a sentence that gets the agreement of everyone in the room.

## ▶ Goals and Objectives

*Have a plan, even a bad plan, but have a plan.*

—Old saying

After crafting your mission statement, the next step is to establish your goals and objectives. The goals and objectives lay out your strategy—your plan for pursuing your mission. The goals and objectives break down the mission statement into progressively more specific levels.

*Goals* identify what you want to accomplish. While you may want to do many things, goals focus on your priorities.

*Objectives* break down your goals more specifically, often numerically. You can evaluate progress on your objectives to see how you are doing. When you write your objectives, identify specific *measures* you will use to track your progress toward meeting each objective.

### Goals and Objectives: Write Them Down!

Like the mission statement, the goals and objectives should be put in writing, because you will have to share your goals and objectives widely in order to build your organization. Your goals and objectives specify where you intend to go. Other people will want to know that.

Don't be afraid of commitment! If something changes, you can always change the goals and objectives. They are written on a word processor, not in stone. So write them down.

### Objectives: Be Specific

In building a powerful community organization, objectives are the place where you get to state exactly what it is that you want to achieve. Just as important, objectives are also where you lay the groundwork for building an *ongoing* organization. Remember—one of the goals of any ongoing community organization is to build up the organization continually. Your objectives give you this opportunity.

Objectives must be specific because they say what you are going to do. This way, the group can achieve exactly what it wants to achieve—and not something else. Work through any differences between members about the details of your objectives when you are writing them. Agreeing on the specifics as you write the objectives can keep your group from divisive and damaging disagreements later on. Remember: Your goal is not only to win a particular improvement, but also to keep the members together to build the organization. Earlier, I explained that you can't compromise on core principles when selecting your core group. However, objectives are the place where you can compromise. Otherwise, differences may come back to haunt you.

## Measures

To maintain your organization, you need to know how the organization is doing. Is it accomplishing what it set out to do? Is it meeting its objectives?

Measures will tell you that. You want to achieve your objectives—so you turn to the information you get from your measures to tell you where you stand. Knowing how you are doing also is important because it will help you to keep building the organization. Organizations that can demonstrate that they accomplish their objectives attract members.

In other words, measures are where the rubber meets the road. Measures state what results you are willing to hold yourself accountable for. Measures name what it will take to meet your objectives, and thereby, to achieve your goal. For example, to elect a candidate to the school committee, you may know that you need fifty volunteers, not ten. Measures tabulate and track what happens in the real world.

The number of votes in an electoral campaign, the amount of money raised toward a budget, the number of people recruited, the number of people who made changes in their lives, the number of people who attended a rally, the amount of media coverage of an issue—all of these are examples of useful measures.

Some measures are easily quantifiable, as in, "number of new people recruited." Others require a qualitative approach, such as, "foster a sense of community, caring, and support." That can be measured too, although it requires in-depth interviewing of the participants.

**CASE STUDY**

# Crafting Your Goals, Objectives, and Measures

*Your mission, goals, and objectives should flow from the general to the specific. You can then select measures that allow you to monitor achievement of objectives. This example is drawn from an organization I started.*

## Mission (excerpt): To create opportunities for young adults to work for justice and social change.

### Goal 1.
To help young adults develop career paths that promote social justice.

### Objective 1:
To recruit young adults into professional social justice jobs for at least a full year.

### Objective 2:
To work with these young adults on career development planning and to support them in their work in social justice.

## Objective 3:

To develop new jobs in social justice in community organizations.

## Objective 4:

To foster a sense of community, caring, and support among these young adults and connect them to a broad network of friends and allies in the city.

*You can see that the goal is more general, and the objectives create more specific targets. Then we specify how we will measure our progress toward our objectives by establishing measures.*

## Selected Measures:

1. Number of new people recruited.
2. Number of people who have found jobs in the past year and who have been assisted with jobs or job development.
3. Number of past participants attending regular meetings or participating in events.
4. Number of jobs created.
5. Number of jobs retained.

*Some groups prefer to assign a specific measure to each objective, or else you can list all the measures in one section, as I've done here.*

# Critique of a Group's Goals and Objectives

*I've already described the Camfield Tenants Association, the group of residents who rebuilt their housing development and then bought it from the government. What issues did they need to think about as they set their goals and objectives?*

## Goals:

The Camfield Tenants Association might set its goals as:

1. To rebuild the development.
2. To allow residents to return to affordable homes.
3. To establish a community center that helps residents.

## Objectives:

A selection of the objectives for these goals could be:

1. To rebuild 100 units of two- and three-bedroom homes.
2. To make sure that the building construction is sound.
3. To set rents at no more than 30 percent of gross income for 80 percent of the residents.
4. To develop a computer center with eighteen personal computers, staffed by a computer professional at least ten hours a day.

## Be Specific!

If you set out to "rebuild 100 units of two- and three-bedroom homes," do you need to specify how big the bedrooms will be? Will your members be satisfied with bedrooms that are six feet by eight feet? Do the bedrooms need two windows and cross-ventilation? Objectives must be specific so that you achieve exactly what you wanted to achieve—and avoid misunderstandings and disappointments that can divide your organization.

If half the people in your organization want all the bedrooms to have cross-ventilation and two windows, but your objectives don't state that design specification, then you may achieve your written objective of constructing new apartments but still lose half your members if all the new bedrooms don't have two windows and cross-ventilation. You met your objective, but the objective was not specific enough to meet the requirements of the members. In setting objectives, continually ask yourself, "Is this all we need to say? Is there anything else we need to put in here to make sure it does what we want?" Play the devil's advocate when setting objectives. With objectives, the devil lives in those details.

## Plans Can Change

Goals and objectives can evolve and change as you confront the results of the work. You have to be willing to learn as you go along. The knowledge you have before you start is different from the knowledge you have once you get going.

In building the Jewish Organizing Initiative, a training program for young Jewish adults in community organizing, one of our early goals was: *"To train Jewish young adults as community organizers and sustain them in this work."* We realized after a few years that not all the participants in the program would become community organizers. This was an unrealistic goal. This became clear as we saw who came into the program and what they did after the program. Participants often went on to other professions, but what mattered was *how they went about their work.* If they went into teaching, politics, the rabbinate, social work, public policy, or law, we could still influence *the way in which they approached* their work in their chosen profession.

So we changed our goal. It became: *"To help young adults to incorporate and sustain a grassroots organizing perspective in their lives and work."* A "grassroots organizing perspective" meant the understanding that those closest to a problem need to actively participate in planning and implementing any solution to the problem.

The new words were important. No longer were we solely in the business of "training community organizers"— which meant something specific and limited. Yes, we did that. But we also helped young adults "to incorporate and sustain" a specific approach to working for social change in many professional settings—employing a "grassroots organizing perspective" and community organizing skills. This perspective is missing from much professional training. If we could accomplish this, it would be valuable. The goal evolved as we observed the likely trajectories of the participants' careers and evaluated what we, realistically, could contribute.

## Story: Leaders Listen, Learn, and Are Willing to Change

Sometimes you change your objectives—your step-by-step strategies—when you realize that what you thought people needed is not what *they* think they need.

*Gladys Vega and others in Chelsea, Massachusetts, saw that many Latinos had little power in the city. So they set out to register low-income Latino voters, most of whom were from Puerto Rico. As Vega went door-knocking, urging people to register to vote, she heard that people really wanted a Spanish-language cable TV show. This frustrated her. She wanted them to register to vote! But she kept hearing about how much people wanted Spanish-language TV.*

*So Vega's group changed its campaign. They negotiated with the local cable television company—which had a contract with the city—to set up a new Spanish-language TV show. They won that issue and then went on to register many new voters. But first they had to listen to what people said was their priority, rather than only sticking to a pre-written plan.*

Sometimes a plan that seems eminently sensible to your core group can get in the way of improving people's lives if you stick to it rigidly in the face of new information. The group's mission—to increase the power of Latinos in the city—did not change. Vega and her colleagues showed that there are many paths (many goals and objectives) to follow that will help you to pursue your core mission of improving people's lives.

## Story: "Enemies" Can Become Allies

Sometimes you change plans when you realize that the people you thought were your enemies turn out to be friends.

*Many of the parents at a school were angry with their children's teachers. These low-income parents thought that the teachers were not teaching their children well or treating their children with respect. They thought that the teachers did not recognize the potential in their kids. But as they fought with the teachers, the parents slowly realized that many of the teachers really were committed to quality teaching and that the teachers respected their children. The parents changed. They shifted their strategy from treating the teachers as enemies to joining with the teachers as allies. They began demanding better conditions for their children <u>along with</u> the teachers, instead of working <u>against</u> the teachers.*

*It was not an easy change. It came about because the parents did not rigidly stick with their original plan. Instead, the parents kept learning as they went along. When they saw that the teachers' attitudes did not match up with the group's original assumptions, the parents changed the way they pursued their goals. Their goal didn't change, but their objectives—how they went about pursuing their goal—did.*

Community organizations operate in the world as it is, not as we wish or imagine the world to be. Part of the job of building an organization is to continually reflect upon our goals, objectives, and assumptions. That is why we write out objectives and measures of those objectives. From the mission to the goals to the objectives, we constantly ask ourselves: Is this where we want to go? Then, is it *possible* to accomplish that goal with our limited resources, the conditions we face, and the power we have?

We also have to ask ourselves: What are we learning as we go along? Sometimes the situation changes, and sometimes our understanding, knowledge, or assumptions change.

## CHAPTER 4

# Structure: How to Build Your Organization to Last

*Contrary to what we would like to believe, there is no such thing as a structureless group. Any group of people of whatever nature coming together for any length of time, for any purpose, will inevitably structure itself in some fashion. The structure may be flexible, it may vary over time, it may evenly or unevenly distribute tasks, power and resources over the members of the group. But it will be formed regardless of the abilities, personalities and intentions of the people involved. The very fact that we are individuals with different talents, predispositions and backgrounds makes this inevitable. Only if we refused to relate or interact on any basis whatsoever could we approximate structurelessness and that is not the nature of a human group.*

—Jo Freeman, "The Tyranny of Structurelessness"

How do you develop a structure that meets your group's needs?

Building a new organization or strengthening an old one requires work on the organization's structure. "Structure" includes the group's decision-making rules, meeting locations and times, legal status, funding, membership guidelines and dues, mission, goals, objectives, and group dynamics. Some organizations, like the military or a police department, where important decisions must be carried out in seconds, require tight structures and clear lines of authority. Other organizations can work with more democratic decision-making.

# ▶ Structure Matters

## Uncovering Hidden Structures

Every organization has a structure. The first question may be, "What is that structure?" The second question must be, "Is that structure clear to anyone wanting to participate?"

The organization's structure may not be written down. It may be hidden. But I guarantee you—it has a structure. In "The Tyranny of Structurelessness," Jo Freeman, who came out of the feminist movement of the 1960s and '70s, observes that some early feminist consciousness-raising groups thought they had no structure. But they *did* have a structure. It just was not explicit. People had varied degrees of power and influence within the group, stemming from personal characteristics, charisma, and knowledge. This is impossible to avoid.

Some groups make the mistake of not being explicit about their structure. This allows unspoken lines of authority to exist without acknowledging them. Still, the structure can be deduced from the group's behavior.

**CASE STUDY**

## The "Structureless" Coalition

This story about a well-meaning organization illustrates the importance of making the organization's structure explicit. The organization began with the best intentions. However, inattention to elements of structure may hinder its effectiveness.

*A social service organization providing mental health and other services received state funding to develop a "coalition" (this was the word the grant used) to deal with the drug problem in its town. A mental health pro-*

*fessional called the first meeting. She announced the meeting in the local paper and called people she knew in the substance abuse field. The meeting was set for a weekday at 10:00 a.m. at the mental health center.*

*Theoretically, anyone could come. According to the notice in the paper and the conditions of the state grant, the meeting was open to the public. But the person who called the meeting invited people she knew. It was not hard to get them to attend, with the lure of money possibly going to their agencies. The meeting focused on ways to get more state money to the various alcohol and drug treatment agencies in town to deal with the problem.*

At first glance this group has little or no structure. It's just a meeting of well-intentioned people trying to get needed services in their community. But there is a structure, and that structure determines what the group will accomplish and where its power lies.

Let's examine the group's structure.

*When do they meet?* At 10:00 a.m. on a weekday, a difficult time for community people to attend, but convenient for professional service providers. There is no child care, making it difficult for parents of small children to attend.

*Where do they meet?* At the mental health center. The setting is familiar to the service providers. If they had met in the church basement where Alcoholics Anonymous meets, it would have had an implicit connection to A.A. This way it has a connection to the mental health center.

*Who is a member of the group?* Theoretically, anyone and no one. A notice is in the newspaper in small type. Most people don't see it. There are no dues and no specific membership criteria. There are no requirements that members believe that any method of substance abuse prevention or treatment is any more effective than any other. There is no expectation that anyone is accountable for any decision the group makes. Without any explicit membership criteria, a member is anyone who shows up.

*Who decides what gets done?* Theoretically, "the community." That is the goal of this publicly funded "coalition." There is no written decision-making process announced at the meeting.

Many of the attendees already know each other. The implicit decision-making process is a modified consensus model. The similar world views and experience of the participants allow this.

*Who sets the agenda of the meeting?* The social worker who called the meeting. She frames the agenda around how to get grants to service providers.

*Who pays for the group?* The mental health center pays for the meeting expenses, including the meeting space and the coffee and doughnuts. The social worker calls certain people and plans the meeting on company time. This provides the mental health organization with influence within the group. It has the membership list and the meeting space. (To determine who organizes a meeting, observe who collects the sign-in list and who sends out the minutes.)

## Why Is This Structure Important?

There is nothing sinister or unusual here. Although it looks like there is no structure to this group, there *is* a structure. One must deduce it by observation. It is not written down anywhere.

This is how most groups begin. They run into trouble when they do not decide if the implicit structure, the structure they fall into by default, is the one they want.

The group could ask itself some structural questions:

Does the group want the mental health agency to pay for the group? What does this mean for the group?

Does the group want to meet at 10:00 a.m.? Whom does this exclude?

Does the group want the social worker to chair the meeting, or does the group want to elect a chair?

Should the group allow anyone to attend? Can they exclude the liquor store owner? Do they want the participation of the city councilor who wants to run for mayor?

Do they want to establish some guidelines about conflicts of interest?

If the group pays no attention to its structure it opens itself up to trouble. If anyone can be a member, twenty people can walk in off the street, form a majority at the meeting, and demand that the group ask the City Council to ban smoking in all public buildings in the city, or give a grant to Ms. Lorraine's Dance Studio because she really knows how to keep kids off drugs. If they are a majority of those in that particular meeting, does the group have to abide by that vote?

## Structure and Accountability

Structure may establish rules, but, like any laws, rules need monitoring and enforcement.

### Story: Accountability Means Counting

*I once worked with a federally funded group organized to fight infant mortality in a low-income community. The grant required that half the decision-making body be low-income residents (not social service providers) of the affected community. These were primarily low-income women at risk of giving birth to children of low birth weight, a common link to infant mortality.*

*The group needed to hold itself accountable. It did this by regular monitoring. The first item on every meeting's agenda was to count the number of people present from the groups they wanted to be represented. This simple act, counting and announcing the numbers, helped hold the group accountable. The members did not blame themselves if they did not reach their goals at every meeting, but the simple act of counting at every meeting reminded members to try to reach their goals.*

If they were not meeting their representative participation goals, they could find out why. Did the community people need rides? Did they need child care?

(Don't guess why those not there are not there. *Ask them:* "What would allow you to attend? Exactly what would you need?")

If you only mandate something in the structure but don't monitor your progress, you are not doing your job. If you don't provide the necessary backup (child care, rides, etc.), the meeting is not really accessible—in spite of the clear written structure.

## Structure and Meaningful Participation

If the desired outcome is meaningful participation by the low-income community, warm bodies on chairs are not enough if those warm bodies don't have a clue about what's going on at the meetings. People can be effectively excluded even when physically present. Without adequate coaching and direction you get tokenism, not participation.

In this example, the grant mandated community representatives, but the chair of the group spoke in language only a Ph.D. could understand. Those people with less formal education were effectively left out. The structure is necessary, but it is only a start. You need to make sure that the results are real, not only words on paper.

## Coaching for Participation—Developing a Common Language

Sometimes people with advanced degrees may be leading a meeting. How do you get those with less formal education—but who are the real experts about their own situation—to participate in a meaningful way? Active participation with such varied levels of formal education requires preparation. This often means, before the meeting, coaching those you want to include. If you don't have the background, find someone who is experienced in both worlds who can coach group members.

### How to Coach for Participation— Working Across Class, Education, or Experience Backgrounds

1. Sit down with the person or people you are coaching. Emphasize that their input is important. All members have a right to ask any questions they want. Make it clear that the members are the real experts. (They probably feel this way anyway.) The theory of group behavior endorses this.

2. Start with *their* questions.

3. Over the course of the coaching session, explain the history and background of the organization, where the money comes from, and any obscure terms.

4. Arrange how you will communicate during the meeting, since they will be doing the talking, but may want your support. You might whisper or write notes. Let the person or people know that you will be there as a resource during the meeting.

5. At the meeting, the coach should sit next to the people who have been coached, providing informa-

tion or support as requested. Use the off-to-the-side communication method you have agreed to. The people you are supporting should explain to the others at the table your role at the meeting and why you are sitting with them.

## Structural Elements Can Define Organizations

You may be in an organization or you may want to form a new organization. In either case, it is useful to examine some elements that define an organization's structure. Some common distinctions or boundaries that organizations choose in order to define and focus themselves include:

- Geographic boundaries: Many organizations limit themselves to a geographic area. They may be bounded by a street (a block club), a small neighborhood (a neighborhood association), a town or city, a region, a state, or a nation. Some are international.

- Issues focus: Some organizations limit themselves to one issue. These include organizations that focus on the environment, women's rights, education, health care, gun owners' rights, adoption, etc. The list is virtually endless.

- Membership criteria: Some groups allow individuals or families to join. Others allow only organizations or institutions to join. These are organizations of organizations. Some groups are for professionals only; some are gender-based. There are all kinds of choices groups can make around membership styles. The decision depends on what makes sense with your mission.

## ▶ Key Elements of Structure

If you are going to be smart about creating or revising your structure, you will want to look at all of the elements that go into creating a group's structure. On the following pages, you will work through an extended exercise format to look at the key features that define your group's structure, one element at a time. This exercise should help you to identify what your group's structure is and what you want it to be— and to make sure that the two match. This is an absolutely necessary step in making sure that your organization's structure is helping your group to make the changes you want in the world around you.

**EXERCISE**

### Finding Your Structure

This exercise is designed to help you get the kind of structure you want, rather than letting structure form by default or by assenting to the loudest or most charismatic person in the room. Under each category, you start in the left column, documenting the structure you have now, whether it is hidden or overt. Then, in the right column, you will check to see if that is the structure you want. The columns are sub-divided into boxed-off rows. Each boxed row focuses on a specific line of questioning. Within each row, read across the columns before moving on to the next row. Just follow the question numbers; they will guide you across the rows and down the columns from subject to subject.

With this exercise you:

1. Gather the data by examining how your group actually behaves.
2. Draw some conclusions about what the data says about your organization.
3. Answer the questions: Is this the way you want your organization to be? Is this the organization you want?

The exercise is spread out over the next several sections of the chapter, as we work our way through the various elements of organizational structure. I recommend that you fill in each worksheet as you come to it.

# Finding Your Structure, Part I

| What Your Group Actually Does | Is This What Your Group Wants to Be Doing? Should This Be the Group's Practice? |
|---|---|

## A. Mission, Goals, and Objectives

1. What is your mission statement?

_____

_____

_____

_____

_____

_____

_____

_____

_____

2. Is this what you want your mission statement to be?

❏ Yes ❏ No

3. If you don't have a mission statement, what steps can you take to secure the group's commitment to a plan for getting one written?

_____

_____

_____

4. What are your goals and objectives?

_____

_____

_____

_____

_____

_____

_____

_____

_____

5. Do they match what you want your goals and objectives to be?

❏ Yes ❏ No

6. If you don't have written goals and objectives, what steps can you take to secure the group's commitment to a plan for getting them written?

_____

_____

| What Your Group Does... | What Your Group Wants... |
|---|---|

### B. Size

| | |
|---|---|
| 1. How big is your group? | 2. Is this the size you want for your organization?<br><br>❏ Yes  ❏ No<br><br>3. If not, what size would you like it to be? What is your numeric goal? |
| 4. Do you have any limits on the size of membership?<br><br>❏ Yes  ❏ No<br><br>(My congregation once set a membership cap of 450 families, recognizing that organizations that grow beyond that size have trouble creating a sense of community.) | 5. Would you benefit from setting such a limit?<br><br>❏ Yes  ❏ No<br><br>6. Thoughts or comments about that? |

### C. Staffing

| | |
|---|---|
| 1. Do you have paid staff in your organization?<br><br>❏ Yes  ❏ No<br><br>2. Or is it all-volunteer?<br><br>❏ Yes  ❏ No | 3. Should you have paid staff?<br><br>❏ Yes  ❏ No<br><br>4. Do you want/need more staff?<br><br>❏ Yes  ❏ No<br><br>5. Or less staff?<br><br>❏ Yes  ❏ No |
| 6. What title do you call the staff? (E.g., Organizer? Coordinator? Director? Etc.) | 7. Does this fit your organization?<br><br>❏ Yes  ❏ No |

| What Your Group Does... | What Your Group Wants... |
|---|---|
| 8. What do the staff member(s) do? <br><br> _____ <br> _____ <br> _____ <br> _____ | 9. Are these the primary roles and functions that you want the staff to be filling? <br><br> ❏ Yes ❏ No |
| 10. Who supervises your staff? _____ <br> How? What is the actual supervision process? <br><br> _____ <br> _____ <br> _____ | 11. Is this the supervision process and responsibility chain that you want for your group? <br><br> ❏ Yes ❏ No |
| 12. What is your staff paid? <br><br> _____ <br> _____ | 13. Is this the right salary to get the needed work done and to fit within your resource constraints? <br><br> ❏ Yes ❏ No |
| 14. What are the benefits that your group provides to its staff? (Health, dental, pension, short and long-term disability, vacation, comp time, etc.) <br><br> _____ <br> _____ <br> _____ | 15. Are these the benefits you want to give? <br><br> ❏ Yes ❏ No |

| What Your Group Does... | What Your Group Wants... |
|---|---|

## D. Time Frame

1. How long do you assume the organization will be in existence?

2. How long do you want it to be in existence?

## E. Collaborations

1. Do you have agreements or relationships with any other groups?

   ❑ Yes  ❑ No

2. Do you want to have relationships with any other groups?

   ❑ Yes  ❑ No

3. How would having (or not having) collaborations help you to achieve your goals?

   _____
   _____
   _____
   _____

4. What are your key collaborative relationships?

   _____
   _____
   _____
   _____
   _____
   _____
   _____
   _____

5. Are these the right collaborators for achieving your goals?

   ❑ Yes  ❑ No

6. With what groups or entities would you like your organization to have agreements or relationships?

   _____
   _____
   _____

## Leadership

Take a close look at what happens in your group regarding leadership, authority, responsibility, and decision-making. Whoever calls meetings has formal authority and a lot of influence over what will (and will not) happen. Sometimes a group may make a decision, but someone else later may change that decision. If that happens, it tells you something about the real structure and authority in the group—no matter what it says on paper about your structure. There are steps you can take to build healthy leadership processes into your group. These include setting up formal pathways for ongoing and open communication, creating multiple ways for people to exercise leadership, coming to formal agreement about how meetings can be called, and agreeing on term limits that can foster continual development of new leadership.

**EXERCISE**

# Finding Your Structure, Part 2

| What Your Group Actually Does | Is This What Your Group Wants to Be Doing? Should This Be the Group's Practice? |
|---|---|
| **A. Leadership** | |
| 1. Who call the meetings? | 2. Is this how you want your meetings to be called?  ❑ Yes  ❑ No |
| 3. Who is the chair? | 4. Is this the person who you want to chair the meetings?  ❑ Yes  ❑ No |

**What Your Group Does...**

5. Do you have any committees?

   ❑ Yes ❑ No

6. If so, what are they?

   _____

   _____

   _____

   _____

   _____

   _____

   _____

   _____

10. Do you have officers or other specified leaders?

    ❑ Yes ❑ No

11. If so, what are the leadership position titles? (List them)

    _____

    _____

    _____

    _____

    _____

    _____

13. How do you choose officers or board members?

    _____

    _____

    _____

**What Your Group Wants...**

7. Are these the committees you want?

   ❑ Yes ❑ No

8. What committees would you add?

   _____

   _____

   _____

9. What committees would you remove?

   _____

   _____

   _____

12. Are these the leadership positions you want?

    ❑ Yes ❑ No

14. Is this how you want to choose officers or board members?

    ❑ Yes ❑ No

| What Your Group Does... | What Your Group Wants... |
|---|---|
| 15. What are the lengths of service of your officers and leaders? | 18. If you don't have term limits, do you want them? ❑ Yes ❑ No |
| 16. Are there term or time limits for leadership? ❑ Yes ❑ No | 19. If you have term limits on leadership, are these the terms you want? ❑ Yes ❑ No |
| 17. If so, what are the term limits? | |
| 20. Who decides things around here? (Who makes proposals? Who follows up?) | 21. Is this who you would like to have making the decisions? ❑ Yes ❑ No |

## Story: Structure Saves the Day

*The City's Department of Health and Hospitals (DH&H) received a six million dollar federal grant to lower infant mortality in a low-income community. The grant required DH&H to develop a community group to advise and guide the effort. I was hired to set up a Memorandum of Agreement between DH&H and this new community council.*

*One of the initiative's first tasks was to hire a director for the project. I knew that a key issue would be how the Memo of Agreement structured responsibility for the hir-*

*ing, evaluation, and potential for firing of the director. That was where the power would lie.*

*DH&H wanted control over the hiring and firing of the director. They argued that they were legally responsible for the grant and needed control over the director. But the grant also specified that they were supposed to be guided by the Community Council. The grant said nothing about who had control over the director. The Community Council understood that the hiring and firing of the director were critical issues in the Memorandum of Agreement.*

*We had many meetings and many arguments over the language of the Memo. I was adamant that the Community Council have veto power over the hiring and potential firing of the director. After long negotiations, both the community people and DH&H officials agreed to hire or fire only if both parties could agree. Both, in effect, had veto power. There were other issues in the Memo, but I knew this was the critical one. Structure matters.*

*A year or so later, the DH&H officials wanted to fire the director. The structure of the organization—the hiring and firing power detailed in the Memo of Agreement—stopped them from doing so.*

## Meetings

The way you set up meetings is about structure. The structures you use in your meetings will affect how successful and powerful your group is. This is especially true when it comes to organizing meetings that are welcoming to members and that foster a sense of member ownership of the organization.

### Turf Counts!

In building community organizations, it matters where you meet. Some people are more comfortable in certain locations. Location says a lot about who counts in the organization. Is the location in the city or suburbs? Corporate office or a church basement? Is it in a place where Black folks (or White folks, or Latinos, etc.) feel at home? If in doubt, ask.

## With Meetings, Timing Matters

If it is the norm in your group's culture to start on time, then start on time. More important, end on time. You want people to come back. Otherwise, you will create some very annoyed members. Questions about time can be culturally driven. Some cultures say four o'clock and people normally come at six. You need to learn the territory. Not all cultures or people run by the clock—but some cultures and some people do. Any group that wants to succeed needs to know its members' expectations around time.

## Recurring Gatherings Can Hold the Community Together

One effective way to build community cohesion for your group is to create shared rituals. Holding regularly recurring meetings is a very basic and very powerful ritual that some groups use. These are events that occur every week or month at a set time and place. There is no need to check your appointment book to see if you can attend. It just gets built into your schedule.

Religious congregations do this. Every Saturday or Sunday or some other day, from a set time to a set time, you know the congregation will be gathering. The same people are likely to be there. No need to call ahead to make an appointment. Most congregations seem to have settled upon seven as the magic number—they need to gather every seven days. Not six, not eight. Every six days would mean we would not be getting our work done. Eight days would be too much of a stretch—too much work and too little rest.

Outside of religious congregations, it often is tough for a new group to meet weekly for more than a year. Members typically just don't have the time to set aside for the meetings. But weekly meetings provide a model of how to build a sense of strong community into an organization. Even if the group can't meet weekly, you can at least make a point of talking weekly with someone from the group.

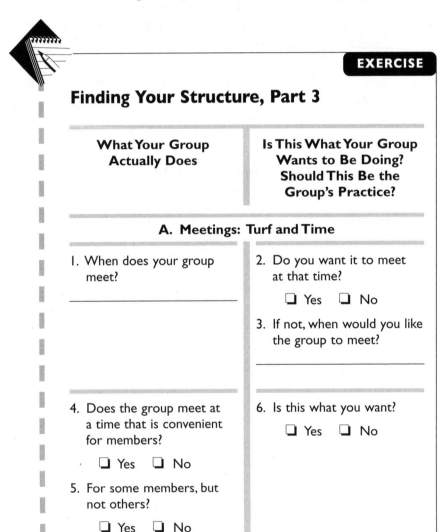

**EXERCISE**

## Finding Your Structure, Part 3

| What Your Group Actually Does | Is This What Your Group Wants to Be Doing? Should This Be the Group's Practice? |
|---|---|
| **A. Meetings: Turf and Time** | |
| 1. When does your group meet? | 2. Do you want it to meet at that time?  ❑ Yes  ❑ No  3. If not, when would you like the group to meet? |
| 4. Does the group meet at a time that is convenient for members?  ❑ Yes  ❑ No  5. For some members, but not others?  ❑ Yes  ❑ No | 6. Is this what you want?  ❑ Yes  ❑ No |

| What Your Group Does... | What Your Group Wants... |
|---|---|
| 7. Where does the group meet? | 8. Is this where you want the group to meet?<br><br>❑ Yes ❑ No<br><br>9. Would alternate locations make meetings more accessible for some members?<br><br>❑ Yes ❑ No<br><br>10. If so, where? |
| 11. How long are the meetings? | 12. Is this the right length?<br><br>❑ Yes ❑ No |
| 13. Do your meetings start on time?<br><br>❑ Yes ❑ No<br><br>14. If not, how late or early do they start? | 15. Do you want meetings to start on time?<br><br>❑ Yes ❑ No<br><br>16. What strategies can you use to achieve this?<br><br>(One simple method is to set a policy that you will always start at the stated time no matter who is there.) |
| 17. Do they end on time?<br><br>❑ Yes ❑ No<br><br>18. If not, how late or early? | 19. Is this what you want?<br><br>❑ Yes ❑ No |

| What Your Group Does... | What Your Group Wants... |
|---|---|
| **B. Meeting Procedures** | |
| 1. How are your meetings run? <br><br>_____ <br>_____ <br>_____ | 2. Is this how you want your meetings to be run? <br><br>❏ Yes    ❏ No |
| 3. Do you have ground rules for meetings? <br><br>❏ Yes    ❏ No <br><br>4. If yes, are they explicit or just assumed? <br><br>_____ <br><br>5. What are the key ground rules (if any)? <br><br>_____ <br>_____ <br>_____ | 6. Are these the ground rules you want? <br><br>❏ Yes    ❏ No |
| **C. Decision-making at Meetings** | |
| 1. Who is eligible to vote/make decisions? <br><br>_____ <br>_____ <br><br>2. Is this in writing? <br><br>❏ Yes    ❏ No | 3. Is this who you want to be vested with decision-making authority? <br><br>❏ Yes    ❏ No <br><br>4. If this is not in writing, how can you secure the group's commitment to put it in writing? <br><br>_____ <br>_____ <br>_____ <br>_____ |

| What Your Group Does... | What Your Group Wants... |
|---|---|
| 5. Do you vote and use majority rule? (This may be efficient, but can create bad feelings among the losers.) <br><br> ❏ Yes ❏ No | 8. Is this the way you want to make decisions? <br><br> ❏ Yes ❏ No |
| 6. Or do you make decisions by consensus? (With consensus, the group deliberates and discusses until everyone agrees, or at least is willing to go along for the sake of the group. This method may produce fewer losers but it can take much longer to make decisions.) <br><br> ❏ Yes ❏ No | |
| 7. Or do you use some other method? If so, what is it? <br><br> _____ <br> _____ <br> _____ | |
| 9. Do you have bylaws? <br><br> ❏ Yes ❏ No | 10. If not, do you want them? <br><br> ❏ Yes ❏ No |
| 11. What is considered a quorum for your group? <br><br> _____ | 13. Is this working for your group? Is it the way you want it to be? <br><br> ❏ Yes ❏ No |
| 12. Can members vote by proxy? <br><br> ❏ Yes ❏ No | |

### Story: You Can't Please All of the People ...

*Most of the members of the Maverick Square Neighbor-hood Association wanted to visit the District Attorney who had taken away their walking beat patrolman. One member of the group did not want to go. She thought it might alienate the D.A. This was a small group. They had never decided how they would make decisions. They did not want to offend one member, so they waited for months, as the neighborhood felt less and less safe each day. Finally they decided to visit the D.A. in spite of this one member's concerns. By trying to please one person, they had made life worse for many others.*

*"We were a small team. We felt we couldn't lose someone," Don Nanstad, a leader of the group said later, reflecting on what had happened. But not deciding how they would make decisions hurt the group and their neighborhood.*

### Story: Don't Count Your Votes Unless You Know Who Can Vote

*A colleague thought he had the chairmanship of a politi-cal caucus sewn up. He did, until the evening of the meet-ing when the election was held. A competitor for the chairmanship walked into the meeting with twenty of his supporters. These supporters had never been to a meeting before. The rules of the group were loose. Anyone in the room could vote. My colleague lost the election. The group had no restrictions or qualifications for voting privileges.*

My town's local Democratic Committee, in contrast, has specific qualifications for voting privileges: One has to attend several evening meetings before becoming an Asso-ciate Member. Then one has to pay dues. Then, to become a Full Member, one has to be voted in by a certain number of existing members at a following meeting. Only after becoming a Full Member can one vote on committee policy.

## Legal Status

At first you may think that questions about legal status do not seem very relevant to the work at hand, but someone in your group needs to think through your legal structure so that you can be as effective as possible. It is all about designing a structure that will make you the most powerful.

Many groups start out all volunteer, and only later, as they grow, hire paid staff. Similarly, community groups often start off informally, without any legal status. As they grow, they may discover that they need more money. They can incorporate as a non-profit so that they can accept tax-deductible donations and are eligible for government and private foundation grants. This status, called 501(c)(3) status in reference to the specific IRS code that guides non-profit tax law, also qualifies a group to be exempt from paying taxes. See the Appendix for a fuller discussion of becoming a 501(c)(3) organization. I will just mention here that the process of acquiring this designation can take at least six months and requires the work of a lawyer with expertise in this specific area of the law. After you become a 501(c)(3) there are a number of legal, fiscal, and reporting requirements with which your organization will need to comply, so many groups wait a number of years before incorporating.

If you are not prepared to incorporate, you can still qualify for tax-deductible donations by asking another non-profit organization to act as your fiscal agent. A fiscal agent is a tax-exempt organization with IRS 501(c)(3) tax status that accepts tax-deductible contributions on behalf of the group. This allows donors to make tax-deductible contributions to the organization. The fiscal agent generally takes a percentage of those contributions, typically five percent to fifteen percent, for its administrative work.

Note: Groups whose primary function is lobbying or campaigning for an election may not be eligible for 501(c)(3) status. The IRS or a non-profit lawyer can guide you about this. But you need to know what the law says you can and cannot do if you have 501(c)(3) status.

## Finding Your Structure, Part 4

| What Your Group Actually Does | Is This What Your Group Wants to Be Doing? Should This Be the Group's Practice? |
|---|---|
| **A. Legal Status** | |
| 1. Do you have your own non-profit status as determined by the IRS, often known as 501(c)(3) status, which allows the organization to accept tax-deductible contributions? ❑ Yes ❑ No ❑ Pending – Or – 2. Do you have a fiscal agent? ❑ Yes ❑ No 3. Who is it? _____ – Or – 4. None of the above? ❑ Yes ❑ No | 5. Is this the legal status you want? ❑ Yes ❑ No |

## What Your Group Does...

6. If you have a fiscal agent, does this agent influence your organization's activities?

   ❏ Yes   ❏ No

7. If so, how?

   _____

   _____

## What Your Group Wants...

8. Are you satisfied with the nature of that influence?

   ❏ Yes   ❏ No

9. Do you want this entity to be influencing your activities?

   ❏ Yes   ❏ No

## B. Money

1. Who pays for what?

   _____

   ("He who pays the piper calls the tune." Whoever provides money has influence.)

3. Where do you get your money?

   _____

   _____

   _____

2. Is this who you want to be paying?

   ❏ Yes   ❏ No

4. Is this how you want to get your money?

   ❏ Yes   ❏ No

5. If not, do you have any plans to get it another way?

   ❏ Yes   ❏ No

6. If so, what are those plans?

   _____

   _____

   _____

   _____

7. Who is following up to make sure that it happens?

   _____

   _____

| What Your Group Does... | What Your Group Wants... |
|---|---|
| 8. How much money do you have? _____ | 9. Is this the amount you need? ❏ Yes ❏ No<br><br>10. How much do you need? _____ |
| 11. What do you spend most of your money on? (What are the biggest areas of annual expenditure, e.g., Personnel? Food? Rent? Something else?)<br><br>_____<br>_____<br>_____<br>_____<br>_____ | 12. Is this how you want to spend your money? ❏ Yes ❏ No |

## ▶ Members

### Basic Membership Criteria

Most organizations start off informally. People get together to accomplish something. They don't think about who is a member, who is in, and who is out. It may seem unnecessary or obvious. "The members are us"—whoever is in the room. But when you build an organization, you need to think: What does it mean to be a member of this group? What does a member need to do? What does a member have to believe in? What kind of person do we want? Do we take just anyone who walks in the door? If we do, what might that mean in the future for our organization?

You need to know what constitutes membership. You may define a member any way you want, but at some point your organization needs to set boundaries. You need to distinguish a member from just anybody who walks in the room during your meeting. Membership might have its privileges. It should also have its responsibilities and criteria.

The membership criteria will depend on your group. If you are trying to build a democratic organization, two basic criteria for membership might include:

1. All members have to agree with the mission of the organization.
2. All members have to agree with and act according to the values of the organization.

I like the three values that Gregory Pierce describes (from *Activism That Makes Sense*):

1. *Equality:* All people—regardless of race, sexual orientation, gender, ethnic origin, religion, culture, disability—are allowed to become members and are treated with respect.

2. *Democracy:* All members agree that they will abide by the will of the organization, democratically decided.

3. *Accountability:* All members agree that they will do what they say they will do for the organization. They will be accountable for following through on their word.

These three easy-to-understand general agreements for all members—equality, democracy, and accountability—help to build an organization that is democratic. They express values that make the expectations of membership clear. Potential members will know up front what the group stands for, and what the group will not stand for. These agreements will screen out people who want the group to be exclusionary. Potential members will also know how the group will make decisions. They will know that the group will expect them to do what they say they will do and that the organization expects them to participate, not only to receive benefits from membership in the group.

## Membership Dues

Some community groups ask for minimal or no dues because they want to make it easy for people to join. They think people won't be able to afford more. This can lead to low commitment of members.

Ask yourself: How will the amount of dues affect the level of ownership and commitment of the members? Groups that require more significant dues often (but not always) find their members more committed. Personal investment often follows financial investment. You want members to feel invested in the organization.

### *Story: Don't Sell People Short*

*A colleague tells the story of founding a community organization of low-income people in the 1980s. He suggested that the dues be $10, thinking, "These are not wealthy people. They can't afford much." He was surprised when they came back to him and said, "We want to pay $25 a year." They knew that if they paid so little, they would have less influence over the organization. They knew that if they cared about something, they would have to pay for it. The dues became $25. My colleague learned an important lesson: If you want people to feel a sense of ownership and to hold the organization accountable, ask for a significant donation.*

# Finding Your Structure, Part 5

| What Your Group Actually Does | Is This What Your Group Wants to Be Doing? Should This Be the Group's Practice? |
|---|---|

## A. Becoming a Member

| | |
|---|---|
| 1. How does someone join? <br><br>_____ <br> _____ | 2. Does this process work for your organization? <br><br> ❏ Yes ❏ No |
| 3. What are the membership criteria? <br><br>_____ <br> _____ | 4. Are these the membership criteria you want? <br><br> ❏ Yes ❏ No |
| 5. Can anyone join? <br><br> ❏ Yes ❏ No <br> (E.g., Some community groups bar elected officials from membership to avoid the risk of becoming a vehicle for an individual official's political or electoral goals.) | 6. Is this what you want? <br><br> ❏ Yes ❏ No |
| 7. Are people required to agree to any rules of behavior upon joining? <br><br> ❏ Yes ❏ No | 8. Are these the rules for behavior you want? <br><br> ❏ Yes ❏ No <br><br> 9. If not, how could you institute new ones? <br><br>_____ <br> _____ |

| What Your Group Does... | What Your Group Wants... |
|---|---|
| 10. Are there membership dues?<br><br>❑ Yes  ❑ No<br><br>11. If so, how much are they?<br><br>_____ | 12. Are these the dues you want?<br><br>❑ Yes  ❑ No |
| 13. How do you think the presence of dues or the dues level affects the organization and its work? (E.g., Might the dues affect how involved your members are, the size of your membership, or how independent your organization is?)<br><br>_____<br><br>_____ | 14. Is this the result you want?<br><br>❑ Yes  ❑ No |

## ▶ Values and Group Norms

Values give your organization a direction; group norms give your organization the guideposts it needs to travel on that route safely and effectively.

### Values Are Key

The values that undergird an organization are key elements of the organization's structure. As much as membership guidelines, bylaws, and leadership structures, they form the foundation of the organization. You cannot build an organization to work for equality, respect, and fairness when these values are not present in the organization's daily workings.

## Setting Group Norms

How does an organization develop its core values? How does it set norms for group behavior? Successful organizations know their core values and model appropriate ways for members to treat each other.

### Story: Setting Group Norms In Real Time— The Brockton Interfaith Community

It is not enough to *say,* "We respect all people," if the group allows personal attacks at meetings. This story illustrates why it is important to pay close attention to group norm formation as well as to the overall and immediate goals of the organization.

*Thirty people sit on folding chairs in a church basement in Brockton, Massachusetts. There are a priest, a minister, and a rabbi among them, and members from thirteen churches and synagogues in the city.*

*Before them is a list of demands that they intend to present to the mayoral candidates at their upcoming annual convention. They call it "BIC's [Brockton Interfaith Community] Rebuild the City Plan."*

*Talking about the issues, one member proposes a value for the group, saying, "I'd like no potholes. I have an old car. But I'd rather have money for schools and libraries."*

*One choice now for the BIC members, in this city besieged by budget cuts, is clear. Do they fix the potholes or fix the schools? The organization's priorities reflect the group's values.*

*There is a question about the tax rate, and then one man says that another is "talking like a demagogue." Suddenly, an awkward silence fills the room. No one has ever personally attacked another member like this. In the silence, it seems that no one is sure what to do. It's a key moment for the organization to affirm its values and establish its norms for group behavior. Even if people don't agree with one another's positions on some issue, there has been a tacit understanding that members don't attack each other personally. The silence hangs heavy in the air for several moments. Then the meeting moves on to cover the business and decide on the agenda for the annual meeting.*

*At a break I ask Marty, BIC's president, to step into the back hallway for a moment, where we can speak privately. I mention the "demagogue" comment and suggest that she, as president, should say something to indicate that such comments are unwelcome at the meeting. She can explain that it is okay to criticize an idea or policy, but not to attack each other personally.*

### Forming Group Norms

*When the group reconvenes, Marty explains that the comment is not in the spirit of BIC. Then several members say that they have come together around their understanding that the spirit of God is in everyone, and it is wrong for anyone to attack another's motives or to attack someone personally. A murmur of approval spreads across the room. A group norm for conduct in meetings is affirmed. The power of the group to express its values weighs on the man who made the attack. He senses the displeasure of the others in the room and remains quiet. He now knows that such comments are not welcome and he, and others, will be less likely to make such comments in the future.*

The values of the organization include not only its political goals, but also the norms about how people treat each other in meetings.

### What Does the Organization Stand For?

Is the organization only about extracting specific, concrete improvements from politicians? If the organization interrupts the meeting's immediate task (in this case, deciding on the agenda for the annual meeting), then it is making a clear statement that *how* the group gets to its goals matters. Alongside its civic agenda, the organization also stands for respecting each member, for building a sense of community and caring among its members. That is also part of its business. If the organization had let the "demagogue" comment go by without opposition, then it might have drifted into a different kind of organization, one focused solely on winning specific improvements, without clear values about how it wins them.

## Story: Linking Social Change Activism with Shared Religious Values

For some types of groups, especially religious groups, the values and norms are clear.

*Everyone involved in the desegregation campaign in Birmingham, Alabama, in the 1960s was asked to sign a commitment card.*

### Each signer pledged to:

1. Meditate daily on the teachings and life of Jesus.
2. Remember always that the non-violent movement in Birmingham seeks justice and reconciliation—not victory.
3. Walk and talk in the manner of love, for God is love.
4. Pray daily to be used by God in order that all [people] might be free.
5. Sacrifice personal wishes in order that all [people] might be free.
6. Observe with both friend and foe the ordinary rules of courtesy.
7. Seek to perform regular service for others and for the world.
8. Refrain from the violence of fist, tongue, or heart.
9. Strive to be in good spiritual and bodily health.
10. Follow the directions of the movement and of the captain of a demonstration.

# Finding Your Structure, Part 6

| What Your Group Actually Does | Is This What Your Group Wants to Be Doing? Should This Be the Group's Practice? |
|---|---|

## A. Values

**1. What are the values your organization expresses?**

_____

_____

_____

_____

_____

_____

_____

**2. Are these the values you want the organization to express?**

❑ Yes   ❑ No

**3. If no, what values would you like it to express?**

_____

_____

_____

_____

_____

**4. What are the specific behaviors that demonstrate those values?**

_____

_____

_____

_____

_____

_____

**5. What are some key behaviors that would demonstrate the values you would like for your group?**

_____

_____

_____

_____

_____

| **What Your Group Does...** | **What Your Group Wants...** |
|---|---|
| 6. What are the behaviors that would demonstrate the opposite of those values? | 7. What are some key behaviors that would demonstrate the opposite of the values you want to have? |

## B. Group Norms

1. What group norms do you want for your group?

_____

_____

_____

2. Are they written down anywhere?

   ❏ Yes   ❏ No

3. Do members of your group agree with them?

   ❏ Yes   ❏ No

# POWER MEANS MOBILIZING YOUR RESOURCES

*Power . . . is the ability to achieve purpose. It is the strength required to bring about social, political, or economic changes. In this sense power is not only desirable but necessary in order to implement the demands of love and justice. One of the greatest problems of history is that the concepts of love and power are usually contrasted as polar opposites. Love is identified with a resignation of power and power with a denial of love. . . .What is needed is a realization that power without love is reckless and abusive and that love without power is sentimental and anemic.*

—Dr. Martin Luther King, Jr.

Getting anything done in the world takes power. This is a basic law of physics. It takes power to make the world, or some part of it, a better place. Power is the ability to act and to accomplish what you want. Power is neither inherently good nor bad. It simply allows you to accomplish things you can't accomplish without the power.

Where does power come from? Power in a democracy can come from various sources. Legal authority, organized money, organized people, and good information are all sources of power.

Legal authority refers to public, corporate, and institutional officials and the laws that govern our daily lives. This legal authority allows those in official positions to affect the lives of thousands of people. Community groups rarely have the legal authority to control the conditions that affect their lives.

Power can come from money. Money can buy relief from many problems. If the neighbors are noisy, money can buy a new house in a quieter neighborhood. If the schools are unpainted and the books old, money can buy a private education or pay for a new school and a new library. If crime is a problem, money can buy a private security force. If you run for office, money can buy advertising and professional staff to help you get elected.

Without access to money, your power is more likely to come from other sources, or from an amalgam of sources. In this book, we look at the power that flows from an organized group of people, some money, good information about the details of the problem you face, and a clear plan of action. Over many years I have asked hundreds of people what they most want to learn about the process of building powerful community organizations. Most answer, "How to recruit people and keep them involved." Since that is what people want to learn, this book emphasizes recruitment. As the stories in this section illustrate, once you have an organized group of people, the group can use the other sources of power—especially information and organized money—to solve their problems and make a difference.

CHAPTER 5

# Developing Power: Why Recruit?

## ▶ The Reason We Organize is to Develop Power

### Story: Organized People Can Organize Money

Even when no one in the group has a lot of money, people can achieve power by pooling their money together.

*Many new immigrants to the United States send money back home to their families. Companies charge high fees for these money transfers: It often costs $100 to send $1,000. The Greater Boston Interfaith Organization (GBIO) organized many of its member congregations to put their checking accounts into one bank, becoming together a $10 million customer of the bank. By combining their business in one bank, the members of this group had greater power to persuade the bank to provide a new low-cost wire transfer service. This saved many immigrants hundreds of dollars on international money orders. It brought new business to the bank (a win for the bank) and relief to the new immigrants wanting to help their families overseas.*

Organizing all these disparate groups was not quick or easy. It took years of patient organizing and relationship-building. Not all GBIO congregations and organizations had immigrant members who directly benefited from this new service. Before GBIO could enlist the congregations to combine their money to become a $10 million customer of Citizens Bank, the organization conducted thousands of one-on-one personal meetings among congregants in homes and coffee shops. As these relationships were woven into the fabric of the organization and the fabric of individual members' lives, the direct benefit to some was felt as a benefit to others as well.

## Story: One-on-One Recruiting is the Foundation for Success

*Hammond, Indiana, 1991. Like many cities in America, Hammond's downtown declined in the 1970s and '80s. In 1991, local federal judges announced plans to demolish the downtown federal courthouse and build a new one far away, in the suburbs. Members of the Interfaith Citizens Organization (ICO), a coalition of local congregations, realized that this would mean the death of their downtown. ICO decided to fight the move.*

*Before the people of Hammond, Indiana, went up against the federal judges, they conducted hundreds of one-on-one meetings. In one congregation they talked with over 200 members in a nine-month period. "We heard a lot of concerns about family struggles and the future of our community," one pastor said. One leader in the campaign reflected, "We could always rally the troops, but these one-on-ones gave us depth. They were penetrating. People really came to understand each other, and it created a dynamic. It gave us legitimacy and a base."*

*Over many years, ICO built a strong coalition of downtown businesses, local banks, and religious congregations to demand accountability from their elected representa-*

*tives and federal officials. It took research into federal regulations, road trips to Washington, negotiations with Congressional representatives, and a strong organization to keep all their supporters together over many years.*

*They won their fight. The new courthouse was rebuilt in downtown Hammond.*

ICO and the people of Hammond, Indiana, were strong because they had done the slow, one-on-one recruiting and relationship-building that allowed them to turn people out for meetings. This showed their strength and the depth of support for their cause in the community.

### Information is Power, Too

The leaders in Hammond also did their research. They needed to find out who really had the authority to make the decision to relocate the courthouse. This turned out to be quite complicated, involving the Federal General Services Administration and several committees in Congress. Having the right information gave them some power, too.

## ▶ Why Recruit People to Your Organization?

Building organizations requires constantly mobilizing resources. People are a key resource. Finding good people is one of your most critical jobs. It will take a lot of your time.

### Start by Knowing Why You Are Doing What You Are Doing

How do you recruit people and keep them involved?

First ask yourself: Why do I need to recruit? The answer may seem obvious, but since it takes so much time and work to recruit people, you should have a clear and specific understanding of why it is so important. If not, you might not do all the work it takes. Even if you think you know the answer, ask yourself: Why recruit?

Some organizations think they already have their members. They develop a small group, get comfortable with each other, and stop recruiting. These are organizations in trouble. They may not look troubled now, but they will be. *Organizations that want to improve conditions in the world but are not always bringing in new members lose strength.*

What about your organization?

**EXERCISE**

## Why Recruit?

**Why are you doing this recruiting?**

Some reasons often mentioned:

- There's strength in numbers.
- With more people we can get better ideas.
- We can have more skills.
- We need a critical mass to be effective.
- Those in authority won't listen if there are only a few of us.
- I can't get what I need from the system by myself. I need the group's power and influence.

Write down your reasons to remind yourself why you are bothering to recruit. People will not return your calls. They won't meet with you. Others will join and then not follow through on their commitments. If you have a written list, it will encourage you when you are feeling discouraged.

Why are you asking people to join? Why do you need them?

_____

_____

_____

## Recruiting Is Different From Making Friends

In addition to strengthening the organization, recruiting also may bring personal benefits to you. The personal reasons are an important part of what *motivates* people to recruit others. However, while your personal gain from recruiting may be nice, this is not the principal reason to recruit. You can get the same personal results without recruiting people into an organization. To keep you focused on recruiting, it is important to have a numerical goal of how many people you intend to sign up. Otherwise, recruiting can lapse into friendly conversations and making new personal friends. That is pleasant, but it does not build your organization.

**EXERCISE**

## Personal Reasons for Recruiting

Understanding the personal gain you receive from recruiting members will help you to keep your personal benefit and your organizational goals separate. It is okay to enjoy recruitment and to benefit from it. Personal benefit can motivate you to keep recruiting. Just don't substitute your personal needs for your organization's goals.

Some personal reasons that people often give for recruiting include:

- "I like to hear people's stories."
- "I enjoy being with people."
- "I get new ideas when I talk to someone else."
- "I know that other people think differently than I do and they will help me to see things in ways that I can't see."

What do *you* get out of recruiting? What's in it for you?

_____

_____

_____

## The Importance of Numbers

Sometimes the need to recruit will be obvious. In a "Get Out the Vote" drive you may have to phone 5,000 people to win on Election Day. No matter how fast you dial, you can't do it yourself. If you recruited people ahead of time, you have 100 people. Each person can call 50 voters on Election Day. You reach your goal and win the election. If you did not recruit enough, you have only ten people. You can call only 500 or 1,000 voters, and your chances of winning go way down. In this case, the need to recruit and the capacity of one volunteer is clear.

### What Kind of Members?

Generally, building powerful community organizations requires active member involvement. This is what is usually needed to make change in the community or in the world.

However, there may be times when you are looking only for more dues-paying members—not necessarily more members who are actively involved. Publicizing the number of dues-paying members in the organization can help you to demonstrate the support your group enjoys in the community. That's okay, as long as you know why you want more members of this type.

In addition to helping you to make your case today, these recruits can be a source of future active participants and leaders. Today, someone may write a check. Later, he or she may do more.

## Build the Organization

You may not have an election coming up. The need to recruit may not be obvious. It may seem like you can manage better by yourself, or with one or two trusted friends. But that does not build your organization. It does not build community. In the long run it does not build effectiveness.

You will burn out when the tasks pile up and your friends have other demands. In the short run, it seems efficient to do it yourself. In the long run it is deadly to the organization—and to you.

## Organizations That Are Not Growing Are Dying

Organizations always need to recruit to replace members lost. Members leave for different reasons. Some people lose interest. Some move away. Some develop new relationships that are more interesting than the organization. (Some may have joined the group looking for a relationship or romance.) People burn out. Some find more interesting challenges. Some resolve the issue they came for and move on.

The community changes, too. You need new ideas for changing times. Organizations with only veteran members may be less willing to try new technologies or strategies to meet new challenges. Strong organizations bring in new members to challenge the ideas of existing leaders. It helps to bring in new people, not only for the added numbers and power, but also to ensure that the "in group" does not get too complacent with itself and with how the organization runs.

New members demonstrate that your organization still means something to people today. Recruiting people is a test of an organization's worth and present importance.

## ▶ Who Should You Recruit?

### People Who Are Representative

If you are trying to build an organization that will represent a certain broad group (parents in a school, employees in a workplace, residents in a city or neighborhood), you need to recruit *people who are representative of the whole group—now.* Your organization may need large numbers of people in order to win important improvements in people's lives. This means that every person you need will have to feel welcome in the group. Every group you want represented should have a hand in establishing the organization and developing its goals and plans. You cannot do this by starting only with those whom you already know or with whom you already feel comfortable. Once the organization's membership and culture represent only a certain segment of the community, it takes tremendous focused effort to become more inclusive. When you try to "diversify" the membership later, people from such "diverse" groups will know that they are being used and will not join. So take the time and be systematic from the outset about getting a truly representative group as you build the membership.

You may believe in diversity philosophically, or you may enjoy being part of a diverse community, or you may have an ideology or an idealism that embraces diversity. Or you may not. Either way, you may need the diversity—because you can add. You know that you will need a certain number of supporters to achieve your goal. For example: How many people (gathered in a meeting, voting in an election, or boycotting a product) will it take to achieve your objective? You do the math. If your group is a powerful majority, then you may have no immediate need to bring together a more diverse group. But if the numbers don't add up or in the near future are not likely to add up to the number you need, you should strive for inclusion of diverse groups of people. You aren't doing this to be nice or for an abstract ideal. You do this because you can count and you want to win.

# Values, Self-Interest, and Passion

In addition to recruiting people who are representative of the group you eventually want, you want people who share the organization's values.

There are many ways to gauge people's values. How do they treat their children? Do they bring them to the meeting where they help them with their homework? Do they listen to others? Do they talk all the time? Do they clean up the cups after the meeting is over? Do they show up when they say they will? Use your observations and intuition about people. Is this someone you feel comfortable with? Do you allow people who make racist, homophobic, or anti-Semitic comments to be members? If you do, what does this say about your values? What will this do to your ability to get all points of view? How will it affect your ability to bring in all the people you need to achieve your goals?

*If I am not for myself, who will be for me? If I am only for myself, what am I? And if not now, when?*

—Rabbi Hillel the Elder (1st century),
*Sayings of the Fathers*

You want people who care about the issue, but not *only* about the issue. You are looking not simply for people who have a personal self-interest in the issues you are working on, but people whose self-interest is deeply motivated, not narrowly defined. What are their stories? What is their motivation? Beware of people who say that they are *not* at all personally motivated, who are doing it only to help others. They are not likely to last long in your organization. Also beware of people who seem to care *only* for themselves (to get *their* raise, to lower *their* water bill, to get rid of the abandoned cars on *their* street.) You *definitely want* people who care deeply about the issue your group is working on. But you also want those who think about others as well as themselves.

## Anger: Hot and Cold

The place of anger in recruiting people is important and complex. People who are the angriest about the problem your group wants to solve might appear to be good recruits, but if you are interested in building a lasting organization, anger can be a problem more often than it is a source of strength.

Kris Rondeau, an organizer with the Harvard Union of Clerical and Technical Workers, describes the place of "hot anger" this way, as reported in John Hoerr's book:

*"I think anger is the enemy of union organizing. It's the union's responsibility to create an environment in which you can be part of a union and believe in self-representation and worker's voice without being mean, without being aggressive, without being merely oppositional. If you introduce anger into a drive, you can kiss the drive goodbye."*

—John Hoerr, *We Can't Eat Prestige,*
*the Women Who Organized Harvard*

People who are *all* anger probably are not going to build your organization. If they are only angry in a hot way that continually leads to verbal outbursts or borders on violence, they are not likely to be good organization members. But anger, especially the slow, "cold" anger that burns deep inside people—anger about the way they have been treated, about injustices they have witnessed—is often a source of power and sustenance. People who share anger out of memory or experience and who are passionate are likely to be your best members.

Ed Chambers describes how some Black pastors speak about anger. They say:

*Anger and grief are rooted in our most passionate memories and dreams. . . . Anger that is focused and deep and rooted in grief is a key element in the organizing of black churches.*

*—Ed Chambers, Roots for Radicals*

This kind of anger or passion, rooted in memory, nurtured with hope and a sense of right and wrong, can beat back the "You can't fight City Hall" mentality and the cynicism of, "All politics is corrupt, so what's the use of trying?"

Anger does not mean violence. John Lewis, a strong proponent of non-violence and chair of the Student Non-Violent Coordinating Committee (SNCC) during the early 1960s, describes it this way:

*Faith, hope, and courage—these were all essential ingredients for the work SNCC was doing in the Deep South in those early years. And anger, too. Yes, there was anger among us in SNCC, but it was a good anger, a healthy anger, at least in the early stage. It was a positive, constructive type of anger. We were rebels, absolutely. We were all about rebellion, but it was a rebellion against an evil thing, the whole system and structure of segregation and racial discrimination.*

*—John Lewis, Walking with the Wind*

## Story: Memory Can Move Us

*When I was working as a volunteer for the Brookline Tenants Union, we were in the middle of a fight over rent control. An election for the town's Board of Selectmen was coming up, pitting two slates against each other, one pro- and one anti-rent control. I lived in an owner-occupied two-family house, so my apartment was not rent-controlled. Still, I threw myself into the campaign as a volunteer, working many hours a day, coordinating the work of fifteen precinct captains for the "Get Out the Vote" Campaign.*

*I remember visiting one elderly woman down the street who lived in a small rent-controlled apartment. If rent control disappeared, she would most likely have to move. I sat in her kitchen and listened to her. She reminded me of my grandmother. I remembered all the stories my mother had told me—how as a girl she had to move from one apartment to another in the Bronx every year, and only could take with her the belongings that she could fit into two shopping bags. I was angry with the people trying to get rid of rent control. They had never sat in the kitchen of the elderly woman down the street. I was angry that an elderly woman, all alone, might have to move and about how hard that would be on her. I remembered that when my grandmother was very old, the landlord had taken out the heat from the entryway of her apartment building to force her and the other tenants to move. At the time, my anger at what could happen to me, at what could happen to the woman down the street and hundreds like her, at what had happened to my mother, father, and grandmother, simmered together in a cold, steady, slow-burning anger. That cold anger kept me going throughout that election campaign. When we won we had a big party and I knew I had made a difference. I was doing it for my mother and my grandmother. I was also doing it for me.*

## ▶ Why People Join Organizations

*Everyone wants two things, to be seen as an individual and to be part of something greater than themselves.*

—Source unknown

People join community groups for a variety of reasons. If you want to get people to join and get involved in your group, you need to understand why someone would join.

**EXERCISE**

### Recruiting Exercise: What Led You to Join?

*Most people you want to recruit are like you in their reasons and willingness to join and get involved in an organization. Think back: How did you get involved in a group?*

1. Think of a time in your life. (It could be any time—far back in your childhood or just last week.) What group or groups did you join?

Group 1: _____

Group 2: _____

2. What led you to join those groups? _____

_____

(I am indebted to Chris Argyris for this phrase, "*What led you to . . . ?*" Asking the question this way helps you to focus *on the behavior or experience* that produced a certain action, rather than on the *thinking* that produced the action. As a leader or organizer, you want to behave in a way that it is most effective for recruiting people.)

3. What was the immediately preceding event?_____

_____

4. Think about the specific event—not your frame of mind, not what you thought about the organization—but what was the *specific action* that led you to join?

_____

_____

5. How did you hear about the group? From whom and in what way?

I heard about the group from _____, via the following method:

_____.

6. If a person asked you to join, how did he or she ask you? Was it in person? Over the phone? By letter? By e-mail?

_____

7. What did the person actually say? What were the specific words used?

_____

_____

8. What else do you remember about what happened just before you joined?

_____

_____

If you are like most people, you joined a group because someone invited you to join. It probably wasn't just "someone," but rather, a specific person whom you knew and trusted. And most likely, he or she asked you to join in person.

I have posed this question—*What led you to join a group?*—to hundreds of people, individuals from many classes, races, and backgrounds. Ninety percent say they joined a group because *a person asked them*. A few join groups after reading a flyer or newspaper ad. Very few, but often highly motivated, people go looking for groups to join. *Most people join because someone they know asks them.* Face-to-face, eyeball-to-eyeball. *This is an important finding.* If you want people to join your group, you have to *ask them,* in person. This is what works. Person-to-person. One-on-one. You can try other things: Letters, flyers, newspaper ads, sky-writing, mass e-mails, direct mail, public service announcements on TV or radio, and other media extravaganzas. But what works, over and over again, is one person asking another person. Your group will likely be no different.

If you are not sure, ask a few friends why they joined a group. It can be the Girl Scouts, the Marines, the bowling team, a reading group, the church or temple. You'll find that it's most often because someone they knew asked them.

**QUICK TIPS**

### *The Secret to Recruitment*

**Q:** What's the best way to recruit members?

**A:** To ask people, one at a time.

> **People join when someone asks them to join.**

You may ask: Isn't this too slow?

It may seem slow, but it's what works.

We are so bombarded by the media that we may think that personal contact is not effective, that we need more modern methods. But how do you feel when someone you know asks you to do something, as opposed to how you feel when you see an ad on TV? Which group will you stick with? You are not selling toothpaste. You are asking people to make a meaningful commitment of their time and money based on their deeply held values.

## What's In It for Them?

Asking people to join is key, but this will not keep them motivated and involved for long. If they know you and like you, they may join as a favor to you. But they need to join for their own reasons and needs. Remember why you joined a group. The deeper reasons you joined are likely the same reasons that will motivate others to stay involved. So, think. What was and is in it for you?

**EXERCISE**

## What's In It for You?

1. Write down the reasons you joined the group you are in:

_____

_____

_____

_____

2. Write down the benefits you have enjoyed from partici-pating as a member in the group:

_____

_____

_____

_____

3. Are those the reasons you've stayed? Or are there other reasons as well?

_____

_____

_____

_____

Most people you recruit will be like you. They will want and need to get something out of the group. What can the group do for them? *You need to learn what is in it for them.* This is complex. People join for many different reasons. Think back to all the things you may have gotten from a group you joined. Some may be personal:

- A chance to enjoy the company of others and the feeling that people appreciate your ideas.
- A chance to express your ideas.
- A chance to use your skills and abilities.
- An opportunity to grow intellectually or spiritually.
- A chance to sing in a chorus.
- A place to meet a mate or a new friend.
- A chance to be with someone you really like.
- A chance to feel some sense of power in your life.
- An opportunity to have some meaning in your life.

Others may be more related to conditions where you live or work:

- A chance to make a difference in the problem of drugs, AIDS, or crime—something that really bothers you.
- A chance to get to know neighbors whom you don't really know. You just wish people were friendlier. You think it would make the street safer and you would feel better knowing the people on your street.
- A chance to lower taxes or a utility bill, or get better medical care, higher wages, better working conditions, or better schools.
- A chance to clean up a park or to cut down the noise in the neighborhood.
- A chance to do something about things you are angry about—the trash in the street, overcrowded schools, the way you are treated on the job, or the way you and your fellow students are treated in school.

### Real Issues and Real People

Many of us have limited knowledge of why other people join a group. It is easier to understand your own reasons. You may think that others are only interested in the issue the group is pursuing. The immediate issue may be better garbage pick-up, higher wages, affordable housing, better schools, getting rid of a drug problem, or getting a traffic light put up. But you miss much if you treat people as interested only in the immediate issue. In fact, if that is all they are interested in, they are not likely to last long in your organization. If you don't look beyond the immediate issue for reasons that people want to join, you may not be able to keep them in your group for very long. You need to be able to get under their skin, to know what makes them tick.

## ▶ The Point is to Build Relationships

Why do you want to find out this information? Because you are building relationships—not just gathering extra hands for a series of tasks.

You also are looking for *leaders*, people who will take responsibility, people who eventually will work on their own initiative. Many people will not take initiative without encouragement. You are looking for openings. You are not looking for full-blown leaders who are eager to take responsibility. You are not likely to find them. (If you do, such leaders are more likely to be out looking to recruit you!) You are looking for people who have some good values, who want to do something, who have some time in their busy lives, and who will do something that advances their own personal interests. You need to find out what they are interested in and get a sense of who they are. They need to get some sense of who you are. In these relationships we can inspire and challenge each other.

## Not Selling, Not Manipulating

New organizers sometimes think that you have to manipulate people in order to recruit them. In the short run this may seem effective. In building long-lasting organizations that can exert power, this is not useful and can even be harmful to your organization.

Some organizers think that being honest and open about their role—that they are trying to get people to volunteer for jobs—will keep potential volunteers from joining. Following this line of thinking, those organizers may try to hide or mystify what they do. This practice obscures a necessary job and makes it harder to build strong organizations.

When organizers mask their recruitment goal behind some other façade, they are unconsciously suggesting that people don't know what is good for them—but that the organizer does. If you believe that what you are doing is in the best interest of people, then there is no need to trick people into that behavior. Given the right opening and encouragement, people will elect to pursue that behavior—because it is in their best interests.

## Strong Relationships Build Strong Organizations

*If we are going to work together, we are going to have to like each other.*

—Horace Small

You are building relationships because strong relationships build effective organizations.

The tasks the organization undertakes are done more efficiently when relationships, morale, and communication are strong. While a common goal is essential, strong relationships are the glue that keeps people working toward that goal.

**CASE STUDY**

# Relationships Keep Groups Together

## Harvard Union of Technical and Clerical Workers

An organization will withstand stress if the personal relationships among its members are strong. Organizers from the Harvard Union of Technical and Clerical Workers were able to convince workers at Harvard University to join the union not so much because the university was seen as "the enemy," but because of the strong personal relationships organizers and union supporters built with other employees. The Harvard union organizers talked to employees about all kinds of subjects—not only about the union. They talked about their personal lives, their families, and the weather. They instituted a Friday afternoon "chat" session for people just to come together to talk. It lowered stress and built the organization. Rumors are harder to start or spread where relationships are strong.

## Strong Relationships Are Also a Reward in Themselves

Remember the reasons you joined a group in the first place. Look at what has kept you in the group. For many, it is the quality of the relationships they find in the group that keeps them involved. Marie Manna at the Harvard Union of Technical and Clerical Workers describes her success in recruiting people to union meetings. After having little luck with sending out flyers and mailing newsletters, she called people up, told them about the meeting and said, "I haven't met you yet, but I'd like to meet you." Fourteen people who never came before showed up. "People want to be part of a welcoming community," she said. "They came because they knew someone would want to meet them."

Some call this focus on relationships a "woman's way of organizing." Some women organize this way, and it is very effective. Men do it, too. I will never forget the six-foot-tall, macho utility lineman in cowboy boots I met from the International Brotherhood of Electrical Workers in Wyoming. In a roomful of men, most of whom spent their working days climbing utility poles in Colorado and Wyoming, he described his method for recruiting and keeping members in his union: "I hug 'em," he said. Another organizer chimed in to explain that he keeps his members connected to the union by taking them bowling every month. Everyone in the room nodded. These methods made sense to them.

# CHAPTER 6

# How to Recruit:
# The Nuts and Bolts

Finally! Now it's time to go out and bring in members.

In community organizing, the best way to learn is often by observing, practicing, and reflecting. In this chapter I will walk you through two recruiting situations—door-knocking (short visits) and one-on-ones (long visits). Then we'll look at two important reasons for recruiting—recruiting for a specific task and recruiting with a general focus on building a democratic organization. Along the way, we will listen in on a few recruiting sessions, we'll role-play, and we'll critique what we have observed. If you can, read and discuss the sample dialogues in this chapter with a colleague or two, or do some role plays of your own before you go out recruiting. Talking about it will help you to learn more. You can use the same practice and critiquing methods you'll see in this chapter.

If you've never recruited before, it would be terrific if you could find an experienced organizer to shadow for at least a few hours, so you can observe someone recruiting before you do it yourself. If you can't, use this chapter as a print version of an apprenticeship and jump in from here.

Either way, the first time you recruit you may feel like you are diving into ice cold water. So just take a deep breath and get started. Every time you do it, you'll learn something that helps you do it better the next time. I've been organizing for decades, and I'm still learning. So try not to feel too intimidated. Remember: The reason you are recruiting is to give people an opportunity to pursue their interests. You're not coercing people, you're giving them an opportunity. If you enjoy meeting people, you'll find out that recruiting can be a lot of fun. So have fun!

## ▶ Listen. Don't Sell.

The most common mistake people make when they try to recruit people to their organization is talking too much. They talk a lot about how wonderful the organization is, all the good things it has done for them, and how much it means to them. This is probably all true. But it is not useful in recruiting. Listening is better.

You want to find out who the potential recruits are and why they might stay in the organization. So, *listen.* By listening you can discover what the organization might mean to them. You can discover how they can best participate in the group, what role or task they can best manage.

### How to Listen When You are Recruiting: Two Methods

How do you listen? That depends in part on how much time you have, where you are, and how much time you want to spend right now with each person. There are a great many situations where you will be recruiting. I will cover two basic situations. Your particular situation may be different, or perhaps it is a mix of these two.

## ▶ Method One: Short Visits, or "Door-knocking"

You may decide that a short visit is what you need now, or it may be all you have time for. Some call this "door-knocking," since it originated with door-to-door neighborhood organizing. This short visit can be done in a wide variety of settings where you meet people for a short period of time. It allows you a short (five- or ten-minute) conversation. You can talk with a large number of people this way. This lets you identify those whom you may want to re-visit for a longer conversation in the future.

### Before You Go: Preparation for Doing Short Visits

#### Practice First!

You will have about 30 to 40 seconds to establish a connection and credibility with each potential recruit. So before you go out, practice exactly what you are going to say. It gets easier as you do it. The exact words matter. Have someone you trust listen to you or else record yourself and then play back the tape or video to critique yourself. (Later in this chapter I discuss in more length how you can use an audio or videotape recording to practice recruiting. Take a look at that section, "Recruiting to Build a Democratic Organization: It Takes More Than Learning a Rap.") If you don't get it right the first few times, don't worry. No one was born knowing how to recruit. Keep trying until you feel that you can say your opening lines easily.

#### Look the Part

The person at the door will size you up in the first few seconds. Dress appropriately. Don't let your clothes or appearance be an obstacle. It may help to wear a button or badge identifying your organization. In some cases you might want a photo identification badge to assure people that you are a legitimate representative of the organization.

### Go With a Buddy

When you do short cold-call meetings with strangers, whether you are knocking on doors or standing in a mall or in the center of downtown, do it with a partner. Go in male and female pairs if possible. This makes people feel most comfortable talking to you. Going in pairs is also safer than going alone.

**QUICK TIPS**

## *Membership Cards for New Recruits*

Before you go, create membership cards to hand to people when they decide to join. That way the organization can immediately begin building its connection with the people you recruit.

### *Figure 1: Sample membership card*

> This certifies that _____ [write in name]
>
> is a member of the
>
> Orange Grove Improvement Association.
>
> Membership expires _____ [write in date]

### *On reverse side:*

> Mission: The Orange Grove Improvement Association is a membership organization that works to improve life for all residents and businesses in Orange Grove City. It is open to all, regardless of race, nationality, religion, or sexual orientation.

## A Flyer to Leave Behind

Prepare a one-page flyer to leave behind at houses where no one is home. Make sure the flyer is very direct and easy to read. Most important: Make sure you put your name and phone number on it, so people who are interested know how to contact you.

*Always put in the day of the week.*

*I often put in the year, so that when I find the flyer years later, I know when it was used.*

*Always put in start and ending times.*

*If someone in authority is coming, put this in, so people know who to expect and possibly to give them more incentive to show up.*

*Always put in contact information for at least one person. Several is better.*

*Mention the basics of the organization, including the dues, so you don't surprise people later when you ask for money.*

---

**The South Street Improvement Committee stopped by.**

**Sorry we missed you.**

We would like to know what YOU think . . .

# Come to Our Next Meeting:
## Thursday,
## March 16, 2007
## 7:30 to 9:00 p.m.

Topic: How to Clean up Everett Park

Guest: Recreation Commissioner Paul McCarthy

—— • ——

For more information:
Contact Michael Brown, (781) 999-9999
or Mbrown@website.org
Check out our website:
www.websitename.org

The South Street Improvement Committee is a group of concerned citizens in our neighborhood.

Membership is open to all concerned residents (except elected officials) who support our goals. Dues are $50 per year.

# Door to Door, Step by Step

So you have all your materials, you have a partner, you have a plan, and you're at the first door. What do you do now?

Knock!

Once someone answers the door, here are the steps to follow:

1. **Smile,** look the person in the eye, and say your name and the name of your group.

2. **Authorize or legitimate yourself.** This can take many different forms. If you are a neighbor and you are trying to get a neighborhood organization going, just being a neighbor may be legitimacy enough. If you are part of a group, say what the group has already done. ("We are the group that got the city to clean up the lot across Broadway last month.") A local leader may have referred you. This also gives you some legitimacy. (For example, "I work with Father Mahoney," or "Rabbi Salzman suggested I stop by." *Always* double-check first that it is okay to use someone's name. The fastest way to de-legitimate yourself is to use someone's name without permission!)

3. **Explain why you are there:** "We are here to find out about what *you* are concerned about." Say "you" rather than "people in the neighborhood." You are not conducting a survey. You want this person to know that you care about what *he or she* thinks, not about what everyone thinks. You recruit people one at a time. Remember, this is what works.

4. **Then listen.** Your job in the short visit is to find out a little about this person. Don't talk a lot. You are not a door-to-door salesperson, although the person you are visiting may think you are. Some people will likely be bewildered that someone who is not a salesperson or census taker is at their door and is asking them what they think about something. This does not happen to them very often. They are used to a different approach.

5. **Try to follow up on their answers with open-ended questions.** These are questions that can't be answered with "Yes" or "No." If they say, "I don't really know," when you ask what they are concerned about, mention some of the things that you have heard from others. ("Some other people have been concerned about the traffic on Broadway, how hard it is for the kids and elderly to cross in the crosswalk near Everett Street. Other people have been concerned about the garbage pick-up. They say it's really a mess after garbage day. Others have been concerned about all the smoke that the tire factory is putting out every night, or that the schools don't have enough money to educate our children. Are these things that you are concerned about, or are there other things?")

6. **Engage the person in some dialogue**—hopefully getting some agreement that something should be done about the problem and that, yes, it would be good to have a group that would take the lead on this.

7. **If your group has membership dues,** make sure to tell each person you visit. People often feel misled if you don't mention dues up front.

8. **Invite the person to join.** If the answer is yes, fill out a membership card right then and hand it to the new member. If the person declines, say that you understand and thank the person for spending the time talking with you.

9. **Ask for each person's name and phone number,** "If you don't mind giving it to me." Make sure to record the name and phone number along with the street address.

10. **If no one is home, leave behind the one-page flyer** containing all the relevant information, including your phone number and address, so that they can contact you.

**QUICK TIPS**

### Bring Your Notebook

If you are out on the street or are meeting many people, keep a record of where you have been, the names of those you saw, whether or not someone was home, and whether you left a flyer. It's amazing how quickly you can forget where you have been when you door-knock at many houses in a short time. I have made this mistake too many times—returning to the same person at the same house, asking the same questions. It's embarrassing. I have an aversion to taking notes, thinking that I have such a good memory that I will not forget which houses I have visited. But I've often been wrong. Good notes on where you have been only slow you down a little, and keep you from wasting your time with unnecessary repeat visits. You can keep the notes on file cards, in a notebook, on a street map, in your Palm Pilot, or right on the address roster you're using. It doesn't matter where you do it, just so you can read your records and use them to keep track of your visits and of subsequent follow-up.

## ▶ Method Two: Longer Visits— The One-on-One

This method is for developing relationships and finding leaders. It involves a longer visit—40 to 60 minutes, sometimes more, depending on the culture and context within which you are working.

**QUICK TIPS**

## Use Your Judgment About Time

The number of minutes I suggest here, somewhere between 40 and 60, is meant as a guideline. The organization needs many people. To recruit many people you have to visit many people. If you spend too long with one person, even if he or she seems to be a good prospect, you may miss out on someone else. You can always revisit someone. Use your judgment and common sense.

# The 80/20 Rule

You recruit by finding out about the other person and his or her interests and seeing how this person's interests overlap with the interests of the organization. You want to learn about the other person—so that means that most of what you need to do is *listen*.

Remember, you are not trying to manipulate anyone or sell anything (not even ideas). You are there to learn about the person and to find out if there is a connection between your group and the person's self-interest.

The rule of thumb in such meetings is to listen about 80 percent of the time and talk about 20 percent of the time. If you are doing more than 20 percent of the talking you are probably selling rather than finding out about the other person.

This is not chit-chat. You are there with a purpose. You are there to find out what the person cares about, what his or her values are, what his or her community connections are, how much time he or she has, what other organizations he or she has been in or is now involved in, what his or her self-interest is, and what makes this person tick. You can't find out everything in one brief meeting, but you can find out a lot if you ask the right questions and listen carefully.

## Go With a List In Your Head

Before you go for the visit, have in mind a menu of possible tasks you can ask the person to do for the organization. These may include:

- Attend a meeting of your group.
- Distribute a flyer for the meeting.
- Make a phone call.
- Bring cookies to the meeting.
- See if so-and-so would like to help with the annual dinner.
- Set up an appointment for you with his or her minister.
- Arrange for the group to hold its next meeting at the person's church.
- Stuff envelopes.
- Volunteer at the office.
- Host a coffee, where you can come to tell the person's friends all about the organization and listen to their concerns.
- Introduce you to Mazy, across the street, by going to visit her along with you.

You get the idea. In your visit, as you listen for the person's limitations and interests, be thinking about what a good first task for this person might be.

## Don't Be Mechanical

You can't fake interest. You can't do this kind of listening mechanically. This is not a clever technique to recruit more members. You have to be genuinely interested in who the person is. If you are not, *stop!* Don't have the meeting. You have to honestly believe that you are there to build community and to find out about this person. If you are not, take a break. Go home. Ask yourself why you are doing this in the first place.

## *Eating and the One-on-One*

When I do this, even if I meet someone over a meal or coffee, I do not order much food. I want to pay attention to the person, not the food. Even if I am only talking 20 percent of the time, I don't want to talk with my mouth full of food. It is also hard to listen when I am hungry. Sometimes I snack beforehand.

**EXERCISE**

# How to Plan a Visit

All this good advice is worthless unless you go out and do it! Start with someone easy, someone you know. Before the visit, make a plan. Fill in the following information about the person you are going to see. What do you already know about this person?

1. Organizational affiliations: _____

_____

_____

_____

2. Past activities: _____

_____

_____

_____

3. Family: _____

_____

_____

_____

4. Networks: _____

_____

_____

_____

5. Current activities: _____

_____

_____

_____

6. What can you ask the person to do for the group?

_____

_____

_____

## Listening In On a Model Dialogue

Here is a dialogue of what such a conversation might sound like. In this model one-on-one visit I am trying to recruit someone into a hypothetical group, "Interfaith in Action." This is an organization of congregations that works to improve the schools, build affordable housing, and improve other conditions in the city. Your organization may be different. The issues may be different. You may meet in a kitchen, a pizza parlor, an office, or workplace. However, the principles of listening, not selling, remain the same.

In this example, I ("Organizer") am a member of a religious congregation, and I am recruiting someone I have seen at services but do not know well. Let's call her Alix. During the after-service coffee, I invited her to meet me at a diner for a cup of coffee. So I am in the diner with my coffee.

The dialogue might go something like the following. My commentary on the dialogue is boxed.

> *Your body language counts. Be relaxed, but attentive. You also want to share enough about yourself so that the conversation is two-way. You cannot expect the other person to reveal much about herself or himself if you don't share much of yourself.*

**Michael (Organizer):** Hi, thanks for coming. I know I have seen you in church often, but I have never really gotten to know you. I have been a member here for about twelve years now. I grew up in New York, but this is now my home. My wife and I have two children, and I like this place, but I wish it would be more of a community—although I know at times it has been. When our last child was born, my wife was pretty sick and a lot of people in the congregation helped us, cooking, bringing groceries, dropping them off on the porch. But I worry about the schools, with the state budget cutbacks; they now charge for band and sports at the high school and my third grader's class has 28 kids, which I think is too many. Could you tell me a little about yourself?

> *You want to leave off with a simple open-ended question to start her talking. An open-ended question is one that does not take a yes or no answer. You are looking for clues about what she says about herself.*

**Alix (Potential Member):** Well, I moved here from Detroit, and have worked mostly for public relations firms in advertising. I always liked to draw and put together ideas on paper. I have worked for Morris & Morris for about eight years now, and I live with my husband and two sons, ages six and ten, in East Cloverdale, near the racetrack. I have been coming to the church for about four years.

**Michael:** And what brought you to this church?

> *She has stopped talking. You want to get her talking again, so you ask her about something you have in common. Again, ask an open-ended question. You ask this because you want to find out something about her values. Why did she join the church? Is it a major family tradition? You are trying to find out more about her and what the church means to her.*

**Alix:** Well. I was looking for someplace that was spiritual and community-oriented—nothing too fancy—and I liked this place.

> *She made some crucial points: "spiritual and community-oriented." This indicates that "spiritual" things and being "community-oriented" are important to her. This is a good sign that she might be interested in a community group. She might have said many other things. She might have said she joined for her husband or for her children. You need to listen between the lines. You are trying to understand what matters to her. She isn't talking much, so you will have to gently pry a little more. Go easy.*

**Michael:** What did you like about it?

**Alix:** Well, the people were friendly and I liked the fact that the minister and some of the members were interested in social action sorts of things.

> *Here's a big clue. She said members were interested in "social action sorts of things." This gives you a good idea that she is interested in the community and possibly the political situation. She looks like someone who might be good for your organization. So you can follow up with a more specific question to clarify the social action business.*

**Michael:** Oh? Does that interest you?

**Alix:** Oh, yes. I have always tried to get involved in the community, although it's harder now that I'm working full-time and I have the two kids.

> *Another big clue. She is interested, but her time is limited. She is giving you a clear indication that she will not like to have her family time heavily invaded. Go slow and show her that getting involved with your organization won't jeopardize the relationship with her two children. This also indicates that her two children are important to her. She is very open about this.*

**Michael:** I can understand that. I have two children myself. I know how much time it takes and how important it is. The older one has been interested in politics, at least for a while, but now she seems to be exploring her artistic side. You never know where they will end up. I only hope that they do what they are meant to do. But, tell me, where did you get *your* interest in social action?

> *Don't remain an aloof stranger. You are a real person with a history, self-interest, and story of your own. You want her to get to know you as well. You should share enough of yourself to help her feel comfortable talking about herself. The relationship should be two-way. On the other hand, don't draw the conversation primarily back to yourself.*

**Alix:** Well, actually it comes from meditation I do and some reading, as well as from my parents, who always were involved in the community. My father was a banker, but the old-fashioned kind, the kind

who loaned money to people because he knew them
and knew they would pay it back.

*Another clue. You are interested in her values. Your
organization is based on values and sustained by the
values of its members. You are looking for people who
have values that you share: concern for the community
welfare as well as for one's own welfare.*

*This clue tells you that she learned something from
her father. Many of us learn our values from our families. Not good lessons all the time, but the values that
we learned from our family are often deeply held. You
need to understand where she learned her values, as
well as what those values are. People who acquired
their values in childhood from their family often have
values that last. This also helps you to know how to
motivate her. If she received values from a teacher of
literature, then literature may be a way to her heart. A
comment like the one above tells you a lot. You would
do well to follow up. Again, she is not talking very long.*

**Michael:** Really? What my parents told me still
sticks with me to this day, too. My mom, who was a
social worker, always told me how there was a right
and a wrong, and that was that. Not much middle
ground. Some things were just right, and you did
them. Other things were just wrong and you did not
do them. I also watched them work hard, so just
from their example, I think I learned something
about the value of hard work. What kinds of things
do you think your parents taught you?

*Again, another open-ended question to find out more
about her family values. You want to find out if she is
interested in community issues out of a sense of charity
or if she is out for herself as well. People who do well
in organizations care about their own welfare. They are
not selfless do-gooders who only think they are doing
good for others.*

**Alix:** Well, they always told me that we should try to give back something to the community. Whatever we had, we shouldn't just hold onto it for ourselves.

**Michael:** So have you done things like that in the past?

> Here you are trying to find out what she has actually done in the past. Does she only talk a good game, or has she actually done anything? One of the best indicators that someone will contribute to your organization is whether they have done something similar in the past. You want to know whether they have put their values into action before.

**Alix:** Yeah, with the church in the last place I lived, before my husband got laid off and we had to move back here. But lately, no, not so much. I've really been too busy. With the kids and work, my husband, the family, and my mother hasn't been too well lately. Since my dad passed away, I've been trying to spend more time with her.

> Again, here are more important clues about her availability. All this information about her helps you to think about her and her needs and also about the organization's needs. How can they both be met?
>
> Part of the job in building a community organization is to build the community part. This includes caring about what goes on in people's lives beyond the issues of the organization. As a member and leader of the organization you should check in with people about their lives. This information about her family is valuable. You will want to remember that her mother is sick and that she wants to spend more time with her. You may want to find things for her to do within the organization that she can do at home. She could stuff envelopes or make phone calls from home.

**Michael:** Oh, I'm sorry to hear that.

**Alix:** Oh, it was a couple of years ago, and he was very sick for a long time.

**Michael:** Well, what do you think of the city here? You said you haven't been here that long.

> *You want to draw her back to the present and her concerns and opinions. Another open-ended question can do this. It helps to show that you have been listening.*

**Alix:** Well, when I was little I actually lived here. My grandparents were from here, used to be farmers. We moved away when I was about ten. I still have some cousins nearby, but I don't see them much.

> *More good information about her roots in the community. These roots give her credibility in a community that values personal history. Now you move to another area where your organization has been very involved.*

**Michael:** You said you have two children. What do you think of the schools here?

**Alix:** Oh, they are okay, although my oldest, I think, has too many children in his fifth grade class—there are about 28. I think that's too many. I like the teacher, but I don't see how she can pay attention to all those kids.

**Michael:** Have you been involved in the PTA or anything?

**Alix:** I actually looked for one, but I don't think there is one in the school.

**Michael:** Sounds like you might like to make things a little better there, if there were some way to do it.

> *This is a leading question. I am stretching here, trying to see how much she might be willing to do.*

**Alix:** Well, maybe, but I'm not much for that. I might help out, but I'm not really going to do much, especially now, with my mother sick. I really still need to pay attention to her. She is really pretty sick.

> *Time to back off, although she said she might "help out." You should be thinking about how she could do this and still not draw too much attention away from her mother.*

**Michael:** I am sorry to hear that. I know what that can be like. My aunt is dealing with some health problems, and I know at any time I might be called to take care of her. *[A brief discussion about Alix's mother's health follows. Then I direct the conversation back to the purpose of this one-on-one.]* You said you went looking for the PTA. Which school was that?

**Alix:** The Garfield School.

**Michael:** I know that school! What do you think of that school in general?

**Alix:** Oh, I like the principal and most of the teachers I've met. I think they try hard, but with so many kids I am not sure there is that much they can do to make things very much better.

**Michael:** I know you said you went looking for the PTA, so I thought you might like to know that I am involved with Interfaith in Action. We worked to get the city to open the swimming pools in summer for the kids and are trying to get the voters to pass a bond issue to fix up the high school and two of the elementary schools. We're also trying to get the banks to fund more affordable housing. You know they could do more to allow people to buy homes and make the neighborhood more stable. Are you interested in any of that?

> Here you are looking to match her interest with the work of the organization. This is a pretty direct question. You are testing out what kind of work she might be willing to commit to.

**Alix:** Well, I am interested in the schools of course, because of my kids, but I really hadn't heard much about the bond issue. I don't know much about housing, although my dad used to talk about loans and mortgages, but I never really listened much to the details.

**Michael:** Well, there is a short discussion group after church in two weeks for about an hour, with some of the people from Interfaith in Action, including me. Would you like to come to that?

> Here you make an explicit pitch for her to take some action. It is not an outrageous request. She is already a member of the church. The discussion group is a low level of commitment. It is only an hour. You make that clear. You know she guards her family time closely.

**Alix:** When did you say it is?

**Michael:** In two weeks, that's Sunday, March 20, from 11:00 a.m. to 12:00 noon. It's right after the service, in the basement. You can get to know a little more about these things then.

**Alix:** That sounds okay, I'll see you then.

## Debriefing: What Did the Recruiter Do?

The recruiter (in this example, it was me) modeled specific strategies in the sample dialogue. These techniques will be useful as you conduct your recruitment meetings. Let's highlight a few of the key principles:

1. I spoke about what we had in common (our children), although I did not focus the conversation on my interests and my life.

2. I followed up on my questions, encouraging her to think about herself and talk about herself.

3. I did not force her to commit to anything or pressure her. I simply suggested a specific follow-up action that seemed well within her area of interest and her time constraints.

## When You're In Someone's Home

In someone's home, the kitchen table is a good place for conversation. (Life insurance salespeople say this, too.) Notice the little things of their lives—pictures of family on the walls, basketball trophies, or wall hangings from far-off places. Home decorations tell you a great deal about the people you are visiting. If something is in open view, ask about it—if it is in plain sight, this is not prying. "Oh, are those your children?" "Is that a recent photo?" "Who is the basketball player?"

Sometimes what you see in a home provides openers for a conversation about people's values. Are they just out for themselves? Do they think everyone deserves a fair chance? Have they volunteered to coach girls' basketball? Why is it that some schools have big gyms and nice athletic fields and some have only a parking lot for the kids to play in? Why is it that people in some neighborhoods breathe fumes from diesel buses and others get good train service? There are lots of ways to uncover how people think about what is right and wrong in the world.

## Food and Drink

**Accept all offers of food or drink**, unless it is against your religious or other strong beliefs or you have a medical reason not to. Food and drink, even a glass of water, whatever is offered, invoke the ritual of breaking bread together. This is an age-old bonding tradition. But beware: Recruiting can be fattening. If your host offers you something that you really don't like, ask for a glass of water. Even if you are stuffed from your last visit, you can always accept a glass of water. Alcohol is not advisable. Remember, you are working. Keep alert.

## Cultural Differences

Be aware of cultural differences. You need to understand the meaning of different foods, even of water. For example, some Haitian-Americans will not accept a glass of tap water, having experienced this as inferior or even dangerous in their homeland. Offering it could be insulting. Similarly, cultures vary in how directly people speak about personal issues, in how close you should stand (or sit) during a conversation, in the significance of eye contact, in use of first names, in how you address somebody much older than you (or much younger than you), etc. Pay attention to these unspoken signals. If you aren't sure of the cultural nuance, find a mentor from that culture and ask him or her. Or, better, do the visit with a partner who is from that culture.

## *Story: Culture Matters*

*One of my first organizing jobs was in Revere, Massachusetts. There were a lot of Italians there, as well as Irish and some Jews. The Italians always fed me. One day, I was sitting in the kitchen of an Irish family. I was hungry. There was a basket of food on the table right in front of me. Just then, my host said, "We're Irish, we just put the food out. We don't ask you to eat." I said thanks and asked if it was okay to take something. He said yes, and I ate.*

I had been oblivious to the cultural dimension of the inter-action. I was lucky that this man explained it to me.

## After the Meeting

### Keeping Records

After a recruitment conversation (but not during it—remember you are not taking a survey!), make notes to remind yourself of the important things you heard about this person. Do this right away. Your memory of the person will begin fading *immediately* after the meeting.

When I was doing a lot of one-on-ones and I was driving to the visits, I would immediately go to my car and write down the important things I remembered.

**QUICK TIPS**

## *A Simple 3 x 5 Card System Works Well*

3 x 5 cards work well. Not high-tech, but reliable. And the cards fit nicely in file boxes. Keep them in alphabetical order. For the sample dialogue, the 3 x 5 card might look like this:

**Figure 3:** *Sample Record of a One-on-One Visit*

> *Visit: 2/23/02*
> *Alix Smith 54 Mason Terrace, Cloverdale,*
> *(h) 889-6756, (w) 878-6750 ext. 352, two children,*
> *6 and 10, Garfield School, dad died, mom sick,*
> *busy with her mother, Our Lady Church 4 yrs,*
> *from Detroit in '82, Pub. Rel., Adv. (Morris & Morris)*
> *Married (Gene), dad banker, meditation, grandparents*
> *farmers here. Issues: classes too big, no PTA,*
> *Commitd: sd wd come to 3/20 disc. grp. Looks good.*

After doing hundreds of these one-on-ones and recording brief notes about each person, I noticed that my memory for details of people's lives improved. Writing down the information on the card seemed to help etch the information in my brain. The cards are also useful because they allow you to refresh your memory, which helps to reinforce it. Remembering the details—children's names, where people were born, what they like to eat—strengthens relationships.

If you have the wherewithal, computer databases are useful for any large list. They allow you to code participants by various categories and to keep track of members' activities and interests.

**QUICK TIPS**

## *Follow-Up: Using Your Notes to Strengthen Relationships*

Most people like to be remembered on their birthdays. A short call or even an e-mail or a note may make them feel appreciated. This helps to build community and models caring for others. An annual list of birthdays helps. I have a monthly calendar good for any year. It hangs in my kitchen. I write in people's birthdays. Then each month I can easily see the birthdays and call to wish everyone on the page a happy birthday. You can also use a Palm Pilot or other personal digital assistant for this task, if you prefer to go higher-tech.

### Following Up

*When you find "live wires," put them to work immediately. Find something they can do—any little thing—and get them started and ready to do more, or you'll lose them for the cause.*

—Fred Ross, Sr.

(Fred Ross, Sr., was the organizer who trained Cesar Chavez and developed the widespread practice of house meetings in the campaign to build the United Farm Workers union.)

I started exploring next steps with Alix, the woman in the sample long visit dialogue, during our very first meeting. I asked her to come to a one-time discussion group after church in two weeks. The best way to get someone started in the group is . . . to get the person started!

If you promised that you'd do something specific after the meeting, do whatever you promised to do. Following up and following through are sure-fire ways to recruit volunteers or members. How many people really do what they say they will do? If you do, you will distinguish yourself greatly.

Reminding helps. Ask if it is okay to remind the person of upcoming meetings or other activities or opportunities. I even ask *how* people like to be reminded, by phone or e-mail, at what time of the day, how late or early I can call. Try to model care and accountability.

**QUICK TIPS**

## *Summary of How to Do a One-on-One Recruiting Visit*

- Talk no more than 20 percent of the time. Listen 80 percent of the time.

- Mention clearly the name of your organization. Make sure the person you are recruiting hears it.

- Encourage people to talk about themselves.

- Be yourself. Be real. Don't fake interest. Disclose enough about yourself to make the other person feel comfortable talking about him or herself.

- Tell the person enough about your organization so that he or she gets the general picture, but not enough to bore your listener or to appear to be "selling" the organization.

- Find out about the person's values and where they came from. (Some basic questions about society can help you to find this out: "Why do you think the situation is the way it is today?" "Do you think there is something basically wrong with society today—how people are living?")

- Find out about the person's networks and connections.

- Find out what other similar work the person has done in the past. Find out about other organizational affiliations he or she has. Find out how busy he or she is with these or other commitments. You don't want to overload your new recruit.

- Ask for some specific commitment, no matter how small—a task the person will do, such as pay dues, come to a meeting, give you the name of someone else to visit, etc.

- Suggest some follow-up, unless the person is not at all right for your organization.

- If the organization has individual membership dues, give people you are recruiting the opportunity to pay dues or contribute money. Let them know that the organization receives money from its members. Don't let this come as a surprise later.

- If you're in someone's home, accept offers of food and drink—otherwise, you may insult your host unintentionally.

- Use what you see in the person's house as a springboard for this get-to-know-you conversation.

- Be sensitive about cultural differences and about what these might signify, especially when you're the guest of someone whose culture is different from your own.

- Record your notes after each meeting. It may be tempting to skip this step. **Don't!** A dozen one-on-ones later, you'll regret it.

- Follow up. If you agreed to do something after the meeting or to find something out for the person, **do it!**

## ▶ Recruiting for a Task

*The duty of the organizer is to provide people with the opportunity to work for what they believe in.*

—Fred Ross, Sr.

Another way to recruit people to your organization is to recruit people to an activity. Many people want to *do* something useful, not just go to another meeting.

### Story: To Be Of Use

*I used to volunteer for the Boston Community Development Loan Fund fundraising committee. Each December, the staff person would invite us to the annual fundraising mailing party. There was food on the table, as well as a list of hundreds of potential contributors. We wrote personal notes on the letters to the people we knew, then folded and stuffed them. We knew we were being useful. The mailing brought in money. A personal, handwritten note on a fundraising letter increased the likelihood of a contribution. I liked writing to people I knew but didn't see often. It also made me feel good to know that the people I wrote would know that I was a volunteer for a valued community organization.*

When you have people who are already interested members of your group, you want to get them more involved and motivated. You want them to take responsibility. There is likely too much work for those who are doing it now. You need the help! There might not seem to be something for them to do. Or you don't think they could do what *you* can do. Your job is to find something for them to do.

## How to Recruit People to a Task: Working for Meaning, Not Money

You are working with volunteers. You cannot tell them what to do, "or else!" You have no formal authority over them. They are working for meaning, not money. You need to find out what has meaning for them. How do you find this out? How do you recruit people to a task?

These are guidelines I have found helpful:

**1. Ask them to help**. This is the first and most important guideline. Just as you need to *ask* people to join, you need to *ask* people to help. People are unlikely to help without being asked. If you don't ask they are not likely to know that you need the help.

**2. Ask them what they like to do.** It doesn't help to ask someone who hates to make phone calls to make phone calls. Maybe he or she will hold a house party, or hand out flyers at the church, or bake cookies. *Find out what the person likes to do.*

**3. Come with a mental menu**. Not a menu of food (although food is vital at most events)—but a menu of things they can do. This menu should be in your head. Don't refer to a paper when you are recruiting people. You want them to look at you and see you looking at them. If you give them a piece of paper, they are more likely to look at the paper than at you. *You recruit people with people, not paper.*

For instance, "We need someone to weed the hedges around the building, bake lasagna for the supper, sell tickets, collect tickets, sign in guests at the dinner, put up signs on the telephone poles along the road to direct people to the dinner, and make phone calls." Ask specifically for what you want. (*Do not ask:* "Can you help us out tonight at the club?" *Do ask:* "Can you help us with the club membership by calling ten people tonight between 7:00 and 8:00

p.m.?") When people ask what they can do, tell them, "It depends on what you like to do. You can choose." (This is probably an opportunity they won't have in a paying job!) Match what the person likes to do with what the organization needs.

**4. Know your overall project**. Know its parts. Divide the whole into as many parts as is reasonable—things people can do without bumping into one another. Make many small tasks rather than a few big tasks. You need as many people as possible in your organization, and each of them needs to feel needed. And they are needed! Before you start recruiting for tasks, take some time to divide up the jobs.

**5. There is something for everyone to do**. Participation breeds greater involvement. Let everyone help as much as they wish, even if it is only a small job. If they don't want to bring cookies to the meeting, ask them to come early to set up the chairs. Try to find something for everyone to do. If they don't want to do something on their own, ask them to help someone else with a task.

## Story: Better Together

*My mother told me the story of how she first met my father. They were students at City College and members of House Plan, a social and political group in the 1930s. The organizer of House Plan was a young instructor, Max Weisman. He recruited them for a task: to get some free cookies from a cookie factory for a party. The factory was a few blocks away. The cookies were not heavy. The task only needed one person. But, Max, the organizer, knew that such tasks sometimes create other opportunities. He thought they were right for each other. So he created a task that might create other opportunities. It did. Lucky for me.*

**6. Don't guess or think you already know what people like to do.** Even if you think you know, ask what they like to do. People like to be asked and like to get their first choice.

**7. Provide a context for the job.** Explain how this job fits in the overall campaign or project. People want to know how important their job is, and where it fits with the whole. Every link of the chain is necessary. No one wants to do busy work.

**8. When someone takes on a task, check how he or she is doing.** Don't assume everything is going fine. Often people won't ask if they don't know how to do something. Check in. You want to let them know you care. ("How is it going? Do you need any help?") But allow volunteers their space. You don't want to be a pest or seem like you don't trust them to do their job. When in doubt about the right distance to keep, you can ask them: "Is it okay if I check in on how it's going every week? Is that too often?"

**9. Appreciate people for the work they do.** Thank them. If they are doing a good job, let them know it. This takes little time and little money, but it is worth a lot. Written *thank-you*'s have staying power.

## Story: Letters Last

*I learned this lesson from a man whose mother complained that he never wrote.*

*"But Mom," he replied, "I call you every week."*

*"But a letter, Alan, that I can read over and over again."*

> *Dear Valerie,*
> *Thank you so much for helping out with the meeting last night. Your brownies were terrific!*
> *All the best,*
> *Alan*

I keep my thank-you letters for years. When I am feeling low, I can pull one out and feel a little better.

**10. If someone is doing a good job, think how this volunteer might take on more responsibility.** Ask if the person wants more responsibility and encourage him or her to take this on. ("You are doing a good job making phone calls. Would you like to take five more, or could you see how Marie is doing with her calls?") Think about what might be a good next step for the person—something that is right for him or her and helpful to the group.

**11. Hand off as much responsibility as possible as quickly as possible into responsible hands.** You want to build the leadership of many people. Leadership means taking responsibility. The group will function better when more people take responsibility.

**12. Keep your word.** If you say you are only going to ask them to do so much and no more, stick with it. Remember that you are building a relationship (and an organization based on relationships), not just getting a job done. Completing the task is not the goal. The goal is building the organization. This is especially true for time limits. If you say work will be completed by 9:00, stop by 9:00, not 9:05 or 9:10. You want your volunteer to return. Don't bait and switch. You do not want them to come home to an annoyed spouse or partner wondering where they were.

**13. Avoid doing it all yourself.** You are terribly competent. You know the job will get done if you do it—even if it takes until 4:00 a.m. This is often the path of least resistance and the habit of many leaders and hard workers. It is also the path to other things: burnout, no personal life, ill health, resentful spouses, no organization, and no members. *Getting others to help develops new leaders—one of your primary goals!*

**14. Keep track of what they say they will do.** Write it down if necessary so that you remember what they said.

**15. Emphasize the need for help**. This is real. "We can't do it without you" is a true statement.

**16. Rule number one. Again: Don't forget to ask people to help.**

## Dividing Up Tasks So Everyone Can Contribute

Since you need a menu of tasks to get volunteers to help, you need to know how to divide up a large task into bite-sized pieces. The following example shows how you can start to divide up the tasks for a project.

### Putting On the Organization's Annual Dinner and Awards Ceremony

This case example outlines a part of what it takes to put on a dinner and awards ceremony. You can see from this example how many different jobs there are for an event like this. When you make your own list, add on to this sampling of responsibilities the entire list of tasks needed for an event or a project. Some activities will have fewer tasks, others more. Almost any event, no matter how small, can be divided into smaller tasks.

***Sample Division of Tasks***

*Overall Project:* The Annual Dinner

*Large Task:* Prepare the dinner and all food
    *Sub-Task:* Buy paper goods
    *Sub-Task:* Buy drinks
    *Sub-Task:* Set up tables and chairs on night of the dinner
    *Sub-Task:* Cook lasagna

*Large Task:* Sell dinner tickets
    *Sub-Task:* Get tickets printed

*Sub-Task:* Sell tickets by phone
*Sub-Task:* Send out dinner flyer announcement
*Sub-Task:* Stuff envelopes on January 17,
7:00–8:00 p.m., at the office

*Large Task:* Awards Ceremony
*Sub-Task:* Get awards speaker
*Sub-Task:* Get all award certificates or award gifts
*Sub-Task:* Do calligraphy on award certificates
*Sub-Task:* Notify all people who will get awards to
make sure they attend

*Large Task:* Dinner Program
*Sub-Task:* Print program
*Sub-Task:* Hand out program on night of dinner
*Sub-Task:* Staff sign-in table at dinner

**EXERCISE**

## Dividing Tasks

This exercise will help you practice. Take a project. Divide it up into all its little pieces.

Your overall project: _____

**Large Task 1:** _____

        Sub-Task: _____

Who will do it? _____ By when? _____

        Sub-Task: _____

Who will do it? _____ By when? _____

**Large Task 2:** _____

        Sub-Task: _____

Who will do it? _____ By when? _____

Sub-Task: _____

Who will do it? _____ By when? _____

**Large Task 3:** _____

Sub-Task: _____

Who will do it? _____ By when? _____

Sub-Task: _____

Who will do it? _____ By when? _____

## This Is An Opportunity for the Individual as Well as for the Organization

When you are asking someone to do something, remember: It is an *opportunity for this person,* not a favor to you or the organization. You and the organization are not only out for yourselves. The group has to accomplish certain tasks. But you also want to provide an opportunity for people to do something that will benefit them. It is a balancing act.

In the sample one-on-one dialogue earlier, Alix, the woman I was recruiting for the group, was involved in the church. The discussion group I invited her to attend will be an opportunity for her to meet other people. It also will help meet her need to get better schooling for her children.

## ▶ Recruiting to Build a Democratic Organization: It Takes More Than Learning a Rap

How do you build an organization that is owned and run by its members? To approach the democratic ideal ("of the people, by the people, for the people"), the organization has to do more than serve its members or advocate on their behalf. Its members must take active responsibility for the welfare of the organization. If your organization wants this to happen, you need to communicate when you are recruiting that you will want members to take responsibility for the organization.

Communicating that members really own the organization is not easy. There may be skepticism and resistance from potential members. Some will find it hard to believe that their participation is valued, that the members own the organization. It may be the democratic ideal, but it rarely happens.

### A Recorded Role Play Can Be a Powerful Tool

When you try to communicate this idea, sometimes the words don't come out right. This may be because you have not fully understood and internalized the need for member ownership. Conveying the concept of member ownership requires that you first look inward.

A tape-recorded or videotaped role play can help. You need to go deeper than a rap or sales pitch. The exact words you use in a role play provide valuable clues about how to communicate the idea of member ownership effectively. The focus on the specific words used in the role play can help you see how your behavior (the words spoken in the role play) may conflict with what you think you believe. You can use the role play format to practice how you'll approach recruitment and to identify and address any conflicts between what you say and what you believe. Examining the conflict can then help you to modify your behavior so that you improve your ability to communicate the values of participation.

## More Than a Script

The recorded feedback provides many clues about the thoughts and feelings of a recruiter, which may conflict with the values and needs of the organization. You must listen carefully for the hidden assumptions in the specific words. Questioning the use of certain words and exploring the thoughts, feelings, and reasoning behind them can help you overcome obstacles to effective communication.

The taped conversation has power. When people hear their own words in their own voice, they can understand how they come across and then can modify their presentation to make it more persuasive. The recorded feedback provides indisputable evidence of what they actually said. It allows people to step outside of what they *think* they are communicating, and hear what they *actually* said and how others hear it. This helps people to better understand the effect of their words.

To do this role play, you'll need three participants: An organizer who wants to practice his or her approach, someone to play the role of the potential member, and an observer, preferably an experienced organizer, who will offer critique as you go along. Then, once you have completed the role play, you can go back and listen to the tape-recorded feedback and refine your approach.

An alternative, especially if you don't have three people, is to have the observer provide the critique and also play the part of the potential member. Another way to structure this is to go through the whole role play as a duo and then go back and listen to the tape, developing a critique together.

The following case study, a critique of a role play, illustrates how this might work. The initial role play enacted a one-on-one visit between an organizer and a potential member, set in the potential member's kitchen. "Davi" is an organizer-in-training. My role ("Michael") is to help him to understand some obstacles he faces in internalizing and communicating member ownership so that he can come up with an effective way to recruit members who will participate in the organization.

**CASE STUDY**

## Using Role Play and Critique to Practice Recruiting

**Davi (Trainee):** Hello, my name is Davi Malcolm and what I am trying to do is talk to as many people as possible here in the neighborhood about what is going on. Some people are upset about the schools, some about health care, some about the hospital. I am trying to talk to as many people as possible—to see what they are upset about, and to see what we can try to do about it. *[He now intends to launch into a discussion with the potential member about that person's concerns, as modeled in the recruitment dialogue earlier in the chapter.]*

**Michael (Observer):** *[I interrupt Davi here]* Davi, when you say you are trying to "talk to as many people as possible," what do you think the impact on your listener would be? I can tell you that it would make me feel unimportant. I would be sitting here worrying, "If you have so many people to talk to, you'd better get going. What are you doing here with me?!" ·

It is important that you convey in a one-on-one visit that you are concerned about *this* person. So, instead, you might say, "I am here to get an idea of what *you* care about." Why would you say, "I am trying to talk to as many people as possible?"

**Davi:** I said it because I feel like it is a little strange that I've asked to come over to this person's house.

**Michael:** You feel it's strange? Did your host do or say anything that might lead you to think it's strange?

**Davi:** No, that always surprises me. Why would I allow this person, whom I don't even know, into my home, to talk about this organization I never heard of?

**Michael:** Well, you might just begin by thanking them. But what do you think is the reason this family let you into their home?

**Davi:** I think they let me into their home because they are used to people visiting—at least, the people who were with the old organization are used to people visiting. There's confidence that I'm not a crazy person wielding a hatchet.

**Michael:** That you're not going to do them any violence?

**Davi:** Yes.

**Michael:** Is there anything that your host said or did that led you to think that he or his family was afraid of you?

**Davi:** No.

**Michael:** So what would make you think they might be afraid of you?

**Davi:** Well, I'm afraid of someone coming into my house. I wouldn't let anyone in.

**Michael:** So, you figure that since you wouldn't let someone into your house, the same goes for this family?

**Davi:** *[laughing]* Why not?

**Michael:** What goes for you goes for them?

**Davi:** Sure.

**Michael:** But is that always so?

**Davi:** Well, no.

**Michael:** Is there anything about these people here in this house that would make you think they feel that way?

**Davi:** No.

**Michael:** So it's mostly that you reason that if you think a certain way, they must think that way, too? Except there is nothing they said or did that would make you think that.

**Davi:** Yeah, I guess that's true.

**Michael:** Here's how you might start off the conversation without getting into that trap:

"Hello, I am Michael Brown from Neighbors in Action, and I just want to talk to you about some of the things you are concerned about. We are a membership organization of people all over the city. I am interested in getting a sense of what you are concerned about."

## Look at the Reasoning and the Feelings

In this case, the new organizer feels uncomfortable about visiting a potential member. So he says he wants to visit "as many people as possible." He feels uncomfortable, and reasons that the potential member will also feel this way. (Psychologists call this "projection.") As a result, he subconsciously communicates to the potential member that the organization is not interested in what he or she thinks. This turns off the potential member.

In theory, the organizer believes in *member ownership*. (He says he does.) However, he feels strange about people visiting in his home and reasons that others will feel the same way. Therefore, he communicates a different value—that the potential member is just one of many whom the organizer needs to talk to. His feelings get in the way of communicating what he says he believes and wants to convey.

The tape recorder or video camera can help you to uncover this. Reviewing the recording, the organizer can see that his words are based on faulty reasoning. Hopefully, this allows him to communicate the value of member ownership more effectively.

Building member ownership is never easy. To communicate these organizational values, we need to learn more than the right words to say. We need to examine our thoughts and feelings so that we are sure to communicate what we intend to communicate.

## ▶ Success Breeds Success

### Recognizing and Rewarding

Successful organizations recognize and reward people. Electoral campaign director Cathy Clement Saleh plastered the walls of Massachusetts State Representative Jim Marzilli's campaign office with the names and instant photos of volunteers. People liked seeing their faces on the wall. They felt important, recognized, and appreciated. It also helped people get to know each other.

*Once you take their picture and put it up, now they're a volunteer and part of the crew, ready to get to work.*

—Cathy Clement Saleh

People like to be appreciated. Verbal *thank you*'s are always welcome. Gifts and other tangible awards also motivate people. Even the simplest paper certificates inspire volunteers. The energy level in a meeting flares up when someone gets an award. The award rewards the individual and also builds the morale of everyone else. When someone is recognized publicly, others can imagine themselves up front next time, receiving an award and the applause of the group.

## Celebrate!

Effective organizations celebrate. People who join organizations come with all their complex wishes, hopes, and dreams. Effective organizations recognize that putting people first—taking time to resolve conflicts, to say thank you, to listen to personal problems, to celebrate—is not a frill. It is an essential part of building an effective organization. Parties, music, dancing, and food (don't forget the food—organizations, like armies, march on their stomachs) are part of any recruiting or organizing effort.

# CHAPTER 7

# The Way to Develop Power Is to Develop Leaders

*The next day Moses sat as a magistrate among the people, while the people stood about Moses from morning until evening. But when Moses's father-in-law saw how much he had to do for the people, he said, "What is this thing that you are doing to the people? Why do you act alone, while all the people stand about you from morning until evening?" Moses replied to his father-in-law, "It is because the people come to me to inquire of God. When they have a dispute, it comes before me, and I decide between man and his neighbor and I make known the laws and teachings of God."*

*But Moses's father-in-law said to him, "The thing you are doing is not right, you will surely wear yourself out, and these people as well. For the task is too heavy for you, you cannot do it alone. . . . You shall also seek out from among all the people capable men who fear God, trustworthy men who spurn ill-gotten gain. Set these over them as chiefs of thousands, hundred, fifties, and tens, and let them judge the people at all times. Have them bring every major dispute to you, but have them decide every minor dispute themselves. Make it easier for yourself, and let them share the burden with you. If you do this—and God so commands you—you will be able to bear up; and all these people too will go home unwearied."*

—Exodus, 18:13-23

After recruiting, a further step in mobilizing resources is developing leaders. Leaders are people who influence others and do the organization's work. You need to find people who will not only pay dues but also will take on responsibility for the organization. How do you do this? For whom do you look?

Leaders come in all shapes, sizes, and colors and from all backgrounds. Some people think only certain people can be leaders. In World War II, the U.S. Army needed to develop many leaders—quickly. They thought the most likely leaders would be tall white men. Better-qualified candidates were overlooked for promotions and success in the Army simply because they were not tall, white, and male. The Army's assumption, of course, was false. Physical traits don't determine leadership.

## ▶ What Do Leaders Do?

In building an organization, even Moses could not do it all by himself. Getting capable help is better for the group and better for the leader.

Leaders make sure things go right with the organization in many areas. Organizations need many and different kinds of leaders. No one leader can do it all.

**1. Leaders think about and develop the leadership of other people in the organization.**
They ask: What does this person need in order to develop his or her leadership? What is his or her next step in taking responsibility for the organization?

**2. Leaders also think about the whole group and what it needs.**
What does the group as a whole need to be stronger? How can a group find its power and voice?

## A Circle of Leaders

Jane Sapp, who is a musician and song leader as well as an organizer and educator, once described to me the African American tradition of "call-and-response" music in terms of its leadership style. Call-and-response underscores the need for many leaders and the fact that many people can and must lead—perhaps at different times—in order for a group to succeed:

*For call-and-response, the group forms a circle. Someone steps in the center of the circle. That person's role is not to tell people what to do but to facilitate how the group can find its voice, find what it has in common, and then act— to sing, clap, march. And you are not the only one who can do that. Someone else can step in. You have something to offer in that moment, but that moment can run out. There is always someone else in the circle who can con- tribute. The leader is someone who stands in the circle for that moment.*

*Sometimes a person leads for just a few minutes, and sometimes, it is for an extended period of time. There are recognized song leaders in this tradition who bear that role for many years. The role is bestowed by the commu- nity on someone whose voice and leadership inspires, dares them to imagine (as when people create different verses), gives hope, and sounds the call for action. What is special is that the circle is always open to new leadership, to someone willing to stand in the circle for that moment, bringing energy, imagination, and willingness to act.*

## The Leader's First Job is to Develop Leaders

Many of us see a problem that needs solving and believe that we may be able to fix it quickly. Developing leaders, rather than solving problems, often involves changing old habits, changing our "default" behavior in many situations.

It can be very challenging for us. The act of building organizations by developing leaders makes us radically rethink what it means to be "helpful" and how we "help."

The following story illustrates some of the complexity of helping. The kind of helping it focuses on is not solving a problem, but developing leaders. The assumption with this kind of help is that the absence of strong leadership in the community is a more important problem than the lack of garbage pick-up, and that a longer-lasting kind of help involves developing leaders rather than more quickly solving the immediate problem.

This is a simple story, maybe too simple. It reminds me also how complicated and difficult it can be at times to remember to develop other people's leadership when we have an ego, when we can so easily focus on the "issue" or problem at hand, and when we want to be "helpful." It is not easy to watch a problem fester when you know how easily you could "fix" it.

## Story: Of Dumpsters, Old Friends, and New Leaders

*An organizer I knew was once working to organize some low-income people who lived in a section of their city that had not been incorporated and was therefore not legally part of the city, even though it was situated right in the middle of the city. Sometimes it was referred to as "the hole in the doughnut." Services were not good there. Roads were full of potholes or not paved at all. Streetlights were not repaired. There were no sidewalks and no trees. There was no garbage pick-up.*

*When the neighbors got together to talk about their problems, the lack of garbage pick-up seemed to be their number one problem. They figured that getting curbside garbage pick-up would be expensive, but they thought that getting some dumpsters would not be as hard. It would not cost the city as much.*

*Joey, the organizer, had grown up in the city. He had a close personal relationship with one of the city councilors. He was almost certain he could make a quick phone call to his friend and get the dumpsters set out in a week. The neighbors would be happy. The garbage would not be piling up in their yards. Summer was coming soon. He knew that the smell could get pretty bad.*

*He did not make the call, tempting as it was. He knew that his first job was to build the organization and develop leaders of the neighborhood group, not to get the garbage picked up. If he had called his friend and asked for a favor based on his personal relationship and history, the neighbors would have learned the lesson that those with connections can get favors done, but others are at the mercy of the decisions of those in power.*

*It certainly would have been simpler and much quicker for the organizer just to make the phone call. It would have "solved the problem." But—and this is the crucial "but"—it would not have built any organization or developed any leaders.*

*The organizer is always looking to **build the organization** and develop other leaders. Every act goes toward this end. Organizers know that if they take charge and "take care of the problem," other problems will arise later and the community will be no better off than when it started.*

*So Joey looked for people from the neighborhood who could go to City Hall and ask for the dumpsters. Then, the relationships of power might begin to change. People who previously were off the trash collection route, people who had little clout in the town, might start to speak up for themselves and win something for themselves, rather than having someone else do it for them. Organizers don't do it all for you. They find ways to let you do it for yourself. This builds leadership, responsibility, and the organization.*

## ▶ Leaders and Self-Interest

An important element of identifying leaders is knowing who is likely to become a leader and why. The traditional model of community organizing pointed to individual self-interest as the basis for identifying, recruiting, and developing leaders. Saul Alinsky, who developed much of modern community organizing technique and theory, understood that self-interest moves people to action. Successful organizers help people identify their self-interest and then organize groups of people to negotiate for their collective self-interest. Alinsky understood that low-income people were unable to advance their self-interest and meet their needs without the power of an organized group. This self-interest often involved problems common to people in a geographic community: poor housing, pollution, unsafe traffic conditions, poor municipal services, etc. Alinsky's approach was based on the model of union organizing that united workers of a company to achieve power against the authority of the owners of the business. Various tactics, generally involving bringing many people together to demonstrate their unity and to negotiate with those in authority, were the hallmark of this kind of organizing. This approach makes sense in many situations.

For Alinsky, self-interest was distinguished from selflessness, to avoid do-gooder types who wanted to "uplift" the oppressed. Alinsky was intensely opposed to such a social service mentality. He knew that such an attitude would alienate the "have-nots." It would not empower them to change the relationships of power that made them have-nots in the first place. He knew that the have-nots or the "have-a-little-want-some-mores" (as he put it) would only be effective in improving their lives if they designed solutions to their problems. He advocated agitating (Alinsky's phrase was "rubbing raw the sores of discontent") to encourage people to fight their own battles, in their own self-interest, and with their own associations.

Traditional organizing also distinguished self-interest from selfishness—which focuses only on the individual's needs, without any consideration for others. Selfishness was too limited. Self-interest is healthy. If you won't stand up for yourself, who will?

If you haven't read Alinsky and you want to do community organizing, start your education there (after you're done with this book, of course!). The Bibliography at the back of this book has information about Alinsky's writings.

## Self-Interest: Not So Simple

Yet, self-interest is not so easy to define. Alinsky was talking mostly about better living conditions and economic self-interest. But I don't believe that is the whole story. I have known people who worked in a wide variety of community organizing efforts. Parents lobbied to put up "Watch Out for Children" signs on their streets. Neighborhood leaders visited City Hall to research tax records. Others organized public hearings to lower the utility rates, worked for years to create affordable housing, and fought for other improvements.

On one level it was in their self-interest, just as Alinsky understood the concept. Their children might be safer crossing the street. Their taxes might go down. Their gas bills might go down. They might have a stable place to live.

But the reasons the specific leaders of these efforts were involved were more complex than economic self-interest or personal safety alone. For many leaders, narrow definitions of self-interest do not fit. People also seek to make meaning of their lives. Making a difference matters to them. Living by their values and speaking out for their beliefs is an important part of their identity. These can be a powerful part of self-interest.

In other words, self-interest rarely is one-dimensional. For people who join organizations, especially those who take leadership, their motivations draw from a deep reservoir of family history and longing for meaning, community, spiritual fulfillment, and connection—as well as from their economic self-interest.

Two leaders I knew in a campaign to improve the schools were elderly grandparents who had raised their children long before and whose grandchildren no longer lived in the city. They lived on Social Security and modest pensions. Yet, they worked to raise taxes to improve the schools in their city. Their motivation came from their basic decency and concern for all people, not from their immediate economic self-interest.

**CASE STUDY**

## Self-Interest at Work in Leadership Development

The resident leader of the Camfield Tenants Association worked for years to rebuild the low-income housing development where she lived. Her journey into leadership started one morning in 1992 when she awoke to find a note tacked to the door saying that HUD was selling the building. As she said later,

*When I saw the notice, I thought immediately of my five kids, and I thought, "Where will we go?" My husband and I both had mediocre jobs. I remembered all the displacement that had happened in Boston—this city has a history of displacing minority people.*

*I knew what could happen if you sit back and do nothing. I grew up at a time when the issues were Civil Rights and Vietnam. Activism was not looked down on.*

*I had heard about Jack Kemp's HOPE program. Kemp thought communities would probably develop if resi-*

*dents had a vested interest in the property. I had talked with two of my daughters about why their friends did not come over. They said, "Who wants to come over when you have a big dumpster sitting in the parking lot?" Kids have enough problems they have to face. They shouldn't be ashamed of where they live. I thought it would be nice if more families could achieve something and move into the mainstream. They just needed a stable and comfortable place to live.*

So she stuck with the fight and over the decade she and her group achieved their goal.

By the time the development was rebuilt, it would have been in her own financial self-interest to move out of the Camfield Gardens development, buy a home, and build equity, rather than continue renting in the development. She could have done that. But her family's history of involvement in the Civil Rights struggle taught her to give back to her community.

She certainly was not selfless. The skills and confidence she acquired during the ten-year campaign to rebuild the development helped her to earn a Master's degree and advance from the position of school secretary to schoolteacher. She gained other leadership skills and built relationships with government officials and other professionals that might enable her to earn more money in other professional settings.

But her "self-interest" was not so apparent all the time. It was a complex web of family history, meaning-making, personal advancement and efficacy, and connection to others.

My own motivations are a web of self-interest, yearning for meaning, the satisfaction of making a difference in people's lives, money, security, power, interesting work, spiritual fulfillment, a connection to my family's history, friends, public recognition, and more. Understanding self-interest involves cutting away layers of self to get at the core of who we are and what we want. That is why stories are so important. That is why relationships are important. The organization builds networks through the ties of relationships, based on our knowing each others' stories—as much as through our own economic self -interest.

We can't ignore economic self-interest in looking for leaders. But we miss many opportunities if we make narrow judgments about someone's self-interest.

Self-interest, in all its complexity, is essential in identifying leaders and building any community organization. The emphasis on self-interest helps to avoid the trap of organizing people who only want to help the other. Some people or organizations envision their work to improve the world as only helping others—the whales, the wilderness, the poor children in Brazil. If the organization's action is not connected to its members' self-interest, then such action or organization is likely to be short-lived. People are unlikely to sustain an effort that is not connected to their own self-interest.

*If you come to help me, go home. But if your liberation is bound up with mine, then you are welcome here.*

—Brazilian peasant

One may want to save the whales, protect endangered species, or end slavery in faraway places. If we delve for the personal stories that motivate people to do this, if we uncover the self-interest in a seemingly distant project, then we have a better chance of building a stronger organization. If not, the organization's action is likely to be another "do-good" project; it is liable to be swept away when some other issue comes along.

## Listening for the Real Story, Uncovering Self-Interest

*Nothing has stronger influence psychologically on their environment and especially on their children than the unlived life of the parent.*

—C. G. Jung

To identify self-interest, it helps to get people to tell *their* stories. Why have they come into the organization? Where do they come from? What motivates them to be in the group?

Although we may cover up painful parts of our past, they remain with us. The stories of the hard times of our parents or grandparents...we inherit these. They have a powerful hold over us.

The positive side also affects us. The values we learned and the behavior we observed in our families continue to influence us. Wonderful moments of our own experience also motivate us—our ambitions, hopes, and dreams; those times when we have felt at one with ourselves, with others, with the universe; moments when we knew we were doing what we were put on the earth to do. We want to get that feeling back.

Telling our stories gives us a chance to remember the good and the painful, the successes and the losses. It allows us to better understand our own self-interest and the self-interest and motivation of others. We need this understanding to have the strong relationships that allow us to trust others.

For these reasons, organizers go for the stories. Sometimes we need to push to get at what motivates someone. We do this because we need people to understand their *own* self-interest. We also need to understand their stories to believe that they will stick with the group. We need people who will be around for the long haul, people upon whom we can trust and rely.

# The Archaeology of Organizing: Digging for Stories, Meaning, and Motivation

### *"I Care About the Homeless"—A Mother's Tale*

This case study illustrates how a leader or organizer might uncover a piece of someone's story:

I am at a dinner party at a friend's home. I meet a woman who tells me that she is interested in becoming more politically active. She explains that she is concerned about homelessness and is thinking of getting involved in that issue. I ask her why.

"I just think it is wrong that there should be people who don't have a home to live in."

I say, "I agree, but why do you think that?"

"Well," she says, "it is just wrong. It is unethical, immoral. I just don't think the world should be like that. There is no good reason for it."

At this point, I am thinking that there must be some reason that she is so interested in homelessness. She is speaking with a passion that indicates something personal, something more than theoretical. Her voice is intense. Her eyes narrow a little, like she is trying to remember something. Her body tenses.

"Yes," I respond to her, "I agree, but why do you think this? What is the story behind your strong feelings about homelessness and your pull to work on this issue?"

She looks me in the eye. She has some idea of what I am up to. "What is the story?" she asks.

"Yes," I say, "Why you? Why do you care about this and not about something else? Why is this so important to you?"

"Well," she says, "years ago I was divorced. I had three children and almost no money, and I thought I myself might become homeless. I am remarried now and doing fine, but there was a time when it was not like that."

She is telling some of her story.

"Good," I say, "that is important, because if you are going to be effective in helping anyone else, anyone who is homeless, you need to know what is in it for you."

Some may object to the prodding or pushing modeled in this case study. How much to push depends on cultural norms, the setting, and the length of time you have known the person, as well as on your own feel for the person. When in doubt about how far to push, you might ask: "Do you mind if I ask you this? Am I being too pushy? I am asking you because I think it is important for both of us to know what lies beneath your interest in this issue so that you, and I, can be more effective in our work. Is it all right if I continue to ask you about this?"

No one homeless is going to want your help if they think you are only doing it for them. *If you are not doing it for yourself, they will not trust you.* You will not be very effective in gaining their trust or even in bringing any but the most superficial help to them. Your help also is not likely to last very long if you are not doing this for yourself. Help that is not long-lasting is not going to be effective, since homelessness, poverty, and the lack of affordable housing are not quick-fix problems. If you are not doing this for yourself, then you are vulnerable to being distracted by some other cause that comes along.

### You Need to Be Able to Tell Your Story

You not only need to know why you are doing this for yourself, but you probably also will have to be able to explain it clearly to others, including those whom you hope to help. So you have to practice telling your story in a way that anyone can understand. The woman at the dinner party may have the passion and self-interest to help someone who is homeless, but no one will know this. Often, our reasons for wanting to help may not be so clear to ourselves. We may have inklings, but we need to weave together the memories and reasons so that we can be honest with ourselves and also can explain our motivations to others. It is easier to dance on the surface, but if we are serious about helping, about being effective, then we have to understand ourselves and get to what really drives us.

### Beneath the Surface

Self-interest includes our whole selves, our stories and memories and the relationships we have with close friends and family. It involves all that makes us tick and why. We may want the traffic slowed on our street, a reduction in our tax bill, or a better school for our children. But while our economic self-interest is key, memory and meaning also play an important role. Self-interest, fully understood, lies beneath the surface and beyond outward appearances.

## ▶ Opportunities for Middle-Class Activists

### Not Looking for Self-Interest Misses a Chance to Connect

The failure to examine self-interest in its broadest sense also masks the problems of people in economically advantaged communities. Many people in such communities encounter overwork, family stress, economic insecurity from corporate layoffs and globalization, domestic violence, substance abuse, and other problems. A culture of wanting to appear fine and the reluctance of some organizations to examine their own members' needs, in the pursuit of helping the "disadvantaged," mask problems that exist close to home.

Economic self-interest also may not be so easy to detect. People with substantial economic means may have close relationships to others in economic hardship—parents, neighbors, fellow congregants, or others. For most people, self-interest extends beyond their own individual self— at least to their immediate family, to their friends, and to others close to them.

The tendency of those with more economic advantage not to examine and extend the boundaries of their own self-interest also limits their lives in ways that they themselves may not want. It makes it harder for them to see what they have in common with those in more obvious need. It makes it harder for them to develop honest relationships with those in need. If one thinks, "I am okay. It is only those *other people* who have problems and I am going to help them," one loses an opportunity to connect to those who may seem to be, but may not really be, so different from oneself.

Economically advantaged people sometimes recognize such limitations by lamenting the "lack of diversity" in their networks and relationships. They recognize that they are missing something in their lives. Examining the complexity of their self-interest can help to overcome such limitations.

## Making the Connection

The reluctance to look at their own self-interest and the preference for more charitable work also leads to the continuation of the very problems that more economically advantaged people want to fix. Often the most effective help can only come from government action or new policies. For example, the increase in family homelessness since the early 1980s resulted from a federal decision to withdraw from the support of low-income housing. (In the 1970s, over 625,000 new low-income housing units were added every year. In 2003, only about 115,000 were added.) Even the best-intentioned efforts to spruce up existing homeless shelters or to house individual families can't address this problem to the extent that government action can.

The focus of more privileged people often is on charity, which is other-oriented. If these people would look at their own pain and broader self-interest, they might then be better equipped to empathize with other people's pain. They wouldn't feel so separate from "the other." Identifying their own needs and self-interest would help them to make connections between themselves and people who seem to be unlike them or who have fewer financial resources. They would then be more likely to develop or join political efforts or politicized initiatives that seek to address the root issues underlying the problems that they hope to ameliorate.

## ▶ How to Develop Leaders

### Developing Leader(s) In Your Organization

Most people become leaders because someone asks and encourages them. Someone along your way probably asked and encouraged you to take responsibility. Now it is your turn to do for others what someone has probably done for you.

### The First Step: Remember Your Role

To start or strengthen a grassroots organization, you need to develop other leaders, people who will take responsibility for the group. In developing leaders, the first step is to recognize that *this is your job*!

> # The job of a leader is to develop other leaders
> •

We get so involved in various organizational tasks—raising money; planning and running programs and meetings; arranging rides, food, and room space—that we overlook the fact that one of our main jobs is to develop leaders, to get other people to take ever-increasing levels of responsibility for the organization. If we are not doing this, we are not doing our job.

Like any job, developing leaders takes time and focus. We need to constantly ask ourselves, "Are we sucking up so much responsibility that we are providing no room for others to take it? Are we doing tasks others could do? Are we practicing the 'Iron Rule' of organizing—never do for people what they can do for themselves?"

Developing leaders is a process. Leadership in organizations is a role (a job), not so much a personal quality or characteristic. We *develop* leaders. We don't find them fully formed.

**CASE STUDY**

## One List of Agreements

One way to help members take on more responsibility is to make those responsibilities explicit.

A leadership group I worked with at a tenants' organization came up with the following guidelines:

*1. Attend all meetings unless you call the office to say you can't attend or will be late, with a good reason why—sickness in the family, for example.*

*2. Come on time and stay until the end of the meeting.*

*3. Tell residents about upcoming meetings.*

*4. Do not promise to do any work you can't do or doubt you can do.*

*5. Accept no kickbacks for contracts.*

*6. Bring concerns of residents back to the Board.*

*7. Get help if you need more writing or speaking skills.*

*8. Provide staff with a schedule of your availability.*

*9. Don't abuse your authority.*

*10. Practice understanding of others. African Americans and Hispanics should understand each other. [This was a group of African Americans and Hispanics.] Ask if meeting days are a conflict. Check on the food people like and on religious observances. Put flyers into understandable language.*

*11. Maintain confidentiality. Do not spread information someone tells you in confidence.*

*12. Use a respectful attitude in meetings and at all times. This means: Don't behave in a loud or disruptive manner. Don't talk down to people. Don't use swear words.*

*13. Care for the property. This means: Prevent vandalism. Pick up papers on the ground. If you see kids on the fence, tell them to get off. Tell other residents to pick up trash and glass.*

*14. Continue to learn and to educate yourself. Attend workshops and other ongoing education for residents and future residents.*

*15. Exercise leadership. This means: Speak to members before the Board meetings. At Board meetings, talk about residents' specific concerns. Help others to become leaders. Support the positive recommendations of others.*

At the beginning, it may not be necessary to make such detailed agreements. But after people have been involved in the organization for a while and have agreed to accept leadership (responsibility), you will need to establish some group norms and clear expectations for members, and especially for leaders.

# Follow Through

Years ago, my colleague Anthony Thigpenn told me:

*"Organizing is one percent inspiration and ninety-nine percent follow-up."*

It is relatively easy to get people to agree to guidelines. Follow-through is tougher. It helps to write the agreements on a large piece of paper with magic marker in big block letters. Tape the paper up in the room where your group meets so people see the guidelines often. Visual reminders help.

## Make a Leadership Development Plan for Someone In Your Group

Leadership development happens one leader at a time. One way to develop leaders is to create a simple plan to develop that person's leadership within the organization. Set aside some quiet time to think about a specific person who has shown some leadership ability.

Paul Osterman quotes one woman as she describes what it felt like to be developed as a leader by a community organizer in an Industrial Areas Foundation organization:

*Judy Donovan (an organizer) has been instrumental in helping me keep the fire lit and challenging me and putting me in situations where I can apply what I've learned, putting me in leadership positions. She would say, "I need some help. I need a co-chair. I need somebody to run this meeting, and I need you to say a little about this. Talk about what you learned in training and share it with the other people." She would ask me to attend state rallies where we were focusing on a variety of issues and then come back and report to the group. Basically it was through action, putting me in situations where I had to apply what I had learned. It has become very comfortable for me because I've done it so many times, and it's become part of the fiber of who I am.*

—Paul Osterman, *Gathering Power*

After I have a strong relationship with someone, I am often transparent about what I am doing. I may even say something like:

"I am trying to develop your leadership. It is nothing mysterious or manipulative. This is what I am trying to do now, as we sit here in Dunkin' Donuts. I am thinking what might be a good next step for your leadership. What do you think? What do you want to do?"

The longer I work in this field, the more I find myself having conversations like this. One of the roles of an organizer is to demystify the role of the organizer. One way I develop leaders and teach leadership development at the same time is by explaining what I am doing while I am doing it and why. I don't do this early on or with everyone, but once rapport is developed, it can be useful.

**EXERCISE**

## Creating a Leadership Development Plan for Someone In Your Organization

Organizers and leaders are always making plans for the organization or for a specific project. It is just as important to make plans for how people in your organization can develop their leadership. This exercise helps you do that.

This exercise should take about ten minutes. Once you've completed it, keep it where you can see it and refer to it frequently. Monitor how you are doing. Modify your plan as you go along if needed.

### Leadership Development Checklist

Date completed: _____

By: _____

Name of leader: _____

1. Who recruited this person to the organization?

_____

2. When recruited? _____

3. Background: _____

_____

_____

_____

4. What are this person's core values? _____

_____

_____

_____

5. Where and how did the person get these values?

_____

_____

_____

(You should have some idea of this person's story. You should know the outline of why this person cares about certain things, and where he or she received these basic values—whether it was from parents, teachers, or experience.)

6. Issues this person is concerned about: _____

_____

_____

(Although people are more than bundles of the specific issues that affect them, you should have a general idea of the person's more immediate self-interest and what might move him or her toward action *now.)*

7. Networks: _____

_____

(Does this person have networks? Family, friends in his or her congregation, workplace, or other organizations? If not, you have to question the person's ability to be a leader. With whom does the person have relationships? Who could the person bring to a coffee at his or her house or to a meeting at work?)

8. Past organizational work: _____

_____

_____

(What work has the person actually done in the organization or elsewhere? Is she or he all talk and no action? Has the person ever hosted a house party? Brought people to a meeting? Made a flyer? Made phone calls? Helped out at the office? Contributed money? Helped plan a program? This will give you an idea of what this person might like to do and what else he or she might do with encouragement.)

9. Next step for leadership: _____

_____

_____

(What might this person do to develop his or her leadership? The next step may vary. It might make sense to ask what the person thinks might be a good next step.)

10. What leads you to think that this should be the next step?

_____

_____

_____

(If you find that there are gaps in your knowledge about this person, that's okay. Have another conversation with the person to find out what you need to know.)

## Follow-Up

Comments: _____

_____

_____

## ▶ The Iron Rule of Organizing— "Never Do for People What They Can Do for Themselves"

Like many rules, the "Iron Rule" is complicated and subtle in practice. The Iron Rule does not spell out what people can or cannot do for themselves. It does not mean that people can do everything for themselves at any point in their lives. It does not tell us when or if people need encouragement or a push to do what they think they cannot do.

Leaders develop through experience and action. Following the Iron Rule develops leaders because it encourages action and fosters new experiences. This case study illustrates how I pushed a leader to take on greater responsibility and learn a new skill. The push was not so hard as to make her give up. I wanted her to succeed.

**CASE STUDY**

### Next Step—Knocking On Doors

Elizabeth grew up in Revere, Massachusetts. After her father died, she lived alone with her mother. She attended Immaculate Heart of Mary, the local Catholic School, and inherited the Catholic concern for justice and the poor. In her early 20s, she phoned the community organization where I was working. It was unusual to get a call from someone. (We mostly went out to find people who might be members.) I went to visit her. We sat in her kitchen, talked, and drank tea. It was the first of many cups of tea I would have there. Elizabeth joined the organization and started coming to some of our small meetings.

After several months, I suggested to Elizabeth that she could help recruit new members by going door-to-door, as I often did.

She was reluctant. "I couldn't do that," she said. "Knock on someone's door? On my own street!?"

I thought she could. She was a little shy, but I also sensed that she wanted to learn, to grow, to make a difference in her city. To do this I knew she would have to gain some skill in speaking to people. Going door-to-door with me was one way for her to start. She seemed nervous, but not totally intimidated at the prospect.

"Okay, Elizabeth," I said, "how about if you just come along with me? I will knock on the door and do all the talking. I may introduce you as a neighbor, but you don't have to say anything, unless you want to. If you want to later, that is up to you. All right?"

By this point she trusted me enough to know that I would not put her into a situation that she would find intolerable. (Perhaps a little uncomfortable, but not intolerable.) I watched her body language for clues. I did not see tremendous fear, just a little reluctance. My taking the lead and going with her made door-knocking more manageable for her.

One early evening we went out door-knocking on her street. I knocked on the door and waited.

"Hi, my name is Michael Brown and I work with Revere Fair Share. This is Elizabeth Migliozzi, your neighbor. She lives at 101 Park.* I just wanted to hear what you think about the electric company's new rate increases, the new statewide tax law, or if there are other things around here that concern you. Are you concerned about those things, or about anything else like that?"

And so the conversations went. Sometimes we were invited in. Most times, we just stood outside at the door for five minutes, listening. Elizabeth was gradually getting the hang of it.

"Do you want to introduce yourself this time?" I asked.

"All right," she said.

And at the next house she introduced herself.

"Do you want to say anything else?" I asked. "I think you could probably say some of the things I said."

"Okay, I'll try."

"If you don't want to, that's all right. Just do what you are comfortable with."

"Okay," she said.

So at the next house she said a little more. And at the house after that, a little more. By the end of the evening she was getting more comfortable with going door-to-door.

Elizabeth could not go door-to-door by herself. It helped her to go with someone. Watching me, being asked to do a little bit at a time, got her comfortable with this activity. She needed to be encouraged—pushed a little, but not too much. Each step along the way, I would ask her if she was comfortable with doing a little more. I had to be willing to accept her answer, even if she chose to say no.

*The name and address given are fictional.*

## No Simple Rules for the Iron Rule

There are no simple rules for how you can know what someone "can or must do for themselves." Asking is a good start. "Would you feel comfortable introducing yourself?" was one of the first questions I asked Elizabeth. People will do for themselves when they are ready. They often surprise you with how much they are ready to do.

One goal of the Iron Rule is to get members to take as much responsibility as possible. This is why you give people the opportunity to do more.

Finding the right job takes judgment. Asking Elizabeth to go door-knocking was one possible job. I thought it was an appropriate next step for her. She had come to a number of our small meetings. She felt comfortable with the other members. But if she was going to develop her leadership, I thought she would also have to be more comfortable talking to strangers. I thought she could do this with a little help and encouragement. Turned out she could.

## The Iron Rule of Organizing: Why and How

Following the Iron Rule encourages members to take more responsibility for the organization. The organization will be stronger if many of its members, rather than only a few leaders or paid staff, take responsibility for the organization.

The Iron Rule not only builds the organization, it also helps individual members. They develop new skills and confidence. Underlying the Iron Rule is an assumption about people: They will feel better about themselves and have a greater sense of personal efficacy if they take responsibility for the organization, rather than acting primarily as consumers or clients. The Iron Rule assumes that people naturally want to take leadership and be effective. They only need the encouragement and opportunity to do so.

How might this work in practice? It begins with the little things.

## An Easy One: The Iron Rule of Supplying Refreshments

When I first tried to use the Iron Rule, I started with the little things. It meant I did not bring all the refreshments to the meeting. I relied on the members. This was something members could "do for themselves."

I divided up the job of bringing the coffee and doughnuts to as many people as possible, since it was something almost anyone could do. One person brought the coffee, another the sugar, someone else the milk, and someone else the cups. It took a lot longer to arrange this than doing it myself. I resisted the temptation to do it all myself (even though I knew it would certainly get done if I did it). I spent a lot of time on the phone asking people what they could bring. Since I wanted everyone to be involved, I tried to break down the refreshments into very small bits. My goal was to give everyone a job and make everyone, even in this little way, as *interdependent* as possible.

It was sometimes hard to find something for everyone to do. But I persisted. There was always something someone else could do. I did not want anyone who could do a job to feel that they did not have one. Sometimes it was tough, especially when people got annoyed at me when no one brought the doughnuts. Sometimes we had coffee but no cups.

It was a small matter with a larger meaning for the group. It let members know, at the beginning, how life would be in the organization. The organization is not in business to serve you. It is *your* group. *You*, the member, are responsible.

## It Shows Who Comes Through

When you start asking people to participate, some people come through. Others do not. They offer excuses. Asking people to take on tasks allows you to see who follows through.

If you start with the little things (like the doughnuts), you can see who does what they say they will do in a situation with little potential for major damage. See if people can accomplish the little things before asking them to take on greater levels of responsibility.

Once you move beyond the coffee and doughnuts, the Iron Rule becomes riskier and more complex. But the principle remains. Do not do for others what they can do for themselves. In the long run, doing for others what they *can* do for themselves just gets you—and the organization—into trouble.

## Moving Beyond the Doughnuts

It is not always easy to know what people can "do for themselves." For example, a colleague was arranging a fundraising house party for an organization that worked through religious groups to raise money to build afford-able housing. She had been trying to develop local "town teams," groups of individuals representing the various congregations in the town. She wanted to get them together, build town pride, and develop a sense of community and organization. She also thought they would raise more money if they were involved as a group, rather than only writing checks in the privacy of their own homes.

A key person in one town had agreed to host a house party. A house party is also a good way to test someone's leadership. Someone who can bring people to his or her home has leadership skills.

> A "house party" is a small event where someone invites friends into their home to raise money for an organization or to discuss an idea of common concern.

My colleague, the organizer, wanted to invite several key individuals from a dozen congregations in the community to the house party. Inviting the congregational leaders required calling up the priests, rabbis, and ministers in the town and asking them for the names of their key lay leaders.

## Who Should Make the Calls?

Generally, the host invites the guests to a house party. In this case, the staff organizer was in a better position to do the inviting because she had relationships with the local religious leaders and the denominational leaders of their churches. So she made the calls, because these were calls that the host could not have made efficiently by herself. The organizer applied the Iron Rule, but with judgment and sensitivity to the overall situation.

> *There is a constant push in organizing to encourage people (volunteers, members) to do tasks for themselves (such as making the calls, in this instance). Some jobs they can clearly do. But for others, the organizer may not be sure. Perhaps they could do the job, with a lot of help, but what people can "do by themselves" always involves a judgment call. The judgment may be about how much time it will take to get the people to "do it themselves." If it would take many hours of work with each member, can we really say that the members are able to do it themselves? Is it worth your time to get the members to do this job themselves? How effective would the calls be? What will happen if they do not do the calls well? What are the risks? With the refreshments at the community meeting, the risk is small: No doughnuts at the meeting. With the calls to the clergy, the risk is greater: Very few people come to the party and those who do come get demoralized.*
>
> *Each situation requires a judgment based on an analysis of complex dynamics such as these.*

### The Team Did This Task For Itself

After this house party, the town team decided that it wanted to go on a driving tour of the neighborhoods in the city where the organization had helped build affordable housing. This was something the town team members thought they could arrange themselves. They did. They made the flyer for the tour. They hired the bus and driver. They brought the people. The organizer found the locations to visit, but the members did most of the work of organizing the tour.

> *In this situation the organizer also followed the Iron Rule. The organizer realized that this was something the members could do and do well. Staff people or more experienced leaders often take over tasks without first asking, "Can someone else do this?" When we give in to this temptation, the task gets done, but no new leadership is developed and the staff or leader risks feeling overworked.*

## The Iron Rule Gets Us to Stop and Ask the Question

The Iron Rule encourages us to ask, "Is this something someone else can do?" It contrasts with the maxim, "If you want something done right, do it yourself." That is a recipe for ego-boosting and burnout—not to mention no organization-building or leadership development.

Take every opportunity to hand off tasks in the day-to-day activities of the organization. This builds member ownership and new leadership. This is so important because so much in our daily lives inculcates passivity and sucks away the urge to engage in civic life.

Organizers repeat the Iron Rule, like a mantra, to themselves and to others. It helps to contradict all the opposing messages that bombard us in our culture.

---

## The Iron Rule of Organizing

— • —

### Never do for people what they can do for themselves.

---

## What Stops You From Letting Go?

As hard as it may be for members to take responsibility, it also helps to recognize the difficulty that *you* face in implementing the Iron Rule.

One of the hardest parts of practicing the Iron Rule is changing your own mindset about the business you are in. You are not helping others, at least not the way "help" is commonly understood. Your goal is to develop leaders. You do everything you can to get others to take responsibility for the organization—and for themselves. It takes time and practice to develop a different habit.

Many of us who work to improve the world do so because we want to help others. Our desire to help can itself become a problem in building associations. Watching a little child struggling to open a big door, our natural reaction is to help. We see the child trying. We sense his or her frustration. It is hard to stand there, wait, and not do what *we* can so easily do.

### What Is Going On With Us?

It's often more about what's going on inside us, our feelings and desires, rather than thinking about what the other person and the organization need.

## Accept Offers of Help

The flip side of the Iron Rule is, "Always accept offers of help." It trains us to "not do for others what they can do for themselves" by allowing *others* to do for us what we can (probably) do for ourselves.

## Story: The Iron Rule in Reverse

*I was pushing my three-year-old daughter in her stroller. Getting on the subway, I had to go down a flight of steps. Now, I could carry her in the stroller by myself. As I was about to pick up the stroller, a young man ahead of me asked me if I wanted help. My initial reaction was, "No, I can do it myself." But I caught myself and instead said, "Yes" ("Always accept offers of help"), and I allowed him to hold the bottom of the stroller as he backed down the steps. He told me how he enjoys being with his seven-year-old daughter.*

This was a small incident. I tell it to remember to accept help, just as we need to learn how to ask others for help. Practicing the Iron Rule can be difficult, especially for those who want to help others. It may go against your instincts or your habits. Be sure to accept offers of help as often as possible, so you will get good at it. It will help to train you to not take on all the responsibility yourself—the essence of the Iron Rule.

## Screwing Your Head on Backwards

I sometimes describe the organizing orientation and the Iron Rule as "screwing your head on backwards." It can feel that painful and unnatural. People who want to help others often have trouble letting others do what they can do. Those that have ability and resources often feel the very human reaction of wanting to help and share. If you are competent, it can be difficult to not exercise your competence, to watch someone else struggle with a job.

## Story: Not So Easy Not To Do It Yourself

*When I was about twelve, I had to do a science project. I wanted to make a cloud chamber. It involved drilling through a glass peanut butter jar. My dad could do this, so I watched as he showed me how. Then it came to my turn. I started drilling and broke the jar. We had a lot of peanut butter jars I could have practiced on, but he took the drill out of my hand and did it for me. It was a natural reaction. But I never learned how to use a drill until many years later.*

**EXERCISE**

## Questions for the Iron Rule: Look Inside Yourself

One way to start to "screw your head on backwards," to internalize the Iron Rule of Organizing, is to examine your own thoughts and feelings. If you have read this far you are probably a person who has a habit of taking responsibility for making sure things go right. You have probably figured out somewhere along the way that not everyone is like you. Not doing for people what they can do for themselves can be a constant battle. This exercise might help. You may want to do it many times, for different projects and tasks. If so, just write your answers on a separate piece of paper.

1. Think of a specific project or job that needs to get done in your organization:

_____

_____

2. What stops you from letting go of a job or responsibility you can do, and letting someone else do it?

_____

_____

_____

3. What might happen if it does not get done right?

_____

_____

_____

4. Or if it does not get done the way you would do it?

_____

_____

_____

5. What is the result of your doing everything?

_____

_____

_____

6. Even if you can do it right, where does this lead you?

_____

_____

_____

7. Other thoughts and reflections:

_____

_____

_____

## ▶ More On the Iron Rule: Don't Suck Up All the Responsibility

### Story: A Time to Challenge

Sometimes you have to challenge someone to develop his or her leadership. There are risks, but also potential benefits.

*Rebecca was a student in a congregation's youth group. The group went off on a retreat for a weekend. Later, she told me:*

*"I was a teenager with an attitude. There I am, smoking off to the side. Well, the retreat sucked. And coming home on the bus from the retreat, the youth group leader asked me, 'What did you think of the retreat?'*

*"'It sucked,' I said. I was brazen. I was not going to tell him what he wanted to hear.*

*"He came back at me. 'So what does that matter? What are you going to do about it?'*

*"I said, 'Nothing.'*

*"Then he got up and walked away. And that pissed me off.*

*"So I ran up to him as he walked away, and said, 'What do you mean? What can I do?'*

*"And then he mentioned that I could do a project about AIDS, and asked me if I believed in this cause—AIDS activism. He asked me if I would lead a program with the youth group about that.*

*"This really took me aback," she remembers. "His asking me what I was going to do about it got me going. He didn't want me to just attend some lame adult program. He wanted <u>me</u> to do it."*

## Don't Make It Easy for People

Organizers put the responsibility onto their members. They do not suck up responsibility at the top.

Barry Oshry, the founder of "Power and Systems," a training program in organizational power dynamics, often talks about how "tops" in organizations "suck up responsibility"—rather than developing partnerships with those on the "bottom." (Read *Seeing Systems*, by Barry Oshry. Better yet, take one of his workshops.)

Organizers do not fix problems for others. (Remember the Iron Rule.) They challenge. They confront. This is not always easy. It is not even the right thing to do in all situations. Timing is important. It takes a close enough relationship so that you have a sense of *when* such a challenge is likely to bring positive results. You cannot fruitfully challenge everyone this way at all times. You need a trusting relationship and a person strong enough to be challenged.

In this case, the youth group leader, Larry, knew Rebecca pretty well. He took a chance. Rebecca said later, "It could have gone either way."

"What are you going to do about it?" is the kind of phrase you can use effectively only when you have built up a solid relationship with the person and know that he or she can take such bluntness. But you need to move in this direction, pushing responsibility onto those who are most affected by whatever the problem is. Organizers ask others to take risks. To do that, you have to take some risks yourself.

# Developing Leaders: Reminding

*The essence of organizing is reminding.*

—Fred Ross, Sr.

Remind people of the organization's needs, of events, and of the tasks they have agreed to do.

People often ask: "Why should I remind them of the meeting? They *said* they were going to come." Yes, but people forget. Something comes up. It rains. They remember an errand they have to do. They are used to people letting them off easily. They are not used to people holding them accountable or reminding them.

## On Being a Pest

You may think you are being a pest. Try not to worry too much about this. People usually appreciate reminders, because the reminders help them to be successful. The odds are that your reminder will help them to follow through. It is unlikely that someone who cares about this cause will resent you because you showed how much you cared both about the work and about his or her contribution.

**QUICK TIPS**

### *Humor Helps*

Humor helps. "Hello, this is your friendly pest calling you up, yes, again, just reminding you of the meeting Thursday." "Oh, yes, you are coming, great, see you then. Bye." This is an art. Like any art, it takes practice. If you are reluctant to call people just to remind them, explain that you are calling to see if they need directions, to tell them where to park or when the meeting will end—all those details that make it easier for people to get there and feel good about going. You want people to feel like they are being taken care of and that their presence matters—which it does! They are not likely to be annoyed by such a thoughtful call. Don't let your own fears about how they might feel stop you from reminding people.

## Spread the Work

Since the goal is to develop other leaders, you also want to get others to do some of the reminding. This is often easy to forget when the work piles up, the event is coming up soon, and you know everyone on the list.

Start by giving people lists to call, but you want others to do more than complete a task for you at your request. You want others in the group to feel it is *their* responsibility to remind others. Once you get to know people, you will see if they generally follow through and you will find out what motivates them to feel ownership of the responsibility. Not everyone will follow through. Part of your job is to see who does what they say they will do and who makes excuses. It will take some one-on-one conversations to help each person to internalize this responsibility. There are only so many people one person can be in touch with. Remember that your job is to develop other leaders, not just to get people to an event or to complete a task.

CHAPTER 8

# Mobilizing Resources: Meetings

*Before the Revolution there was a plague of taxes. After the Revolution there was a plague of meetings.*

—Old Chinese saying

Mobilizing people means meetings. Much of your organization's business happens in meetings. Meetings can be productive, useful, and even fun. They can also be dull and deadly. Running meetings well takes skill and attention to the details. Here are some guidelines for making meetings productive.

## ▶ Guidelines for Meetings

### People Bring People

To bring somebody to a meeting, it helps to have a relationship with him or her and to invite the person face-to-face. Next best is on the phone. E-mail is a far, far distant third.

Without a close relationship, flyers, e-mails, and public announcements will rarely bring people. True, flyers or a mailing for a hot issue—like a toxic waste dump or garbage incinerator proposed in the neighborhood—may bring people to a meeting. But these do not build a lasting organization. Use flyers and mailings to *remind* people of upcoming events, but not as your main recruiting tool.

Without a hot issue I have observed that 1,000 flyers attract one person on average to a meeting. Your time is better spent meeting several people face-to-face, rather than handing out 1,000 flyers.

## Story: No Magic Turnout

*A new organizer was working to turn out people for a citywide hearing on increased water and sewer rates. He passed out thousands of flyers. He put the announcement on cable TV. He called lots of people who had signed a petition on a door-to-door canvass. He was signing up hundreds of people to come to the meeting. He enthusiastically told me he expected 100 people at the hearing. Only a dozen showed up, all people he knew personally. He was disappointed, forgetting that flyers and media won't bring people.* **People bring people.**

The media and the mail have a place in a recruiting strategy and can be used effectively. It is helpful to copy any newspaper or magazine articles about your group. The media coverage lends legitimacy to your organization. But it doesn't bring people to meetings.

Some people—a small minority—self-recruit. They show up when they see an announcement. So public service announcements and ads in the media may result in new members. People who self-recruit will often be self-motivated and hard-working members. But they are also likely to be busy with other organizations. If you need more than a few people, *don't make media and mailing your main recruiting strategy.*

# When Should You Call a Meeting?

**The first rule for any meeting is to ask: Is this meeting necessary?**

You can break this question down into its sub-parts:
- Why are you having this meeting?
- What is its goal?
- Where do you want your organization to be at the end of the meeting that is different from where it was before the meeting?

Stop!

If you don't know why you are having this meeting, don't have it! If there is a reason for it, if it has a reasonable goal, go ahead. If not, wait.

# Goals for Meetings

Meetings may have several functions or goals:
- To make decisions.
- To brainstorm ideas about where the group should go.
- To celebrate a victory, build morale, recognize or reward leadership.
- To have a place and time to complete tasks (writing fundraising letters, stuffing envelopes, coming up with names of people to ask for money, etc.)
- To provide opportunities for training or learning.

Know the goal or goals for *this* meeting.

### Goals

Know the goals for your meeting. Writing them down helps—so that everyone in the room will know them.

At the meeting, take a flip chart or a piece of paper and tape it up on the wall. Draw a little box (for checking off once you've met the goal):

❏

Next to that, write:

**Goal:**

Next to that, write down the goal for the meeting.

For example:

❏ **Goal: To brainstorm ideas for group expansion.**

If you have more than one goal for the meeting, list them all in this fashion.

Meetings can have multiple goals. If this is the case, be clear about what they are. Write them all down. Get agreement from those at the meeting that this is in fact what you want to accomplish at the meeting.

## What Is the Right Time and Place for Meetings?

### Rule Number One: Start on Time and End on Time

How long should the meeting be? An hour or two is enough. Do not let your meetings run on.

## Story: Respect People's Time

*When I first worked construction I would get up at 5:00 a.m., drive to work, lug plywood onto the floor joists all day, and come home at 5:00 or 6:00 p.m. It was tough going to a community meeting at 7:00 p.m. The same schedule was typical for millions of people before me. It was an early lesson in how many people are kept in their place. The work tired me out. The exhaustion from the physical labor made it hard to keep my eyes open much past 9:00 p.m.*

One lesson was: End meetings on time. This work gave me an appreciation for anyone who came out to evening meetings after a long day at work. It helps to understand that organizational work for most people comes on top of a working day and other responsibilities.

### Rule Number Two:
### The Five-to-Nine Rule

I have observed that when meetings start at 7:30 p.m., people start squirming in their seats at 8:55 p.m. This is a sign that they want to leave. I call it the "five minutes-to-nine o'clock rule." End your meeting by 8:59. People will come to your next meeting.

### Rule Number Three:
### Make It Pleasant

Make the meeting as comfortable as possible. Pleasant surroundings help. Set up the space to minimize distractions, such as people wandering in and out or phones ringing. Ask everyone to turn off cell phones and beepers.

## Physical Layout

People should be able to see each other at the meeting. There are different ways to do this, depending on your goals for the meeting. Tables for participants provide a more professional setting, especially for a planning meeting where people may want to write or look at papers. Sitting in a circle or horseshoe shape creates a feeling of equality.

Adequate lighting and air circulation help people think.

Set out *fewer chairs* than the number of people you expect. Empty seats demoralize. Putting out chairs is a victory. Have extra chairs ready to put up easily and quickly when more people arrive.

Set clear physical boundaries for the meeting. Close doors. If the room is too large for your numbers, set up a visual divider or barrier so your group does not feel dwarfed by the space. Folding tables work well as room dividers.

## Ground Rules

Any group—especially one that wants its members to have an ongoing commitment to the group—should adopt guidelines or ground rules that express the values and behaviors for participants to observe in group meetings. (Even for one-shot meetings, ground rules for participants' behavior are useful.)

## Using Ground Rules to Guide Effective Meetings

### Sample Set of Ground Rules for Meetings

1. Listen to others in order to understand them. Don't just make sure that others understand you.
2. Appreciate differences.
3. Keep your sense of humor.
4. Take responsibility for focusing on what you care about.
5. It is okay to criticize another person's ideas, but not another person.
6. Don't talk more than your fair share.
7. Don't interrupt.
8. Allow for silence between comments.

You can say:

"I suggest these guidelines. I think they will make the meeting run better. Are they all right with everyone? Are there any others you would like to add?"

(Wait for response . . . allow for silence . . . look around the room . . . taking the time to look at everyone.)

Then write these guidelines down on a big piece of paper in black block letters large enough to be read by everyone in the meeting. Keep the paper displayed on the wall where you meet.

For ongoing groups, you can cover the poster with a plastic laminate to keep it from being ruined over time. Tape it to the wall at meetings so everyone can see it. Visual reminders help.

The sample shown is a fairly typical list of ground rules. Your group can tailor them to your organization. For example, some groups add "confidentiality" to their list of ground rules—that what is said in the room stays in the room. People sometimes need this guideline in order to feel safe in the group. Confidentiality in a group can build cohesion and trust. In other cases it may be irrelevant.

Get agreement about the ground rules. Keeping them visible helps the group to stay with them. If someone strays, you can point to the rule on the wall and remind the participants of their agreement. Since it's written down, it's tougher for any one person to claim that she or he never agreed to it.

## Deciding How You Will Decide

Meetings are, in part, a series of agreements. The group may agree to take on a task. It may agree to elect someone president or secretary. It may agree to go visit the landlord and ask for improvements in the building where all the members live.

Before getting to any of these larger agreements, you need to decide how you will decide:

• Will you vote and let the majority rule?
• Will you make decisions by a two-thirds majority?
• Will you agree to be governed by consensus?

You may run into trouble trying to decide how to decide when you are in the heat of an argument. It helps to make the decision about decisions early on.

Decisions can be tough for a group, just as they are for individuals. Don't underestimate the tendency of a group to put off making decisions. Just like many of us, groups can easily procrastinate. The word "decision" comes from the Latin root of a word that means "to cut off." So whenever we are making a decision, we are "cutting off" something else. This is painful. So, before you set a goal of a meeting to decide something, make sure the group has agreed to make the decision at the meeting and also has agreed *how* it will decide.

**QUICK TIPS**

## *Your Rules Are Better Than Robert's*

Many organizations fail to decide how they will make their decisions. When there is a disagreement, these groups often slide into Robert's Rules. This is a big mistake.

Robert's Rules of Order are a complex, formal system for group decision-making. They were developed by General Henry M. Robert, a U.S. Army Engineer who studied parliamentary procedure. He first published *Robert's Rules of Order* in 1876.

In the absence of an agreed-upon decision-making process, someone at the meeting invariably will "move" such-and-such or "make a motion." Most people don't know much about Robert's Rules beyond first and second motions. Most of us are intimidated by the formal protocol of something we don't understand, so we get quiet and step aside.

The reason groups tend to fall back on Robert's Rules is because many people have learned along the way that Robert's Rules are the "right" way and the "most democratic" way to run a meeting. This is not true. I have observed that the use of Robert's Rules tends to confuse people more than aid in democratic decision-making. Robert's Rules actually can undermine democracy in many community settings, where only a few people (or no people) understand them. This is the last thing that a participant-owned organization needs.

You're better off coming up with your own rules.
That way, you'll understand them and believe in them.
They'll work for you.

Decide ahead of time how you will make your organization's decisions. Don't slide into Robert's Rules. It is a slippery slope.

## ▶ Meeting Facilitation

Sooner or later you will facilitate a meeting. It is one of the most difficult skills in organizational life. Doing it well takes practice.

### The Meeting Before the Meeting

You need to prepare for meetings. Here are some guidelines.

**1. Know who is coming.** Consult with participants beforehand about what should happen.

**2. Anticipate problems.** Know what people are likely to do or say that might cause problems. I call this "the meeting before the meeting." If there is a topic that is likely to be controversial, talk to people about it before the meeting. Ask them what they think. Ask their advice. As a rule of thumb, it takes *at least* four hours of preparation for every hour of a meeting.

You ask people for their time, a valuable commodity. Don't waste it with unproductive meetings. Avoid problems by discussing them *before* the meeting. If there is a committee report, make sure that the person making the report sends out a written report before the meeting, and only summarizes the report. If he or she has a recommendation, make it and ask for questions. If there are ten people at the meeting and a report takes ten minutes longer than it should, that is 100 minutes of people's time wasted. If there are new people at the meeting, meet with them beforehand to catch them up on the history. Do not take everyone's time for questions that only one or two need to know.

**3. Remind people to come.** Make the invitation personal. Ask if there are personal needs people have that would create obstacles—transportation, child care, and accessibility.

**4. Include good directions** if the meeting place is unfamiliar. Provide written directions and a visual map. People learn in different ways. Some do well with words. Others need a picture.

**QUICK TIPS**

## How To Get People There: Provide Good Directions

Good directions alleviate anxiety and make everyone feel welcomed and comfortable.

In written directions include distances between points. ("Go 0.6 miles and then make a right turn.") Include landmarks. ("Go past the big ball field on the right. You will pass a large white church on your left.") Landmarks reassure people that they are not lost. People will arrive at the meeting in a better frame of mind and with more confidence in the organization when these little things are done well.

**5. Make specific assignments for participants.** Ask people to take responsibility for logistics or parts of the meeting. This helps to ensure attendance, spreads the work, builds community, and helps people to count on each other. It builds the organization. It helps people realize that it is *their* organization.

**6. Come early** to set up the room and make sure there are lots of signs pointing the way. If the meeting is somewhere people have never been, assume that they can easily get lost. Just because you know how to get there, don't assume others know or have your great sense of direction.

**QUICK TIPS**

## A Toolkit for Organizers

**Always Carry:** Cardboard and paper to make impromptu signs, dark magic markers, drafting tape, duct tape (for putting up more signs when your room assignment is switched at the last minute or the directions might be confusing). Black type on yellow paper is easy to see—like a school bus. A pocketknife with scissors is useful for cutting duct tape to hang signs or cutting wind-holes in cloth banners on a windy day.

Drafting tape—different from masking tape—is good to use in rooms with painted walls. People may not want you to put masking tape on their walls since it might remove the paint. Drafting tape will not damage the paint. It costs more and is harder to find, but leaves the walls as you found them and keeps your host happy.

## The Opening Portion of the Meeting

**1. Introduce and authorize yourself.** State how *you* were designated to chair the meeting if this is not clear. ("At the last meeting, I was elected to chair this meeting." "At the beginning of the year, we decided to rotate chairing the meetings, and tonight is my turn.") Otherwise, get agreement from the group that you will facilitate. ("Since I think this meeting will run better if someone facilitates it, I will volunteer to do this tonight. Is that all right with everyone?")

**2. Welcome people.** Introduce any special guests and thank anyone who has done special work.

**3. Have participants introduce themselves** if they don't know each other. If they already know each other, some short positive icebreakers help build teamwork and unity. ("Briefly, what is something good that happened to you lately?" "In one sentence, say your name and why you are here." Keep this brief! Have someone start who you know will be brief. If you don't know anyone, start yourself to model how to be brief.)

Name tags also help people to learn each other's names in larger meetings.

**4. Describe the process and ground rules.** (People should raise their hands to speak, etc.) Get agreement on ground rules.

**5. State how the group will make decisions at the meeting.**

**6. Review the agenda.** Make the goals of the meeting clear. A written agenda on a flip chart reminds people of the agenda throughout the meeting. An agenda review also allows people to change or add to the agenda. Introduce each item on the agenda and clarify the goal for that item. ("We have to make a decision on this item today." "This agenda item is for information only." "This item is a report with a few minutes for questions.") A meeting is a series of agreements. Make agreement on the agenda the first agreement of the meeting. Important items should go first. Estimate the time it will take for each agenda item and write the time allotted on the flip chart. This will help you to stop that part of the agenda when needed, to keep the whole meeting from running overtime.

**7. Make the ending time for the meeting clear.** Ask if anyone has to leave before that time. Ask for a show of hands and then ask those with raised hands to say when they have to leave. This avoids someone interrupting the meeting to leave and others not knowing why. Then you can say, "So when Janice leaves at 8:00 p.m. it is not because she is mad. She has to pick up her son." This keeps a sense of humor and builds accountability in the group.

**8. Make sure everyone has signed in.** Don't lose the sign-in list! It helps to have it on a clipboard, which is harder to lose than a piece of paper. You may want to tape it to a table so no one can walk off with it. In larger meetings have several sign-in lists so the sign-in process goes quickly. Remember this rule: The organizer gets the sign-in list.

## During the Meeting

**1. Your job is like being a traffic cop.** You are not there to express your own opinion but to keep the discussion moving and make sure that everyone has a chance to speak and be heard.

**2. Use your authority to keep the conversation under control.** If attacked, remember that your authority to chair comes from the group. If you think you still retain the confidence of the group, you can ask: "How many people want me to continue to chair? Let me have a quick show of hands." If you get most of them, move on. This should re-establish your authority as chair.

If someone is very unruly, use the authority of the group to get them to quiet down. "Our ground rules say that people will not speak until recognized by the chair. Is that still how we want to operate?" Most likely, the group will voice its agreement and that will quiet the unruly person. If that doesn't work, you also can appeal directly to the person, calling upon your authority as the chair.

One person chairs at a time. Sometimes others will start calling on others to speak. Don't let this happen. You can remind the group that you are the chair and that people should raise their hands to speak "and I will recognize them."

**3. Appoint a timekeeper.** This person should keep track of time limits for each item and tell the chair when the time for that item is up. The chair then decides how to proceed, with the advice of the group. The timekeeper's role is to keep track of time, not to cut off discussion. It is up to the chair to decide when to limit discussion.

**4. Try to elicit participation from as many people as appropriate.** Invite quiet people to speak and ask talkative people to allow others a turn.

**5. Make sure the group is in agreement about decisions.** Summarize discussion and decisions as the meeting goes along. If people seem to agree on a decision, say so and test this by asking if the group agrees with your summary. ("It seems to me that everyone agrees we should sell the truck. Is that what you are hearing? Do we need any more discussion on this or can we say it's the sense of the group?") Restate any decisions to make sure they are clear and written down accurately in the minutes.

**6. Keep the discussion focused on the topic at hand.** Encourage participants to avoid repetitive comments. ("I think that comment has been made a few times. Does anyone have anything new to add?")

**7. If you need more time for an item,** ask the group if they want to spend five (or ten, or some other appropriate number) more minutes on that item.

## Three Steps for Facilitating Discussion at a Meeting*

Here is an easy and useful outline for guiding the group's discussion to a decision on a meeting goal or topic. In general, when you facilitate the conversation—no matter the specific topic—you will want to lead the group through each of these three stages:

a. **Present the Proposal.** "The goal for this meeting is to decide whether we should visit the mayor about the conditions in our building."

b. **Check for Understanding.** "Does everyone understand what I mean? Does anyone have any questions about the goal for this meeting?"

c. **Check for Agreement.** "Do you agree that this is what we want to do at this meeting?"

*Thanks to Michael Sales for this simple three-step guide to facilitating meeting discussion.*

## At the End of the Meeting

**1. Review what was decided and accomplished.** Re-state any major decisions. Review the commitments people have made and any assignments that have been given to individual members. People should leave the room clearly understanding any actions that the group is expecting them to complete.

**2. Set a time and a place for the next meeting,** if that has not already been done. It is best to set out the dates for a series of meetings far ahead of time.

**3. Evaluate the meeting.** ("What was good? What could have been changed to have made it better?") Avoid discussion of the evaluative comments. Just note them for future reference.

**4. Close on a positive note.**

**5. Did I say end on time?** End on time.

## After the Meeting

**1. Clean up.** Leave the room as you found it, especially if it belongs to someone else.

**2. Write up notes** or minutes or make sure someone else does.

**3. Send out the minutes promptly.** Ask everyone who attended if the notes accurately reflect what happened. Make any necessary changes after feedback.

**4. Follow up on action steps and begin to plan the next meeting.**

**QUICK TIPS**

### *How to Build or Destroy an Organization through Meetings*

**BUILD:**

1. Stick to the agenda.
2. Support the chair.
3. Mention unifying elements, what everyone shares.
4. Emphasize your trust in people at the meeting.
5. Appreciate each other's work and efforts.
6. Take responsibility for the mission and goals of the group.
7. Mention people's good intentions and attitude.

8. Listen respectfully.
9. See that others have a chance to speak.
10. If you have a problem with an individual's behavior, speak to that person directly and privately outside the meeting.

Add your own here:

_____

_____

_____

## DESTROY:

1. Throw the agenda out the window as soon as the meeting starts.
2. Oppose the chair.
3. Point out the differences between people at the meeting.
4. Say you distrust people in the meeting.
5. Unconstructively criticize each other's efforts.
6. Form a sub-group to subvert the leadership.
7. Tell others that they are not meeting the group's goals or mission.
8. Attack people's motivation.
9. Interrupt. Take more than your fair share of the group's time.
10. Ridicule or criticize people in the group meeting. Talk about them behind their backs.

Add your own here:

_____

_____

_____

For more guidance on running effective meetings, see *How to Make Meetings Work*, by Michael Doyle and David Straus.

# Mobilizing Resources: Raising Money

*Whoever pays the piper calls the tune.*

—Old saying

*Fundraising is an act of will.*

—Source uncertain

All community organizations, except for the smallest and most informal, need money. To build an organization that affects events out in the world takes money—for staff, office space, phone, mailing, computers, food, and supplies.

Money may be a tough subject, but you need to be up-front about it. You need to know where it comes from and how to raise it.

## Story: Early Money Helps You Rise

*When I first thought of starting the Jewish Organizing Initiative it was just a vague idea. I got a check for $25 in the mail from a friend. It was addressed, "Michael Brown, Executive Director, Jewish Organizing Initiative." At the time there was no Jewish Organizing Initiative. There was no group, no members. There was certainly no "Executive Director." Putting the idea in writing and giving it a name allowed someone who liked the idea to send in a check and call me the "Executive Director." Receiving that first check inspired me. It made* *me think, "Oh, now I have to spend this $25 to advance the idea. I can't just blow it on beer. I have an obligation to the donor to spend it on the organization."*

Money helps. It is in the category of real help and is one of the best indicators of support.

Maybe this is why people who start a business frame their first dollar bill and hang it on the wall for all to see. There is something special about that first dollar. It says we have faith in the business. Whether you are starting a grocery store or a community organization, that first dollar is a token of faith in your business's long life and success.

Those who give money influence the organization. If money comes from your members, they exercise influence. U.S. Congressman Barney Frank once joked that politicians are the only group of people who contend that people who give them thousands of dollars exert no influence. Most of us know better.

## ▶ Members and Money

### Whoever Pays for the Organization Runs It

You need to think about funding your organization as much as you think about its mission, its goals, its structure, and its need for members and leaders. Think about money— even if you don't ask for much—at the start. Have the group pay as it goes along. Even if it is only a dollar for cookies or copies of the flyer for the next meeting, ask the group to pay for what it uses. Pass the hat. Some people who start organizations are reluctant to do this. But if *you* pay for it, then it becomes *your* organization. If the members pay for it, then it becomes *their* group. Unless you are building a cult of personality, you want it to be their group.

People value what they pay for. They will expect something from the group. When the issue of dues is raised, some people ask, "But can't we just volunteer our time?" A colleague of mine routinely replies, "Can you volunteer at the telephone company to take 411 calls to pay the phone bill?" If not, and you want a phone, you will need money. If you want stamps, paper, paper clips, transportation, or staff, you need money. You have to get money from somewhere.

Money is not the only way to assess value, but it is one way to do that. Ask everyone for money. It reinforces the idea that everyone has value. Every member should make what is for him or her a meaningful contribution. Those who don't have much money can ask others who do.

People also will work for what they pay for. When people pay what is for them substantial dues, they are more likely to care how the money is spent and more likely to work for the organization. Volunteer work often follows money.

Where you get your money says a lot about your organization. If your members pay for the organization, they run it. If someone else pays for it, that someone else has a big say in what the organization does. If an anti-drunk driving group receives most of its money from a beer company, will the source of its money compromise its actions? One might imagine so. If a civic group receives money from City Hall, will that affect its actions and attitudes toward the city government? Most likely it will. I have heard about situations like these. That's why it is so clear to me: If the members pay for all or most of the organization's expenses, the members decide what the organization does. If the money comes from the government or from some other source with an interest in the outcome that may be different from that of the members, there will be strings attached. The strings may be unspoken or they may be overt, but they will be there. Guaranteed.

## ▶ Effective Organizations Organize Money Effectively

### Organizing for Change Costs Money

Too many community organizations rely on too few sources of money to survive. If your money comes from just a few sources, your group is at risk. Any of those sources could withdraw their support at any time. Then what will you do?

Organizations that start with passion and volunteers can be very powerful. To have more power as they grow, they usually need paid staff. Organizations with money generally are more effective than those without money. Volunteers, no matter how responsible or well-intentioned, get tired. Their jobs or families interfere with their organizational work. For an organization to grow and become more effective, over time it helps to have someone whose full-time job it is to build or to carry on the work of the organization.

### Story: No Results Without an Organization; No Organization Without Organized Money

*In my twenties, when I worked construction, I was building condominiums near a ski resort. One of the guys thought the new buildings were awfully close to a stream that fed into the town's drinking water. We read in the local paper about an environmental hearing on the construction project. We weren't sure exactly what was planned, but we thought we ought to find out. So that day, at lunch, we drove into town to attend the environmental hearing. The room was full of men in suits. In our construction clothes and hard hats, we were out of place.*

*Our construction superintendent was surprised to see us. He was even more surprised when we started to question the building of the development so near the stream.*

*We didn't get fired for our little escapade. The boss was more surprised than angry. Our presence, and our questions about the development, although a surprise, caused little trouble for the developers. That was because we had not done our homework. We didn't know the laws. We could take off one long lunch hour, but not another. We were young and willing to risk our jobs for what seemed to us like the "right thing" to do, but there was little we did to follow up.*

*We were not effective. Even if the development would pollute the stream, we didn't have the organizational backup to do anything about it. We had no group. No money. No ability to make any phone calls during the day. We worked from 7:00 a.m. to 4:00 p.m. We could not afford to miss more work. We had no union or environmental group to back us up or work with. If there had been some problem with the drinking water, we were not organized to do anything about it.*

*The developers had lawyers and experts on their payroll. They could go to the hearings, do the research, talk to the state officials who made the decisions, and do the follow-up.*

*The state officials didn't ever visit the construction site and see what was going on. We were there all day; we saw everything. But they never spoke to us.*

Even if we had been right, without an organization there was little we could accomplish. Organizations need money to run. We had no group, no money, little information. We were not in a position of power to make change occur.

## Your Money Can Be Your Asset— Or Your Undoing

All organizations need to keep good track of their money. First, shoddy accounting practices can imperil your nonprofit status. Second, if finances are not in order, some people will question *everything* you do. One common way that opponents often discredit organizations working for social change is by attacking their finances, looking for money mis-spent or unaccounted for. The way you manage your money can have direct bearing on your success in making the changes in the world that you desire.

### Story: Follow the Money

*In 1960, Martin Luther King, Jr., wanted to prove that money donated to the Montgomery Improvement Association and the Southern Christian Leadership Council in Alabama was not taxable. The money for both groups had passed through his personal bank account. He could not substantiate all his expenses and was hounded by the Alabama auditor when he tried to transfer the money to Georgia. King ended up paying the IRS $500 in back taxes and the State of Alabama $1,667.*

(This was reported by Taylor Branch in *Parting the Waters*.)

Keep good records of all the money you receive and spend, right from the start. If accounting is not your forté, either learn to do it or find someone who can. Get qualified accounting help. This may seem unnecessary now, but it will save you and your organization money in the long run.

# ▶ Asking People for Money

When you ask people for money for your organization, you are giving them an opportunity to do something good with their money. They will likely spend their money on something. Since you know your organization is doing good work, you can feel good about giving them the chance to do something effective and worthwhile with their money. Think of what else they might spend it on. Is anything or anyone so much better than your organization?

Raising money is a big topic. The Bibliography at the end of this book provides a useful list of references about fundraising. My focus here is on key points that are particularly important in grassroots organizing. Over the years I've seen more than one organizer and group get hung up or tripped up in the area of money and fundraising. This chapter tries to anticipate barriers you may experience and offer a structure and solutions to make sure that you are successful at generating the funds you need.

**QUICK TIPS**

## *Things to Remember for Successful Fundraising*

- You get what you pay for.

- If you want to do something big, you need big money.

- Match your appetite for doing with the resources that will allow you to accomplish what you want.

### *Story: Make the Work Fit the Money*

*I once was asked to help an organization of volunteer community mediators. They were wonderful people. Many volunteered hours every week to sit in courtrooms to help* *mediate problems in civil and criminal cases. They wanted to do more. They had one grant from the Attorney-General's office of $30,000 and this paid one part-time coordinator and other expenses. They had big ideas of what they could do.*

*I had to walk them through a process of attaching dollars to what it would cost to do everything that they wanted to do. Project by project, we put their agenda up in writing on a flip chart, with a dollar amount that they agreed it would cost to do each project. The total came to $120,000. They had $30,000. Painful as it was, they realized that they simply could not do everything they wanted. So, they went through another discussion about what their priorities were and—with me holding their feet to the fire—pared down their program.*

- **Every member should pay something.** Even the poorest. Don't let people off from making an investment, even a small investment.

- **Whoever pays for the group controls it.** If you want control to be among your members, don't let a few people or foundations pay for everything.

- **Time *and* money.** One key to success in asking people for money is to feel okay about asking. Many of us feel bad or guilty about asking people for money, even though we are not asking for ourselves, but for an organization that we believe in. If you believe in the organization and know it needs money to be effective, then you are asking people to make an investment in the mission and goals of the organization. Just as the organization needs people's time, contacts, thinking, and ideas, it also needs their money. I often invest both my time and my money in the same organization or campaign. Both are needed. I can knock on doors or attend planning meetings. But only my money can pay the rent, phone bill, or staff salaries.

- **Making an investment.** When you ask people for money, think about it as asking them for an investment in the organization. An investment means giving a part of themselves. If they give money now, other help may follow. They might introduce you to new contacts, come up with new ideas, or bring in new members to increase your power and range of skills.

## How to Ask for An Investment

The most effective way to raise money is to ask people who have some. The cost is minimal: the time and travel for the visit. No need to hire a hall, cook spaghetti, bake cookies, write a grant, hire a band, or pray for sunshine.

**QUICK TIPS**

### *Guidelines for Asking People for Money*

- **You don't ask, you don't get.** Obvious, but important to remember.

- **Find out as much as you can about the person** you are soliciting before you ask him or her for a donation—so that you know how much money to ask for.

### *Story: Do Your Homework*

*I went to a woman's home to ask her for money for the organization I was working for. I knew her first and last name, and her middle initial, "R." I looked around on the walls. She had evidently gone to an exclusive private school. There were many expensive antiques. I asked her for*

*$1,000. She immediately said, "Yes," and asked her husband for her checkbook. Seeing how easily she had said yes to $1,000, I stammered, "Or $1,500 if you can do it . . . that would . . . er . . . be better. . . ." She wrote a check for $1,500.*

*I had failed to find out what her middle initial stood for. It was the first letter of the name of a famous wealthy family. She used her married name. She could have written a much larger check. Had I done my research, I might have gotten $5,000 or more. I felt good about coming back with $1,500, but stupid for not knowing who she was.*

- **Tell the person your overall goal.** People who contribute want to know what portion their contribution is making to the big picture. This also gives them a sense of how large a contribution to make.

- **Say a number.** Ask for a specific number, ask if the person can do that, and then remain silent. Say, "I would like you to invest $1,000. Can you do that?" [Silence.] Wait for the reply. This is the hardest part, but keep silent. Wait until the person answers. If he or she says yes, then immediately express your thanks and ask how and when you can get the check. If the response is, "That's too much," ask, "How much do you think you *can* invest?"

- **People are investing in *you* as well as in the organization.** No matter how good your organization's goals, no matter how much they align with what the potential donor believes, most people also invest money in organizations that they trust will spend their money wisely. How credible, trustworthy, and effective you or others in the organization appear and the relationships you build often determine the fundraising results.

## Story: Collect Money Now, Not Later

My friend and colleague Lee Staples told me this story.

*Lee's organization was holding a house party to recruit members. He was going to make a pitch to the guests to join and to pay their dues. Ahead of time, he arranged with the hostess of the house party that she would respond to his pitch by announcing that she would pay the dues. The others respected her, so Lee figured that they would follow suit. Lee thought all was set.*

*The evening came. The people came. He showed a slide show of some of the neighborhood eyesores and then of how residents in another neighborhood had made improvements. Everyone in the living room was talking and engaged. Then Lee made the pitch.*

*Just as Lee had arranged, the hostess spoke up: "Yes, I will pay my dues. I'll give it to you next month, right after I have done my Christmas shopping."*

*All those invited then followed her lead.*

*Like the proverbial check that is "in the mail," the dues did not arrive.*

The devil is in the details. If someone says they will pay their dues, make sure they give you their cash or check right away, not later.

# Getting Over Your Hang-Up About Asking People for Money

In spite of the fact that asking people for money is the easiest way to raise money, many organizers and organizational leaders fail to do it. They are afraid to ask people for money. They feel guilty and bad. Some think that asking people to give money is forcing these donors to do something that they would not otherwise do.

This exercise asks you to take a few minutes to reflect on your own experience giving money to organizations. See if this helps you to understand how the person whom you are asking for money might feel about your request.

1. Have you ever given money to any organization?

    ❑ Yes   ❑ No

2. How did you feel when you gave the money?

    _____

    _____

3. Have you ever given what *for you* is a lot of money?

    ❑ Yes   ❑ No

4. Who asked you? _____

5. How much did you give? _____

6. To which organization? _____

7. Why did you give? _____

    _____

    _____

8. How did it feel when you gave? _____

    _____

    _____

## Asking People for Money is Like Giving Them Chocolate

Now look at your answers. My guess is that you felt pretty **good** about giving. I have asked this question to hundreds of people, of varied incomes and backgrounds. Almost 100 percent say that giving felt "good" or "great."

Yet, many people don't like asking other people for money, **even though the people they ask are likely to feel good when they give!** The people who need to do the asking worry that they are going to make someone feel bad, even though all the data shows that they are going to make someone feel good!

In spite of the objective evidence, even when we ask this in groups, even when everyone says that they feel good about giving money, it takes time and effort to get over the feeling that you are going to make someone feel bad. You would probably feel good giving them chocolate. *Asking people for money is like giving them chocolate.* It is an opportunity for them to do something good with their money.

Try doing the above exercise in a meeting. It helps to gather the data yourself and hear for yourself how people feel when they give.

## People Can Always Say No

If you still feel guilty about asking people for an investment, remember that they can always say no. You aren't putting a gun to their head. You have no threats or influence, other than that your organization is doing something they might want to invest in. It is their money. The decision is up to them. Your showing up only provides the opportunity for them to do something good with their funds.

## There is More Where That Came From

There is no reason that those without wealth cannot use their influence to raise money among those who have more.

### Story: There's Always More Where That Came From

*One of the largest donors to an organization I worked with gave $50,000 every year. I knew he also gave similar or greater sums to other organizations. A couple of colleagues were starting organizations that I respected. I wrote to this donor on their behalf, explaining in detail why I thought these organizations were doing good work. I encouraged him to meet with them when they called. Both had meetings with the donor and received initial investments of $5,000.*

*I felt that I had an obligation to help those doing good work, and that if I had any influence with this donor, I could use it by putting my name on the line for my colleagues. It would be up to the donor whether he wanted to give or not. I never thought that it would mean less money for our organization—and it didn't.*

*Individuals of wealth often do this themselves. (One old-time Yankee told me that the line he always used at his club was, "What are you interested in these days, John?")*

## ▶ What About Grants?

### Funding from Foundations

Grants from foundations are nice, and they may seem like an "easy" solution to an organization's budget needs. With one grant, you may get enough money to fund the whole project. This can make all the difference in getting an organization or project started or in getting the funding for a one-time expense. Many groups pursuing a better world pursue foundation funding.

But relying too heavily on grant support alone can create a bind for your group's future. That is because foundations that support community organizations typically stop the funding after three to five years (or even sooner).

## Story: "We're No Longer Interested In That"

*In the 1980s I was working for the Jobs with Peace campaign. We had a meeting with one of the Rockefeller Foundations to discuss funding for a campaign to increase federal funding for child care. We had been working on this for a few years. They had been a major funder.*

*"Oh, we are no longer interested in that," the foundation program officer said, almost as soon as our meeting got going. "I think we want to look at doing something about domestic violence. That is getting to be a really big problem."*

*I looked at him. Then I looked out their big picture window high up in Rockefeller Center, overlooking Manhattan. I wanted to throw him out the window. The challenge of finding quality, affordable child care had not been solved over the previous few years. Most low-income parents still could not get quality child care. But apparently, to the Rockefeller Foundation, child care was no longer "in." The foundation was no longer interested in it. They had moved on to another interest. (This was in 1988. It is not much better now, many years later.)*

As long as they were the source of funds that paid for our work, we would live or die on what they thought was important. We had little other financial support for the child care campaign and it soon folded.

Organizations should not rely on just one or two (or even three) funding sources. If you do, you are at risk of destruction at every moment.

## Foundation Practices From An Organizer's Perspective

To understand why foundations often shift priorities and grantees every few years, it helps to use Alinsky's traditional organizing perspective and look at the behavior of foundations in terms of their self-interest:

Foundations with missions to increase equality between society's "haves" and "have-nots" frequently grant funding to community organizations that serve or support people without access to traditional sources of power (such as low-income people). For example, such foundations may fund grassroots efforts to change public policy to increase taxes on the wealthy (people like themselves) in order to re-distribute wealth to low-income people (those often served by their grantee organizations). Their grants do not favor the situations of the wealthy or privileged, even though the wealthy and the privileged are the people who sit on the foundations' Boards.

In other words, the activities that these foundations usually fund are contrary to their own economic self-interest or that of the foundations' founders, endowers, or donors. These activities do not advance the long-term interests of the foundations' balance sheets, so the foundations lack a financial incentive to make long-term investments.

Further, foundations typically hire professional program officers to oversee the application process, to select those organizations they will fund, and then to evaluate how the grantees have done in fulfilling the grant requirements. Program officers earn their pay by finding new programs and organizations. In family foundations, the same dynamic occurs when new family members, who want to make their own mark, join. This means finding something new to fund. Funding new organizations or pursuing new initiatives—not renewing grants to former grantees—is aligned with the self-interest of foundation staff and of new members on family foundation Boards of Trustees.

Bring these two forces together—little institutional incentive for long-term investments combined with great personal incentive for short-term investments—and you get foundations that typically only fund groups for relatively short periods of time. They then suggest that funding organizations for the short term is good for the organizations because it "builds self-sufficiency." There is little data to support this theory. The members of many social change organizations are very low-income and could never support their organizations at the level of foundation grants. However, most grantees are reluctant to challenge the practice, since such a challenge might stop the needed, but short-term, funding.

This dynamic is quite typical of the pool of foundations that usually support community-based organizations. As a result, community groups with long-term strategies to push our society toward greater equality have a tough time planning or implementing long-term strategies based on foundation support. The frequent shifts in focus by foundations can lead unwary community organizations to repeatedly be re-inventing themselves in order to follow the money, or else to lay off staff when the grants dry up. Both strategies weaken the organization.

There are other foundations whose practices are aligned with the self-interests of their backers. These are foundations whose missions help to maintain the status quo or to enhance the situations of the wealthy and privileged. They typically fund conservative causes, such as efforts to influence government to lower taxes on wealthy people.

Ironically for us, these foundations tend to fund the same grantee organizations for years and years. They know that changes in public policy don't happen in three or five years. They are willing to make an investment in an organization that has a realistic long-term strategy because they know that they are likely to get a return on their investment over time.

The impact of philanthropy on organizational success and social change in America is a fascinating and complex topic. See Robert Kuttner's article, "Philanthropy in Movements," in *The American Prospect*, July 15, 2002, for an especially interesting analysis of this dilemma.

## Government Can Also Be Fickle

Reliance on government funding can also present problems, especially when administrations change.

### *Story: Now You See It, Now You Don't*

*In 1980 I was working for Massachusetts Fair Share. A good part of the organization's budget to pay local community organizers came from the VISTA program (Volunteers in Service to America), run by the administration of President Jimmy Carter. On January 20, 1981, at 12:00 noon, Ronald Reagan was inaugurated as President, replacing the defeated Carter. At 12:15 p.m., the organization received a phone call from a Reagan appointee in the Law Enforcement Administration Agency. He told us that a $75,000 grant that had already been granted to pay the salaries for several organizers working on neighborhood safety issues in a low-income neighborhood was now rescinded.*

*Similar phone calls went out that afternoon to community organizations working in low-income neighborhoods and rural areas across the country. In one case, the*

*Federal Emergency Management Assistance Agency had given a grant to a community group in Cleveland. When the Cleveland organizer asked the official in Washington, D.C., why the grant was being taken away, the official replied, "Because we are in power now and you are out."*

(This story is from Larry Cunningham, "Community Organizing in Cleveland," Unpublished.)

# MAKING CHANGE

*You can't organize in an office.*

—Michael Jacoby Brown

If you have read this far, congratulations! You have the skills and resources you need. Now you are ready to solve problems and change the world.

Buckle your seat belt: Now you are ready to make a difference and win some improvements in your world or stop something bad from happening. In this section you'll see how to use the skills and tips covered in earlier chapters to push for change in the world.

Yes, it helps to plan and organize before you act. But you don't want to develop a "paralysis of analysis." All action is premature. But if you wait until you have everything perfectly worked out, you are likely never to act to get what you need. And if you never act you will never learn how to do it better the next time.

So let's go!

# CHAPTER 10

# Organizing:
# Pathway to Change

*It is highly undemocratic to plan, govern, arrange, and impose a program without communication with the people for whom it is designed; it is also disastrously impractical.*

—Saul Alinsky

## ▶ Organizing as a Strategy

### Strategy

Strategy is your overall plan or path. It defines how and why you do your work. A strategy of organizing is based on some basic assumptions and theories about how the world works and about the most effective way to solve problems and improve life for people.

### Problems May "Just Happen." Solutions Don't.

People face many problems in the world: sub-standard schools, toxins in the environment, mediocre health care or inadequate health insurance, poor public transportation, lack of good jobs at decent pay, unfair taxation, health and safety hazards in the workplace and neighborhood, over-priced housing, overcrowding, and more.

These problems don't just resolve themselves. Good things don't just happen.

*If you wait for the boss to raise your pay, you'll all be waiting 'til judgment day.*

—Woody Guthrie

Positive changes don't occur because of the pure benevolence of the powerful. They don't happen because of rational arguments about how such conditions hurt many people. Problems get solved when people (the people affected by those problems, working together in an ongoing organization) have the power to solve them. This is an assumption of the organizing strategy.

## A Theory (Based on Observation): The Imbalance of Power

An organizing strategy assumes that problems exist in the world because of an imbalance of power. Some people have power to control many of the conditions that affect their lives: where they live, how much time they spend at tasks they don't like, the education of their children, their physical safety, their ability to travel, preparation for a secure retirement, and more. Some people, a much smaller number, have the power to control the lives of others, including control over others' work lives, neighborhoods, schools, and environment. This power extends to control over what it costs most people for the necessities of life: health care, transportation, housing, education, heating fuel, etc. Most people, however, have little control over many of the decisions that affect their lives or over the costs of their basic needs. They spend much of their lives trying to make enough money for the necessities of life or worrying about whether they and their families will have enough in the future.

Most of the time we accept this imbalance of power. Low-income mothers from poor cities don't start showing up with their five-year-olds in September to register them for kindergarten at the nice schools in nearby leafy suburbs—even though the mothers know their children would get a much better education there. New immigrants living eight to a room don't show up at the empty second or third homes of the rich to have a better place to live. The people in power rarely have to demonstrate their power forcefully in order to maintain the current situation. The only time those with power need to assert their power to preserve this imbalance is when people challenge the ways things normally are. Think, for example, of Birmingham, Alabama, 1963, when Commissioner Bull Connor ordered his troops to meet Black children singing freedom songs with police dogs and water hoses.

## Story: The Students vs. The University

*As a young person, I saw this imbalance of power clearly enforced in 1968.*

*I was a college student at Columbia University. We staged a week-long sit-in to oppose two university policies: Its position on the war in Vietnam and its decision to build a college gym in a public park.*

*What we learned: That the owner of our classrooms, the university, had the power to call the police to beat us bloody, break our bones, throw us in jail, and haul us into court. In our classrooms, we had studied this phenomenon and learned that its name was "legitimate authority."*

Power can come from making the rules. The rules are then just assumed to be "the way things are," although there is nothing God-given, just, right, or natural about them. They are simply the result of some people having the power to set up rules in their own favor.

I saw this imbalance—in a less dramatic and violent way—when I worked as an elected judge in Rutland, Vermont, in 1975. When cases involving customers and businesses came before the court, my job was to issue judgments based on the regulations encoded in the *Uniform Commercial Code*. It soon became obvious to me that the laws, as written in the *Code*, were biased toward the interests of the owners of businesses.

## Why Organizing?

After my grandmother's mother died in the early part of the twentieth century, her father was often unemployed—as were thousands of other poor immigrants. The only job he could find was mining coal in Pittsburgh. So, to survive, he went to Pittsburgh. He left his six-year-old son in the Hebrew Orphanage. His eight-year-old daughter, my grandmother, went to live with and work for strangers.

*(My grandmother always kept her vaudevillian sense of humor. When I was a little boy I asked her, "Your father went to Pittsburgh?"—which seemed very far away. Minnie replied, "What do you think? Pittsburgh would come to him?!")*

The Hebrew Orphanage (a service, provided by wealthier Jews to help the less fortunate) kept Minnie's brother sheltered and fed. But it was a poor substitute for a family home. If anyone would have given my eight-year-old grandmother good food to eat, that certainly would have been welcome—better than the coffee and stale roll she usually got for breakfast. Helping disadvantaged people is a good thing. No argument with that. Hungry people can't wait to eat until an organization is built.

But to be more effective, it takes an organization with the power to get what people really need. Without the power that organizing can provide, people like my grandmother's brother are stuck in orphanages and eight-year-olds like my grandmother are stuck with whatever food, housing, and work they can get to survive.

If there had been Unemployment Insurance and Social Security survivor benefits at the time, my grandmother's father would have been able to maintain a home for his family. But those improvements came only 30 years later, and only after thousands of unemployed people built organizations to fight for Unemployment Insurance and Social Security. Thousands of people joined labor unions, Townsend Clubs (the forerunners of Social Security), new political organizations, Unemployed Workers Councils, and other organizations to pressure the federal government to provide these New Deal improvements.

## Powerful Organizations Don't "Just Happen"

There are many ways to improve the world. I focus on one way, *the strategy of organizing*—building powerful, ongoing groups that can change the world, or at least your part of it—because I think organizing holds the most promise to be effective. Problems get solved and improvements in the world come from powerful organizations. This book is about how to build those powerful organizations. The details are here because effective and powerful organizations that make a difference in the world don't "just happen." Making a difference takes organizers, leaders, vision, goals, planning, recruiting, experience, money, information, action, negotiation, learning, evaluation, and attention to many details.

## Here Today, Here Tomorrow

An organizing strategy understands that powerful organizations are those that will be around for a long time. They are not just temporarily arranged to solve immediate problems.

There are always going to be problems for people without power. There always will be imbalances of power. Some people will be born with money and power. Others will not.

The world will never be perfectly just—but it can be better. This takes an ongoing organization, so that when the next problem springs up, the organization (the people, relationships, staff, information, phone trees, precinct captains, e-mail lists, etc.) can get to work right away. No need to start from scratch and build an organization. You will already have the skills, experience, regular funding, staff, office, computer databases, mailing lists, networks, relationships, and trust to get to work and solve the problem.

You also need an ongoing organization to ensure that any solution is implemented well—that the devil does not come back in the details to haunt you. You can never guarantee that a solution you plan or negotiate will not run into problems down the road. Most solutions run into unexpected problems over time. You need the organization to spring into action to solve the problem without going through all the time and trouble of building the organization again from scratch.

Too often, too much energy is spent on the specific issue that is urgent right now. It can be easy to focus only on the immediate action needed to solve a particular problem. But you need to divide your time and attention so that you also continue to develop resources to sustain the organization for the long haul. That way, you'll be able to address not only today's problem, but also the next problem, and the next, and the next.

An organizing strategy focuses on building the organization. There may be immediate problems, even critical problems, you want to address. In fact, your organization may well have arisen in reaction to a very immediate problem— like the Camfield Tenants Association's reaction to the threat of the sale of their homes. When you undertake an organizing strategy, your overall path or plan (strategy) is first to solve the immediate problem (you certainly need to do that!) and then to move on to build a powerful ongoing organization.

## Organizing Ignored

I also emphasize the strategy of building community groups because popular culture, the media, and public and professional schools ignore it. Schools of management and public policy train managers to exercise authority in government and teach the analytic skills to develop policies to fix problems from the top down. The "community service" practiced in high schools and colleges provides charity (direct service) rather than building ongoing organizations to solve problems and foster a sense of community. TV and Hollywood depict social change as the work of lone rangers, heroes, heroines, politicians, speechmakers, and brave crusaders.

We see film clips of Martin Luther King, Jr., making a speech before thousands of people. We never see how all those people got there. No scenes of all the phone calls made to the bus and porta-potty companies; all the work to raise the money, publicize the march, set up the sound system; the millions of meetings, planning sessions, and organizational details that brought all those people there at the same time on the same day.

Try this test: Ask someone if they have ever heard of Sigmund Freud, the father of individual psychology. Then ask them if they have ever heard of Kurt Lewin, the father of group dynamics. (In case you skipped Chapter One, you can look there to find out about Lewin.) Then ask yourself: Why do we have hundreds of magazines, news articles, and television shows about what individuals have done, but so few about what groups have accomplished? When you have the answer, send it to me on a postcard. The winner gets a free dinner and a year's supply of spaghetti.

## Story: Top-Down Problem-Solving

*In 1990 I attended the Mid-Career Program at the Kennedy School of Government at Harvard University. After working for more than twenty years, it was a pleasure to take a year off and be in school, studying, reading, and reflecting. In one of my first classes, we read a case study of "the under-funded health center in Central America." In the case, there was a long line of women waiting for care. From the back of the room, I raised my hand. "I think it would be a good idea to go down the line and ask the women waiting in the line what they think would be the best way to redesign the schedule." That seemed reasonable to me: It was in line with my twenty years of community organizing experience, and, as I was soon to learn studying academic research on group behavior, it was in line with organizational theory. The teacher (who later went on to run a major government human service agency), replied, "No, that is the wrong approach. You have the expertise to decide. That is not what you should do."*

*I was stunned. The wrong answer? Who do these people think they are? No one in the class, which included many veteran government officials, thought my approach made sense. The class moved on to discuss ways to rearrange the center's schedule and analyze its budget. The women standing in line were irrelevant. The school taught that analytic tools could figure out the solution from on high, without listening to the people closest to the problem. No wonder so many government services do not work for the people they serve. Schools like this are where government bureaucrats learn their trade.*

## ▶ Organizing Strategy: The Nuts and Bolts

### The Premises of Organizing as a Strategy

*1. Those closest to the problem are the experts in solving their problems.* They know what is best for themselves and must be involved in the details of planning and implementing any solution.

*2. Those closest to and affected by the problem need a powerful ongoing organization to solve the problem.* Without the power of a group to represent them, they can't effectively influence policy and manage the planning and implementation of any improvements.

Organizations with a core organizing strategy may provide services to their members or the public. They may advocate on behalf of members having trouble with complex bureaucracies. They may mobilize people to demonstrate their power. However, in all these activities, building a powerful organization and developing leaders are the underlying goals. The organizers see every service provided, every person advocated for, and every mobilization through this lens. The long-term goal of any specific activity is to develop leaders and to build a more powerful organization—in other words, to be building up the group's power.

# The Tutoring Project

### Story: Ask Why You Are Doing What You Are Doing

*I once spoke to a group of college students who volunteered in a tutoring program in a nearby low-income neighborhood elementary school. Ten college students sat around a table.*

*I asked, "If your children were having trouble reading at grade level, what would you want for them?"*

*Each student said the same thing: They all would want an experienced reading specialist to help their child.*

*"So," I asked them, "why are <u>you</u> doing this? Would <u>you</u> want a local college student to tutor <u>your</u> child?"*

*"No," they all said.*

*I pressed them. "So why are you doing this?"*

*There was a long silence. They looked at each other and then back at me. They said they had not thought about that. I asked them what their goals were in tutoring. More silence. They had not really thought about it in this way, they said. They had no specific goals.*

*After more discussion, they asked if I could come back to talk to them again about what they were doing. They had been doing something that seemed helpful, but they recognized that they had not thoroughly examined their motivations, clarified their goals, or considered the effectiveness of their actions in reaching their goals (whatever they were).*

It wasn't that they needed to cancel their program. They needed to build a set of actions that would clearly contribute toward an identified goal that both they and those being helped could jointly embrace.

## How Was the Strategy Chosen?

When you want to help, it may be uncomfortable, or seem unnecessary, to choose a strategy. It seems obvious that reading to the children helps them. It makes the tutors feel good. However, if they do not clarify the goal of the reading and evaluate its effectiveness in reaching that goal, how helpful is the help? Who is being served?

They might ask: What is the goal of a tutoring program? Is it to help the children read better? To read at the level of children who go to schools in wealthy suburbs? To improve the schools? To evaluate effectiveness, first clarify the goal.

Embedded in their activity (tutoring) is a strategy of how to improve the world. In this case, the students came with a solution, reading to the children, rather than asking those closest to the problem (teachers, principals, parents, and maybe even the children themselves) how the college volunteers might be most useful. This approach assumes that reading to students is an effective way to deal with the problem of an under-performing school. But is it? There was no investigation of the problem or of other possible solutions. The tutoring solution came first.

## Other Possible Solutions to the Same Problem?

There are other solutions to deal with ineffective schools or with children who are not learning to read well. These include: training teachers better, changing formulas for public school funding, developing different kinds of schools, creating smaller schools, increasing parent involvement, supporting multiple teaching styles, and introducing different school management techniques. Before committing many volunteer hours over several years to a project to solve a problem, the students might have investigated the most effective means (strategy) to solve the problem. They did not do this. We may not know the best solution to this problem. We do, however, know that the solution to this or any problem requires the active participation of those closest to the problem.

When I asked two people close to the problems in one city school system what they would ask such volunteers to focus on, they suggested improving the physical conditions of the worst school buildings. In *their* opinion, this would be the best use of volunteers. The two experts also had specific suggestions about how to do this work.

It was not hard to get this information. I just called them, asked for a meeting, and asked them what they thought would be the most helpful use of the volunteers. A simple approach, but one not often taken.

## Story: Ask Before You Act

Chanel Dubofsky, who works at Oberlin College, told me this story.

*Some students at Oberlin College wanted to help the local Boys and Girls Club. They got together and made 250 peanut butter and jelly sandwiches. They brought them over to the club. When they got there, the staff said they did not need the sandwiches. They had plenty of food. They said they wished the students had come and played with the kids.*

The people closest to the problem are the experts. But sometimes it is easy to forget to ask them.

## Analysis of What's Missing

*If one performs an act of kindness for a living person, it is impossible to know if it is indeed such. There are those who think they are helping another person, and in the end it is found that that action was bad for the one they had hoped to help.*

—Ohel Yakov (18th century)

Organizing is the missing piece in the puzzle of how to improve the world. Too much emphasis is placed on good policies or on electing the right people to office. Smart policies and good elected officials can certainly help, but these alone cannot solve our problems. What is missing is the group intelligence of those closest to the problem.

## Business Knows Better

Although public policy managers generally ignore those closest to the problem, the best managers in the corporate world understand the importance of bringing the decision-making directly to those closest to the problem.

## Story: Smart Businesses Know the Real Experts

The story about the under-funded health center case from the curriculum of the Kennedy School of Government is all the more remarkable because just a couple hundred yards away at the Harvard Business School, the for-profit sector—or at least some of its smarter business managers—knows that it makes sense to go to those closest to the problem in solving *business* problems. I heard this story from a professor at the Harvard Business School:

*The entire assembly line of a major auto plant in Detroit had shut down. The engineers and managers came crowding around, trying to figure out what was wrong.*

*No one could get the machines working. The company was losing millions of dollars a day.*

*A consultant was called in. He got out a big bucket of paint and a brush. He painted a yellow line around the entire assembly unit. Then he said, "Only those who work directly on the machines can step across the line to touch the machines." The managers and engineers backed off. Then he said to the assembly line workers, "Here's $10,000. Get the machines working today and it's yours."*

*The engineers and managers watched. The workers got the machines running in a few hours. The managers thought the consultant was a genius. He had just saved the company several million dollars.*

## ▶ Other Strategies for Improving the World

In order to understand organizing, it helps to compare it to other related strategies for social change. Following are brief descriptions of the other major strategies. Although set out as distinct, within real organizations these approaches often overlap. Many real-world organizations use a complex mix of strategies. The definitions are not meant to caricature actual organizations or to limit how we understand them. The definitions are meant to provide a common language. The assumptions underlying the strategies are also key. The definitions and assumptions I describe here can help us to think about why we are using a particular strategy, the long-term effects of an approach on the people we work with, and the potential effectiveness of alternate strategies. This analysis also reminds us to look at how an organization actually behaves—not just at what it says it does. Sometimes it can take a bit of digging to understand what strategy or strategies an organization is using. What matters most is an organization's actual attitudes and practices.

## Some Basic Strategies for Making a Difference

**Service** provides programs or direct, immediate material help to people in need. You have something. Others lack it. You give what you have. It could be money, books, clothing, or furniture. It could be your time to clean up a vacant lot or re-paint a homeless shelter. It could be time spent reading to a child, sitting with an elderly person, or bringing someone a meal.

With a service strategy, if the problem is lack of food, the solution is a food pantry or soup kitchen. If the problem is poor schools, we might tutor children or provide textbooks. People assume personal responsibility to provide what is lacking. Service providers typically come with a solution they have designed, rather than asking those closest to the problem for their solutions.

The advantage of this approach is that it fills an immediate need. Hungry people can't wait for long-term solutions. The disadvantage is that this is not a long-term solution. The next day, next week, and next year, the problem is still there. Another disadvantage is that the need filled may not be what is really needed. You get peanut butter and jelly sandwiches at the Boys and Girls Club when what they really need is people to play with the boys and girls.

**Advocacy** involves well-trained experts speaking on behalf of people in need. Lobbyists do this in legislatures. Lawyers and other experts do this in courts, police stations, hospitals, and government agencies. Advocates often untangle complex webs of regulations and laws to help their clients navigate bureaucracies. Lawyers often exert more influence with businesses, landlords, and government agencies than private citizens do.

## Story: More Than One Way to Heal a Child

*Barry Zuckerman, a pediatrician at Boston Medical Center, had been treating children for years. Many children had come in over and over with the same chronic problems, such as asthma—often caused by roaches and mold in their apartments. One day a lawyer friend of his asked him, "Isn't there a law against that?"*

*Zuckerman, a doctor, had not thought about that. He was a healer, a doctor, not a lawyer. The question led him to found the Family Advocacy Project, where lawyers (advocates) team up with doctors and nurses to use the law to get rid of mold, roaches, and other building code and public health violations, to improve life for children and their families. He has found that sometimes a lawyer going after the source of the problem through the courts or city agencies can do as much to cure children as the doctors can.*

**Mobilizing** brings people (often many people) together for a short period of time to express their opinion. The 1963 March on Washington for civil rights is a classic example in modern American history of an effective mobilization. The Million Man March, Stand for Children, and other marches, vigils, and rallies are more recent examples.

**Community Development** creates homes and new jobs and provides education, loans, and other resources to address inequities in the market economy. The assumptions underlying a strategy of community development are that the free market does not work well for many people and that cooperative efforts can improve their living conditions. Cooperative loan societies, job training programs, development of affordable housing, and micro-enterprise lending are examples of this strategy.

Embedded in this strategy is the assumption that an affordable home and a job with a living wage are central to a better life. This work requires experts in the complex business of coordinating the market and government agencies to create affordable housing or business ventures. The technical nature of this strategy requires highly trained professionals. The time sensitivity of housing development often clashes with the timeline required for leadership development and the slower process of community participation.

**Electoral Politics** are a common strategy to improve conditions in any democratic country. This strategy assumes that the decisions of elected officials affect people in important ways.

Electoral politics in America focus on the person running for office. Personality, charisma, and biography take center stage. Political parties involve people only during a specific election campaign. The lack of a strong ongoing political organization makes it difficult for average citizens to provide meaningful input or to hold elected officials accountable until the next election. Except for the minor public offices, more often it is money, not organizational support, that is the key to electoral success.

*The core problem facing progressives is the declining participation of their constituency: the falling voting rates and declining political activity of people below the median in the income distribution. . . . The solution lies not in crafting a better message to beam from Washington, but rather, in effective local mobilization. What is missing are opportunities for poor and working people to participate and learn firsthand about politics and to become connected in an ongoing way to a political organization.*
—Paul Osterman, *Gathering Power*

*People today are into participatory activities. They
want to have influence over a decision that's made.
They don't want to just sit and passively absorb.
They want to be involved and a political program
ought to realize that.*

—Ken Mehlman, Campaign Director,
George W. Bush for President 2004

**Education and Study** are other important ways of
improving the world. Education includes educating both
the general public and your own organization's members.
This strategy recognizes the importance of understanding
the broader picture and the changing environment in which
we work.

Education can be a powerful tool for changing the world. It
can include classes, public lectures, mass advertising campaigns, and small study groups. Knowledge is power.
Inequities in power often are maintained through inten-
tional mis-education and mis-information. Most schools do
not prepare students to think critically or to figure out how
to change the conditions that affect their lives. The current
interest in many public schools on community service
focuses on charitable acts, often without analyzing the root
causes of the problems. Most people get their news from
the mass media, which provides little in-depth understanding of world or local events.

Self- or small-group study can help us to understand complex systems in health care, education funding, public
transportation, taxation, and other areas that affect our
families. We need to learn the details to know how to
change them.

# ▶ Assumptions, Effectiveness, and Values of the Strategies

Each of the social change strategies described here incorporates implicit assumptions about people and their development, about power, and about how and what we want to change in our world.

## Service

Service delivery rests at least in part on the assumption that people mostly have needs. The service organization's strategy presumes that the service providers are more capable of meeting those needs than the people themselves. The service strategy can shape the views of those providing the service, so that it is easy for them to begin to view those whom they serve as bundles of needs.

### Needs and Assets

Service providers typically conduct "needs assessments" in order to design appropriate services. Needs assessments ignore the *resources* of these same people "in need." A more balanced approach would include an "assets assessment"—to determine what assets, strengths, and resources the same people have. Looking only at "needs" overlooks important resources of a community.

For example, rather than conducting a traditional needs assessment of a low-income neighborhood, organizer Cheryl Bardoe looked at its assets. She reported:

*Grand Boulevard is a poor, mostly African American community of 36,000 on Chicago's South Side. Its unemployment rate was 34 percent and 82 percent of its children were living below the poverty line. . . . A recent survey shows that Grand Boulevard has more than 320 local associations, groups of citizens working together to improve life in their neighborhood . . . everything from*

*a church hand bell choir to a mothers' support group,*
*from a senior citizens' social club to a youth group*
*organized by a local postal worker.*

—Cheryl Bardoe, "Asset Management"

Attitudes and assumptions count. If one assumes that people have needs, then one provides a service to fill those needs. If one focuses on the assets, resources, or gifts of those same people or community, then one looks for ways to use and strengthen those assets and resources.

## Advocacy

Traditional advocacy assumes that people are not competent to speak for themselves. Advocates speak on their behalf. With this assumption an advocate may overlook opportunities for the person to speak up for him or herself, or to learn how to understand and navigate an agency's complex rules so that the person is more self-sufficient the next time.

Such advocacy also blocks the agency from learning the impact of its policies and regulations directly from those closest to the problem. This is counterproductive, especially if we assume that people in authority can learn and possibly change their behavior when personally confronted with information from the most credible source—the people the agency directly affects.

## Mobilizing

This strategy assumes that a public display of large numbers of people will influence authorities or public opinion, and thereby will further the mobilizers' goals. Some mobilizations are very effective. However, it is not uncommon for organizers to make the mistake of substituting mobilization alone for a fuller plan of action that draws upon the mixture of power sources that are needed to make real change.

## Clarify Your Goals

With mobilizations, timing, goal, and target all need to be clear and agreed upon by all involved. Why *this* mobilization *now*? Some may think that the goal is to change the governor's mind. Others may think that the goal is to change public opinion. Others may think it is to inspire those already convinced. Success is elusive if you don't know what you want. A group considering mobilizing as a strategy should clarify its goals and question its assumptions. The group should ask:

*What exactly is the goal of this mobilization? To inspire members? To gain media attention? To enlist new supporters? To influence a public official?*

*How likely is the mobilization to create the intended result? (Or does the group mobilize just because this is what it has always done?)*

If the goal of the mobilization is to influence a public official, the group should analyze how susceptible that official is to public pressure at the time. A mayor trying to attract a political convention might be susceptible to a mobilization just before the convention decision is made. At another time the mobilization may have less influence. A public official in a close upcoming election race can be more influenced by a public mobilization than a candidate with no credible opponent.

## ▶ Real-World Complexities of the Different Strategies

### Groups May Mix Strategies

Organizations may use elements or mixtures of several strategies. A community organization with an organizing strategy may also provide home-delivered meals, rides to the doctor, or legal advice for a member having trouble with an immigration visa. These activities foster mutual support and a sense of community.

Some advocates provide maximum opportunities for people to speak on their own behalf. Legal Aid attorneys used to call this "being on tap rather than on top." This mantra helped attorneys to remember that their role was to educate and empower clients as well as to advocate on their behalf.

An organization may provide home-ownership counseling and also may make every effort to get each participant to contribute time or work to the organization. A group with an organizing strategy strives not only to deliver a service but also to develop members' participation—even in the smallest ways. It assumes that all members can give, not only receive.

**CASE STUDY**

### From Advocacy to Organizing

Strong organizations reflect upon their effectiveness and may change strategies over time. I once worked with a community development corporation that had used an advocacy strategy for years to improve the business district in one low-income neighborhood. The group relied on the expertise of a few well-educated neighborhood leaders and their personal contacts with City Hall. But as the organization grew, its leaders realized that many problems affecting the neighborhood were not being touched by the organization. Women had been raped in a vacant lot. Abandoned buildings dotted the streets just a few blocks from the business district. The main street had some new construction and some of the old buildings had been renovated, but life for most residents was not improving.

Upon reflection, they realized that they needed more power if they were going to make improvements in the lives of most of the neighborhood's residents. The amount of power that was available from the City Hall contacts of a few well-educated people in the neighborhood was not enough. They decided to bring more of an organizing strategy into their organization. This move would require bringing many new residents into the organization as members and leaders—and not just as "puppet leaders."

## Limitations and Challenges of Changing and Mixing Strategies

This change was going to require a new orientation for the organization as well as a significant investment of time and money put into organizing. It was going to take a whole new way of thinking and a willingness on the part of the old "leader-advocates" to relinquish some of their power and status in the organization. It meant that the new organizing staff would have to be paid on par with the housing development staff—something very new. Without the raises, the organizing work would be seen as less important. (And indeed, it would be!) It meant a change in the composition of the Board of Directors and a change of priorities that put the (slower) pace of getting neighborhood input into any proposed development deal ahead of the need to close development deals that could drive new construction. There had to be changes in the culture, communication, and language used in Board meetings and other meetings. It meant more than just adding on a new organizing component. The whole organization had to change. It would not be easy or quick.

The payoff for the organization was greater power, based on many new members who voted, rather than on the less stable power that came from the advocacy strategy of a few neighborhood "advocates" who sometimes could convince City Hall to address neighborhood needs. The new power that grew from the expanded neighborhood base might eventually lead to more and bigger property development opportunities. But this would be a long-term gain that could only be achieved at the expense of giving up business-as-usual practices for the organization.

There were difficulties with this strategy. Funding for organizing is much harder to attract than funding that comes with the development of new housing. Development fees generate income, so the organization has a financial incentive to do more property development in order to generate the fees—instead of attending to recruitment and leadership development. Without a clear commitment from the Board and the Executive Director to maintain and fund an organizing strategy, it would be difficult, if not impossible, to do real organizing.

## Organizing Elements Within Service Agencies

Sometimes there is room for elements of an organizing strategy within a more service-oriented agency.

For example, a homeless shelter, which primarily uses a service strategy, might also have a program to develop the leadership of its homeless guests. The shelter may nurture guests' voices by teaching them how to write and encouraging them to tell their stories in the shelter's newsletter. One homeless shelter created a "Guest Advisory Panel" so that the guests could help to design the services of the shelter. In doing so, participants learned group facilitation, negotiating, and other skills. The shelter also used an organizing strategy when it brought shelter guests into a group, educated them about state and federal housing policy, and supported them in setting up meetings with state representatives and human service agency leaders to advocate for changes in housing policy.

Remember, the primary goals of any organizing strategy are to develop leaders and to practice the "Iron Rule of Organizing"—never do for people what they can do for themselves. Within a service-focused organization, there can be opportunities to practice this kind of leadership development.

## *Story: The Organizer in the Homeless Shelter*

*After working as an organizer for three months at a transitional shelter for Latina women in Boston, Ayla (not her real name) noted that stress was a common problem of the single parents at the shelter.*

*Rather than speaking with all of the guests herself about the problems that she thought they shared and coming up with solutions that she thought would work for them, Ayla decided to speak with a few of the guests and ask them to speak with others. This way, the guests would do the work to uncover if this was a shared problem and what others thought about it. From her actions, the women understood that Ayla trusted them to do this work and to come up with their own ideas about how to address their concerns.*

*As time went by, Ayla got nervous. She thought that nothing was happening to come up with solutions for the pervasive problem of stress. A couple of weeks later, the women decided that they wanted to go to the YMCA and ask for a reduced-cost membership for guests, so that women from the shelter could go to the Y to get exercise. Exercise is a great way to reduce the negative impact of stress.*

*They asked Ayla what she thought of this and whether she would go and make this request for them. She said she would help them practice what they wanted to say, but that she didn't need to speak for them because they would do it well. So instead of speaking for them (as an advocate), Ayla acted as a coach (organizer). She helped the women whom the group chose as representatives to practice what they would say to the director of membership at the YMCA.*

*By serving as their coach rather than their advocate, Ayla helped the group members to understand that they were capable of achieving the changes that they wanted for themselves. Had she spoken for them, they would have learned that Ayla had made it possible and that they were not capable of achieving such a goal themselves.*

*As a result of Ayla's organizing, the group secured YMCA memberships. These women and Ayla created a new opportunity for the women who follow in their footsteps. In owning the power to organize themselves, they were able to see that they can make positive changes in their lives and in the lives of other women like them.*

(From a case study by Emily Weitzman-Rosenbaum. A different version of this case story was published in the Jewish Organizing Initiative newsletter.)

This use of an organizing strategy occurred within a service organization because one staff member had the skills and insight to use it and because the organization allowed her to do so. However, it was not an integral part of the organization's mission or its daily work. Such "organizing" depends on the presence of an extraordinary individual and on the organization's willingness to allow this person to operate outside of normative organizational practices.

## Need to Look Deeper

To understand the *actual* strategy of a group requires careful observation. An organization may appear to be using an organizing strategy, but upon careful examination, may be doing something else. A membership-based community organization may in reality be staff-driven. It may have what my colleague Horace Small calls "puppet leaders."

## Story: Organizing Is More than Skin Deep

*A community group had invited all the city councilors to a meeting to address an issue. Only one accepted. I was her volunteer driver. We arrived at the meeting site and were ushered quickly into the basement storefront. We sat on hard plastic chairs for fifteen minutes before being escorted upstairs to sit around a conference table. The group's leaders sat across from the councilor. A young man, obviously a staff person, was dashing through the group, whispering into the ears of the leaders, and handing out pieces of paper. The "leaders" asked the councilor whether she would support their position. "Yes or No? What is your answer?" they asked.*

*The councilor tried to explain the complexity of the issue. She said that even if she agreed with them, they would not get the result they wanted. The leaders only repeated, "Yes or No? What is your answer?"*

*There are times when an unfriendly elected official evades a question. This was not the case here. It was clear to me that the organizer running around the room was orchestrating the meeting, and that the "leaders" had little or no understanding of how the City Council ran, who this councilor was, or what the issue was. The group, ostensibly a membership-based organization with an organizing strategy, was using a classic direct action tactic. But the leaders were clearly not leading.*

One needs to look carefully at an organization to see what is really going on. A membership-based community organization, like the one described above, might *seem*, on the surface, to be using an organizing strategy, but the homeless shelter, seemingly using a service strategy, might be doing more real organizing.

## Different Strategies for Different Times

Although I describe organizing as the most effective strategy for solving problems and changing the world, there are times when other strategies might make more sense. Time is one factor. No one would ask hungry people to wait to eat until you can build a big organization that can solve the nation's long-term hunger problem. If someone is about to be deported, it would make a lot of sense to hire a good lawyer and use a classic advocacy strategy to help that person avoid deportation.

Some people—and I have seen this especially with middle-class people of faith—will be willing to pay thousands of dollars to fly thousands of miles away to rebuild a health clinic in El Salvador but won't want to drive to their state capital to ask their state representative to support funding for health care for their uninsured neighbors. In that case, it might make sense to go with what people will actually do. Support their motives and their efforts in El Salvador, and during that week in El Salvador, help them to reflect, learn, and plan what they can do back home. Help them to make the connection between what they see in Central America and what they can see back in the U.S.

I have seen this work: I know a number of people who have gone to underdeveloped countries for various "service projects." What they encountered there was starkly different from what they had grown up believing. The trip gave them time away from home to learn and reflect. They came back with a different view of their own government, inspired to change conditions for poor people closer to home. Sometimes it takes serving (and learning) far away from home to learn what it is possible to do when one returns. But this only happens if someone (you!) pays careful attention to the learning that goes on in the service project and extends that learning to encompass intensive and persistent follow-up.

# ▶ For Service Organizations That Want to Move Beyond Service

Some organizations provide services to individuals. You may want to move an organization toward a broader vision of help. How can the group move beyond providing individual assistance to changing public policies so that it can help more people?

## Helping Service Organizations to Embrace a Broader Vision

You start moving an organization from helping individuals to helping groups of people by asking many questions. The questions that follow suggest how you might approach this shift. You will need to walk your group through a process of reflection, analysis, and decision-making in order to identify a new direction (or to re-affirm your existing direction, if that is the choice you make). You can use the methods described in this book to go through this process.

1. Start by asking the basic question:

**Does our organization *want* to do more than provide individual services to our members (or clients)?**

This question gets to the heart of who you are and what you are about, so be sure to devote ample time to it and make sure that all perspectives get voiced.

2. The first question needs to be discussed in the context of the other basic question:

**Is changing the conditions that affect people's lives consistent with the mission of our organization?**

If the organization wants to go beyond service, then it first needs to clarify that such work is a goal of the organization and part of its mission. (If necessary, you may need to modify your mission.)

If you decide that you don't want to expand beyond service, that is okay. It is fine for the group to affirm that it *only* wants to help individuals in its own organization and that it doesn't have the time, interest, or resources to do more. All organizations need to set boundaries in order to be effective. Mission, goals, and limits are critical parts of an organization's structure.

3. If the organization has decided that it wants to affect more people than it can reach through direct service provision and that it wants to have longer-term impact on the conditions of their lives, then its members and leaders need to dig deeper. You need to figure out if you can be effective in organizing, and how:

**What strengths and skills could we bring to creating systemic change for people over the long haul? How can our organization be effective using an organizing strategy?**

For example, if one member of the organization is out of work and his or her unemployment benefits have run out, can the organization extend unemployment benefits for all members who have exhausted their current benefits? Can it help to change the unemployment funding or policies in the state?

If one elderly couple is having trouble staying in their home because of a recent hike in property taxes, can the organization develop a policy in the town that would allow all low-income residents to stay in their homes in spite of the big jump in property taxes?

Figuring out how to move an organization from helping individuals with immediate problems to helping many people come closer to lifelong improvements requires asking the many questions that flow from this major question. Here are just a few:

- What problem or inequity do we want to address through organizing?

- How does this build on our strengths and expertise; how does it flow from what we have done in the past?
- Who else is in the same situation?
- What would be helpful to everyone like him or her?
- What power do we have in our group?
- Can we be effective in changing this specific policy?
- Who else could we possibly join with to accomplish what we want?

4. You also need to look at the risks to your organization if you shift from service to longer-term solutions:

**What might we lose through this shift, and are we willing to accept these losses?**

Questions might include:

- Who in our current organization might we lose if we enter a more political or policy-oriented arena?
- Are we willing to take on a long-term campaign that will not yield the immediate satisfaction of helping those in obvious need right now?
- What will it mean for our funding, and can we manage those changes?

5. If the answer is still *yes* and you want to go ahead and try to create long-term solutions, then you are ready to start planning your approach:

**What might be effective in helping more people in a more systemic way, so that we create change for people over the long haul? What would be the most effective help we can offer?**

To come up with the answer, you should break this question down into many sub-questions, such as:

- What is our goal?
- What are our specific objectives?
- Who is closest to the problem?

- How can we ask them for their advice, suggestions, and experience?
- What do they think is a good solution?
- What would they want us to do?

Once you go through all these questions in a thoughtful manner—and with a major shift such as this it will take your group quite a while to wade through all the questions—you will be ready to incorporate an organizing strategy into your organization's work. One of the powerful benefits of taking the time to answer all these questions is that you have been building "member ownership" in your new direction all along the way, by asking all of the people involved to think through this shift together.

**EXERCISE**

## Personal Reflection on Service and Organizing

This exercise is designed to help you think about your own motivations, the focus of your organization, the operating values and assumptions implicit in your group's structure and culture, and the impact of your work. Compare your answers to the choices listed below each question, which describe how pure service and pure organizing strategies might address the same question. For each question, take a minute to think about the similarities and differences.

Most people and most groups are more complex than the oversimplified opposites printed here. Most likely, you're no exception. The purpose of this exercise is to push you to think about your work in terms of service vs. organizing, so the distinction between the two is highlighted. The intention is not to describe your reality in all its real-life complexity, but to increase your understanding of the strategy or strategies your organization uses.

**1. Why am I doing this?**

Service: For personal growth only.

Organizing: To develop the leadership of others as part of a group.

**2. What skills do I use and develop in others?**

Service: "Technical" skills (reading, computer literacy, health education, etc.).

Organizing: Critical thinking, group process, political awareness, negotiation with public figures, strategy, campaign planning.

**3. What methods do I use?**

Service: Individual volunteers or professionals in agencies helping others who are seen as having limitations or needs.

Organizing: Organizing membership-based associations and groups and developing grassroots leadership to conduct public negotiations, etc.

**4. How are the problems that are addressed identified or chosen?**

Service: By the agency, through "needs assessment."

Organizing: Through priorities that are democratically and publicly determined by the community and by person-to-person interviews.

**5. Who "owns" the project?**

Service: The agency and the individual providing the service.

Organizing: The membership-based community organization.

**6. To whom is the project accountable?**

Service: To the agency and the funders.

Organizing: To the community organization.

**7. What is my self-interest?**

Service: Feeling good by helping others, personal skill development.

Organizing: Feeling good about developing the leadership of others, acting from deeply held beliefs or anger, changing relations of power.

**8. What connection to civic life does the work develop?**

Service: Little involvement or change.

Organizing: Intimately connected to civic life, including developing "public relationships" with business leaders and public officials (City Councilors, the mayor, your senators, police officers, and government regulators, for example).

*Based in part on a discussion tool from the Institute for the Arts of Democracy, San Rafael, CA.*

# ▶ The Minnie Test

*The word I hate most in the English language
is "sympathy."*

—Minnie Jacoby

## Strategy and the Minnie Test

When I think about any strategy I might use to make the world a better place, I use the Minnie test. I ask, "How would this help my grandmother, Minnie?" I mix my love for my grandmother, telling me stories in our house, with my fury at the world that could not make life any better for her as a little girl, or as a young woman. And I know that there were—and still are—thousands like her.

## Sympathy

Minnie never wanted sympathy. It would be easy to pity her, a poor eight-year-old girl whose mother had died. She had no money. She lived with strangers. She worked for people who treated her as a pair of hands to do whatever they wanted for as little money as possible. What would really help her? Who could help her?

What *did* actually help her? Today I might ask, "What strategy would be most helpful to her? Or to people like her today?"

**EXERCISE**

## Identifying Real Help

This exercise is an opportunity to practice figuring out what would really help someone to make permanent life improvements. It shows you how to draw on what you have already seen and already know in order to envision a better future.

1. Think of someone you know who is like Minnie, someone with no resources or family who can help him or her. Who are you thinking about? _____

2. What would be most helpful to him or her? Sometimes history can help us to design a strategy for today. It may help to look at what you judge to have been effective in the past (either in personal experience or in historical experience). Or you can answer with all new ideas.

_____

_____

_____

Unemployment insurance for Minnie's father would have helped Minnie, so he could have afforded a home when he was out of work.

## What Actually Did Help Minnie?

When I go back and look at the specific things that my grandmother told me bothered her, I can see that the labor unions helped. They allowed her bathroom breaks without being timed. They helped her (and many others) get better wages. They stopped the worst conditions in the factories. That was real help, not sympathy.

Social Security and Medicaid helped. That gave her money and medical care.

When she was older, public housing gave her a safe, affordable apartment.

Other things could have helped her when she was a girl. Kind teachers would have helped. A decent-paying job for her father would have helped most of all.

## What Would Help Her or People Like Her Today?

Take the Minnie test. Would any action, project, campaign, legislation, or organization help Minnie or someone like her? What would *she* say? What would it do for that little girl left without her mother? What would it do for the young woman trying to get an education, find a place to live, get useful and safe work, and find some way to use her talents and feel respected in the world?

# CHAPTER 11

# Taking Action, Solving Problems, Getting Results

*If architects want to strengthen a decrepit arch, they increase the load which is laid upon it, for thereby the parts are joined more firmly together.*

—Viktor Frankl, *Man's Search for Meaning*

## ▶ Actions:  Setting Change In Motion

### What Are Actions?

Every organization has a program, often referred to in the organizing world as an "action." Common types of actions include:

**1. Forums or panels**. These are educational. Experts discuss a topic. The goal is to educate those who attend.

**2. Public hearings**. These are opportunities for the public to testify about an issue. Hearings can be convened by public officials or by a community organization. Who runs the hearing is critical, as this group shapes both the process and the outcomes of the hearing. Time limits and decisions about who testifies matter, as do the location of the meeting and the selection of the person who will serve as the meeting's chair.

**3. Research actions.** You can organize an action around getting information. This is often a useful step. Members of the group go in an organized fashion to retrieve information about their problem. This might be a group visit to the Department of Public Health to find out what division controls the drinking water in the town or what acceptable lead levels are, or a meeting with the Housing Authority Director to find out how maintenance budgeting decisions are made and who will be present at the next budgeting meeting. These types of programs are useful because they supply the group with the information it needs to take a more confrontational action later on. In addition, these actions are themselves steps in the mobilization of the group, as they are the interim steps that educate, inspire, and motivate the members of the group. Members can learn a lot about the problem, about the institutions they are fighting, and about conducting actions from participating in research actions.

**4. Accountability sessions.** These are carefully orchestrated public negotiation sessions. They generally include specific questions directed to individuals who have the authority to effect some improvement in the lives of those who attend the session. The action may be a public session asking a mayor to agree to fund school supplies and textbooks. It may be a session where 1,000 people ask a bank president to fund low-interest loans for first-time home buyers. Whatever the topic, the essential ingredient is a clear agenda to ask an individual who has the authority (power) to deliver to make a specific improvement in the public arena.

Such face-to-face negotiations with public or corporate authority are based on the assumption that power is not absolute. Accountability sessions assume that those in authority can be influenced and can change their behavior or decisions when personally confronted by people who make a specific request of them. Accountability sessions further assume that those in authority are more likely to agree to such requests when the requests are made by large numbers of organized, disciplined people. This approach relies on the propositions—which experience bears out—that the public presence of many people influences the person in authority and that the power of the group is directly proportional to the number of people it turns out for the meeting. Such sessions also provide those who attend with a sense of increased power to influence the decisions that affect their lives and an increased sense of confidence in their ability to act in public. This strengthens the group, an important goal of any action.

## Story: Ask For What You Want

*For years, students in Boston's public schools complained about dirty, smelly bathrooms. The stalls lacked doors. There was no toilet paper. They were rarely cleaned.*

*Then the Boston Youth Organizing Project started organizing high school students. Number One on the students' list of concerns was still the smelly bathrooms. After weeks and months of planning and recruiting, they invited the Superintendent of Schools to a meeting at a church, where they turned out over 50 students.*

*The Superintendent came with two of his assistants. The students were orderly and organized. They went through an agenda that included testimony from students about their experience in the bathrooms, with dates, times, and details. They had a very specific request of the Superintendent: to fix the bathrooms in one specific school by a certain date. He agreed.*

The students' research, orderliness, and attention to details, along with their specific request and the presence of a large number of students, plus clergy and other community members, got them what they wanted.

## Story: Accountability Sessions Can Also Help Hold Members Accountable

*I recently attended a meeting of 1,000 people, convened by a group working to pass state legislation to set up health insurance for hundreds of thousands of uninsured people. The plan was to put on a statewide ballot a question authorizing such a health insurance plan. To get the question on the ballot would require 40,000 signatures. At the rally, leaders on stage asked for 200 people to sign pledge cards promising to each get 200 signatures. Such a big meeting, where the power of 1,000 people all in one room is palpable and inspiring, can lead to more accountability. It inspired me: I signed the card.*

*And again, accountability means counting. Since it would take 40,000 signatures—not 20,000 or 2,000 or even 38,000—to get the question on the ballot, I knew that I needed to stick to my word and get my 200, in order for the entire effort to work.*

## It's the Goal

Whatever the program or action, it's the goal of the action that matters. The first rule of any action is to ask: What is its goal? Make the goal crystal-clear and put it in writing. Too many groups conduct a certain kind of action because that is what they have always done. It may not be working, but habits die hard, even when they are no longer effective.

## Story: Winning is Different from Being Right—or Righteous

*A group of affordable housing advocates was angry over rising rents. They went to some sympathetic city councilors and wrote a rent control regulation. Four of eleven councilors supported them. They pressed for a vote, and when the vote came, they lost. They screamed, "Shame, shame!" But they had never lined up the votes to win. They thought that they were right and that those who voted against them were wrong. They did not take the time to try to negotiate a compromise.*

Being "right" did not mean that they would win. Winning is different from being right. In this case, winning required a majority of the Council, which they did not have. Some people may want to be right more than they want to be effective. Unfortunately, their action did nothing to affect rising rents in the city.

## ▶ Actions Cause Tension; Tension Leads to Change

Any social change or improvement project requires action. Action brings increased tension. Without increased tension, nothing changes.

An action may be a meeting with a person in authority, an election, a boycott, a press conference, a rally, a teach-in, or some other activity to affect social change. The organizer's job includes not only teaching leaders how to plan and conduct actions, but also how to evaluate and learn from the action.

### Action Requires Confrontation, Face-to-Face

*Repressive social structures are maintained in part because authorities masquerade as benevolent, define inequalities as too complex for resolution, and hide real conflicts of interest in a fairy tale of paternal benevolence. An organizer, therefore, seeks out confrontations and conflict; for the organizer understands that only in conflict situations do issues become clear, with real interests no longer camouflaged; only in conflict situations does the rhetoric of the powerful lie exposed and the mobilization of a movement become possible. Yet the organizer is also aware that all conflict is partially premature; that in the polarization that ensues some members and potential members will be frightened, choosing the side of authority against their "true" interests. And in the need for instant decisions in crises, participation in decision-making is narrowed. Yet here new leadership is also tested.*

—Richard Rothstein, "What is an Organizer?"

## Actions Bring Contradictions to Light

Organizers, often in dramatic ways, bring to light the contradictions between generally accepted assumptions about how people should be treated and the reality of their living conditions. That's why tenants have brought rats from their apartments to City Hall. That's why people with disabilities have camped out in the State House when politicians have cut needed services. That's why citizens brought samples of polluted drinking water from across the country to Congress. They know it is not socially acceptable in our country for people to live with rats in their homes, with no access to basic services, or with polluted drinking water pouring out of their faucets. Yet these conditions exist. Most people just don't see them. Action makes them visible and makes the contradictions apparent.

## Actions are Experiences for Learning

People learn through action. Without action and the inevitable reaction, no situation improves. No person changes. There is no learning. With organizing, the learning and personal growth happen within a group. The individual member learns and hopefully teaches others in the group. Then the group itself learns, and this learning becomes part of the group's norms and culture.

Organizers facilitate experiences for learning, for people to see the hidden reality. This often happens most effectively with face-to-face interaction.

*People change what they do less because they are given analysis that shifts their thinking than because they are shown a truth that influences their feelings.*

—John P. Kotter, *The Heart of Change*

## Story: Learning the Truth— Even When It Hurts

*I was training a new VISTA organizer at an anti-poverty agency working with low-income people at the Franklin Street public housing development in Malden, a small city just outside Boston. The city government failed to deliver basic services to this neighborhood. Most people in this public housing development were not registered to vote. At that time, to register to vote, one either had to go to City Hall or else get twenty people to sign a special form requesting that a voter registrar come to their location. It took a trip to City Hall to get the form.*

*Because of federal restrictions, the VISTA volunteer could not directly help anyone register to vote. She could, however, inform the public housing residents of the law and tell them where to get the voter registration petition. She did this, and so the resident leader from the public housing development took the bus downtown and went to see the voter registrar at City Hall. The VISTA organizer and I waited for her in a coffee shop across the street.*

*As the woman from the residents' group told us later in the coffee shop, the conversation with the registrar went like this:*

*"Good morning" she said. "I am from Franklin Street and I would like a voter registration petition so we can have someone come down to register voters."*

*"Oh," the clerk replied, "those people on Franklin Street, they never vote. You are wasting your time. They will never vote. They are all so lazy. All they do is sit around all day, drink, get into trouble, and collect welfare. They are all no good."*

*The woman from Franklin Street was stunned. She barely knew what to say. She managed to pick up the petition and walk out of City Hall, a bit dazed.*

*I knew the registrar was likely to say something like this. That was why we had stationed ourselves at the doughnut shop across from City Hall—to go over what happened.*

*The woman walked into the doughnut shop. She was frustrated and depressed. She had never been talked to like that. It took us over an hour to review what had happened and why. We pointed out that the clerk worked for the public, which included her, and that, in fact, she paid the taxes that paid the clerk's salary. We said that no one had a right to talk to her, or anyone, like that. Gradually, the tenant leader became more angry than depressed. She was getting annoyed and wanted to do something. She was determined to get all twenty signatures on that petition and show the registrar that people on Franklin Street did care, did want to vote, and did count for something.*

Organizers seek out such confrontations. From experience, I had a good idea of how the registrar might treat the woman from public housing. I *wanted* her to be treated that way—not because that is the way she should be treated, but because that is the reality behind the image the public officials display. That is what the registrar really thought of her, although it is not publicly declared. The tenant leader would not learn it if I simply told her, "People in City Hall don't respect you." Even if she believed me, my telling her would not have the impact of the registrar telling her to her face.

## ▶ Tips for Making Actions Work

### Action/Reaction

This action allowed the public housing leader from Franklin Street to uncover the masquerade of City Hall benevolence and then gave her a chance to test her leadership. How would she react to being called those names? How would she feel? What would she do?

She went back to her development and got the required signatures to bring the voter registrar out to her street.

We need personal experiences to learn and develop in ways that differ from how we habitually act. Bodies at rest tend to remain at rest. Sir Isaac Newton discovered that. Bodies in motion tend to remain in motion. He also discovered that. Use Newton's Laws of Inertia and Motion to get people moving and keep them moving. We need experiences outside of our normal routine to make change and learn. Then we need to take the time to evaluate, learn from the experience, and move on to further action, more improvements in our lives and communities, and greater learning.

### Ask for What You Want

Action often involves negotiation. Just like in fundraising, if you don't ask, you don't get. The asking creates a tension and reaction from the person you ask. The tension and reaction will be forces for change. Even if the reaction is no action, the tension alone will lead to some sort of change. The change might be in your organization (re-grouping for another action that does lead to change), or in the person or institution whom you are confronting, or in the surrounding community where you are doing the organizing.

This is where Newton's Third Law comes in. For every action, there is an equal and opposite reaction. You have to initiate an action if you want a reaction. If you ask for what you want, you can be sure that something will happen. It may take time to understand exactly what the reaction is, but I guarantee there will be an effect if you take action.

## Evaluate the Experience

Do not let the experience of an action fall on one person alone. Make sure that it is a group experience, even if only a few representatives from your group actually sit face-to-face with the person you are confronting. Before the action, agree to a time and place when you will meet to evaluate the experience. We had arranged the meeting in the doughnut shop ahead of time because we knew that the Franklin Street leader's experience would likely be difficult and that it would be important to evaluate the experience together. We first asked her how she felt. Then we led her through a process to see that she had a right to be angry rather than depressed. Then, hopefully, she would act. In this case, she did.

# ▶ Information Is a Cornerstone of Action

## Information + People Create Power

*Knowledge is power.*

—Francis Bacon

What was good for Sir Francis Bacon is good for community organizing efforts, too. If you look carefully at the stories throughout this book, you'll see that organizers often use information in combination with other strategies when they want to build their power. For example, as you'll read later in this chapter, a neighborhood group in East Boston went down to the State Office Building to get a copy of a grant that was supposed to benefit their neighborhood. They found out the amount of the money that was supposed to be used to benefit their neighborhood, the specifications of the grant, and its term. This information, combined with a strong community organization that successfully mobilized people, provided them with a source of power that they otherwise would not have had.

## The Right Information Can Guide Your Action(s)

Although information is a source of power, simply having the right information is not enough. You need to do something with the information in order to leverage power. Otherwise, you could be right and still be powerless.

### Story: Paying Attention to the Top Dog

*Some of my neighbors have recently come together to oppose a proposed dog park down the block from our house. They started making all kinds of arguments—that a dog park could create a health hazard, that the neighbors don't want it, that it was a threat to young children, that the noise and traffic would disturb the peace, that the dogs could damage the nearby soccer field. Their arguments were interesting, and they certainly fanned the flames of self-righteousness, but no one stopped to find out who in the town had the authority to make the decision for or against the park and what kind of information would be important or persuasive to that decision-maker. Just having a lot of information about dog parks wasn't enough.*

*So I called the Town Hall and asked who has the decision-making power about building the dog park. The answer: Our Town Manager, who operates under the direction of our town's Board of Selectmen.*

*So now we're talking. Now we have a target for our efforts. We may have a lot of interesting arguments, but the only ones that matter if we want to make change are the ones that will influence the Town Manager or the Board of Selectmen. So our next step is to find out what the Town*

*Manager and the Board of Selectmen are worried about. Public health issues? Public opinion? The expense? Once we get this information, we'll be ready to roll out an action plan.*

## Which Information Is the "Right" Information?

The information you need may be more than the simple facts of the case. One of the first questions you usually ask in organizing is: Who has the legal authority to make the decision? That leads you directly to the second question: Who (or what) would likely have influence on that person? You then need to find out what process that person will use for making the decision.

### Story: Getting the Right Information

*A number of years back there was a campaign to raise the minimum wage in California. Organizers found out that the Board with legal decision-making authority over the minimum wage had three members. One member was in favor of the increase, one was opposed, and one was undecided.*

*Now it was clear what information the organizers needed to guide their actions: The campaign needed to know what kinds of arguments would be most likely to sway the one swing voter on the Board. They found out that economic arguments carried the most weight with him, so they recruited a number of academic economists to help them make their case.*

It is possible to collect all kinds of information, possibly even too much. With the Internet, massive amounts of information are readily available. Whatever issue you are fighting, you may want to start by collecting just the informational basics, to give yourself some general background. Then stop and assess where you're at. Ask the questions about legal authority and how to influence the decision-makers. Now's the time to start thinking strategically about what additional information you'll need and how you're going to use the information to shape your actions. Once you have the information, you can link it with some of the other sources of power to shape an action that will have impact.

**EXERCISE**

## Information as a Source of Power

There are all kinds of information that can be useful as sources of power. One very common type is about who has the authority to make the change. We sometimes call this "Decision-maker Research."

**Think of one problem your group is facing right now:**

_____

_____

1. What do you want to accomplish? _____

_____

_____

_____

2. Who has the legal authority to make the decision?

_____

3. What is the decision-making process? _____

_____

_____

_____

4. Who could influence that person? _____

_____

_____

5.  What kinds of arguments would influence that person?

    _____

    _____

    _____

6.  What are the relevant laws that might restrict or support the change you want?

    _____

    _____

    _____

7.  What are the "accepted practices"? _____

    _____

    _____

    _____

8.  Is there any particular history behind this? _____

    _____

    _____

    _____

9.  Write down three next steps you could take right now to get you closer to answering those questions:

    a. _____

    b. _____

    c. _____

## ▶ Action and Learning

### Organizers Evaluate the Action

*The plight is worsened by a network of "citizen commit-*
*tees," "health and welfare councils," and other blue ribbon*
*citizen packages claiming to represent people who have*
*given them no mandate, and, as often as not, are ignorant*
*of the fact that others are speaking in their name.*

—Saul Alinsky

### *Story: Action, Reaction, and Evaluation*

#### Sometimes When You Take Action, the Reaction Is Nothing

In this story, just having the information didn't mean we got
our way.

*The neighbors around Maverick Square in East Boston*
*had worked hard to get a walking beat patrolman assigned*
*to their neighborhood. The patrolman got to know the*
*neighbors and was able to recognize the drug dealers. He*
*worked with Pastor Don Nanstad of Our Saviour's*
*Lutheran Church and some elderly residents in a nearby*
*public housing development to get rid of much of the drug-*
*dealing in the neighborhood. Then the walking patrolman*
*was pulled off the job. The neighbors were not happy.*

#### Getting the Information Helps

*A special grant had paid for the patrolman. The neighbors*
*wanted to know why the officer was taken away. If a spe-*
*cial grant was paying for the patrolman, why would he be*
*taken off this assignment? We decided to do a "research*
*action"—to go downtown to visit the agency that admin-*
*istered the grant, to read it for ourselves and find out*
*what the grant required.*

*(Don was smart: Before we went downtown, he called the*
*agency responsible for monitoring the grant's progress to*

*see if anyone there knew how the grant was going. The woman on the phone said, "I would like to know myself!" Don thought she sounded a little annoyed. He figured he might have found an ally.)*

*So we gathered at Don's church and took the subway downtown to the state office building. We rode the elevator to the office that had given out the grant. The woman from that agency was glad to see the neighbors once she realized what they were doing. She was frustrated, too, because the District Attorney had not made progress reports as required by the grant.*

*As we crowded around the counter, the clerk found the grant application. There it was in black and white: The grant included "$21,000 toward a walking beat patrolman in Maverick Square." The clerk made a copy of the grant application for us.*

*Armed with the information we needed about what the grant required as regards the walking beat patrolman, we took the subway back to East Boston.*

If one state agency is not giving you what you want, don't assume that all the other state agencies are on their side. Each agency has a different bureaucratic responsibility. In this case, one state agency could help citizens to get what they wanted from another state agency. There may well be some internal competition or inter-agency dispute that can work to your advantage—as it did here.

## Go to the Person Who Can Give You What You Want

*The District Attorney's office had received the grant, so our next step, we decided, would be to ask the District Attorney why the money was not being spent on what the grant specified. We tried to set up an appointment with the D.A. We could not get one. The group debated what to do next. Most wanted to go downtown to confront the D.A. about losing the patrolman. One woman in the group refused. She didn't want to upset the District Attorney. The group talked things out and made decisions on the basis of the informal influence of the individual members. They decided to keep this woman happy and not go downtown, at least for the time being. In retrospect, trying to keep one person happy led to a bad decision, because the group lost momentum. In organizing for change, it is important to keep members' energy levels high to empower and propel them to take action that otherwise might feel frightening or overwhelming.*

*In the meantime, the local Assistant District Attorney had set up a new "Neighborhood Advisory Group." The neighbors thought that this allowed the D.A. to look like he was involving the neighborhood when, in fact, he was not. He chose the members of the group, but Don was the only member out of the fifteen who was a neighborhood resident. The meetings were public. The neighbors often showed up at these meetings. The chair would not recognize them to speak. Sometimes the meetings were held in non-wheelchair accessible sites, a problem for the elderly residents and also a violation of the law. The residents complained. Nothing was done. They were getting pretty discouraged.*

*When Don complained, they kicked him off and posted a security guard at the door to stop him from coming to the meetings. (That did not stop him. The security guard played basketball with Don and just waved him in.)*

*After months of attending the local meetings with no results and getting no response to their requests for a meeting with the D.A., the members of the neighborhood association decided to go downtown again to try to meet with the District Attorney.*

## Sometimes You Come Up Empty

*They still could not get an appointment with the D.A., so they trooped down to his office in the musty old courthouse. They knocked on the door and were told, "The Dis-*

*trict Attorney is busy. Do you have an appointment?"*
*They said they had tried to get one. They asked to speak to*
*the public relations officer who often responded to them.*
*They were told that the public relations officer was out of*
*the office. They took seats on a bench and waited. One or*
*two would occasionally go out to go to the bathroom or the*
*water fountain. They asked again if the public relations*
*officer was there and again were told she was not in the*
*office. Then, as they looked out the door into the hallway,*
*they saw her walk down the hall and disappear into the*
*elevator. She had been there all the time and had taken*
*another door to avoid meeting them. When they saw this,*
*they realized that they were not going to get a meeting.*
*They had been there for over an hour, sitting on a hard*
*wooden bench. They decided to leave.*

*I had asked the neighbors to reserve time after the meet-*
*ing to get coffee and talk about what had happened. I*
*knew that, whatever happened, we needed time to talk*
*about it. We found a lunch place near the courthouse and*
*ordered coffee and sandwiches.*

## The Evaluation: What Do You Do With Nothing?

*"How did you feel?" I asked. "Disrespected," they said.*
*Some were feeling pretty down. They had tried to meet*
*someone who could help them and did not succeed. I asked*
*them, "Why do you feel that way?" "Whose fault was it*
*that the meeting did not happen?" "Who does the District*
*Attorney work for?" "Who pays his salary?" (Answer:*
*Their taxes. He works, at least theoretically, for them.)*
*Slowly, they started getting a little angry, rather than*
*depressed, about what had happened. I looked for any*
*sparks of anger I could fan. Isn't this supposed to be a*
*"government of the people, by the people, for the people"?*
*Has it "perished from the earth"? Isn't that what we learn*
*in school? But what happened here? Slowly, instead of*
*seeing their own inadequacies as the problem, they recog-*
*nized that the District Attorney was not doing his job—at*
*least not in the way they thought he should be doing it. He*

*was not even adhering to the grant he himself had written, which they had seen with their own eyes. The knowledge of the grant and having seen it gave them a little more confidence that they were right. Having done their homework helped tremendously.*

*It took over an hour to evaluate what happened. If we had just gotten on the subway and gone back home, we would have left with a sour taste in our mouths, like we had failed. Instead, after evaluating what had happened, the group saw that there was nothing wrong with them. There was something wrong with a system that could not provide the walking beat patrolman, especially when a grant specifically required it. Even though they did not immediately win back the walking beat patrolman, they stayed energized and ready for more action.*

## How to Evaluate an Action

Start by asking how people felt. After an action, some people are likely to feel good about the action, others not so good. Some may feel bad. Explore how everyone felt and why. Make sure everyone gets a chance to talk. Start with the feelings, and then move to what people are thinking and why. Your job is to help them examine their feelings and, if necessary, help them move beyond them. You want them to leave the evaluation with an understanding of what they think about the experience and with motivation to take further action.

## *Checklist for Evaluating an Action*

*Get together after the action to debrief and evaluate. Let everyone speak. Go around in a circle to make sure everyone gets a chance. Suggested questions:*

How did you feel?

What happened? (Get the story straight. People often hear or see things differently. Get an accurate recording of the facts and who said what. If someone misheard something, the group can set him or her straight.)

Did we have a plan of action?

Did we follow *that plan?*

❑ Yes. If yes, great!     ❑ No. If no, why not?

What was our goal?

What was the reaction?

Did we achieve our goal?

Did we get the reaction we expected?

Did anything surprise us?

What did we learn?

Would we do anything differently next time?

Did we need any more information?

Would more information help now?

What is our next step?

What might help us take this next step?

How do you feel now?

## Learning From Action

When we take a public action (going to see the District Attorney), we get a reaction (no one will see us). How we understand that reaction is essential to our learning.

Do we learn that we are not worthy of the District Attorney's attention? Do we have a right to ask the government to do what it says it will do—in this case, to spend the $21,000 on the walking beat patrolman in the neighborhood as the grant specified?

Action makes it possible to win improvements in peoples' lives. It also helps people to move away from hopelessness, to step outside of their feeling that they are unable to change their living conditions. It is often people's *feeling* that they can't act, rather than any innate inability or objective conditions, that stops them from acting. So doing your job often means encouraging people to act. Just as you might do when you are developing individual leaders, think about what the next step might be for the group to develop more capacity and confidence in exercising its power.

## *Story: When No One Listens, Why Talk?*

David Trietsch, who worked as a planner for the city, tells this story:

*It was the first meeting between the newly-formed public housing Tenants' Association and the surrounding community to discuss the future development of a "super" block that was to contain the housing development, a community church, and the surrounding residential neighborhood. When the agenda turned to better integrating the public housing community into the larger neighborhood, local neighborhood residents stood up one after another and talked about "those people." The neighborhood residents stated that the housing development residents "don't care about the same things we do." They went on to say that the people who lived in public housing were responsible for the garbage on the streets and for the run-down state of their housing.*

*To my dismay, not one tenant responded. Not one member of the Tenants' Association demanded to be heard. The public housing tenants looked at their feet and remained silent throughout the meeting.*

*Later that night, I sat with the tenants in their association office and asked, "How could you hear what they were saying and not respond?"*

*Their answer: "Who would have listened to us? What right did we have to talk?"*

*That night began our real work together.*

You have to constantly take the time to ask, "What have we learned from this action?" The evaluation of the action is as important as the action itself. Without the evaluation and the learning that comes from it, the group will lack a common understanding and the basis to plan what to do next. The evaluation provides not only individual learning but also group learning. The group then can learn how the world works and plan accordingly. Action, evaluation, and learning lead to more effective action.

People experience action in different ways. Your job is to help people see any action they take—and the reaction they get—as confirmation that they have the potential to make a difference in the world. You want people to leave actions prepared to continue to act in the future in even more effective or powerful ways.

## Action Means Face-to-Face Negotiation

Sometimes you have no time to build an organization. The wolf is at the door and you have to act fast. Knowing how to do this helps. This story illustrates the importance of face-to-face communication with those who have the authority to give you what you want.

## Story: Asking Face-to-Face

*Cheri Andes, an organizer with the Greater Boston Interfaith Organization, an affiliate of the Industrial Areas Foundation, lives in Framingham, Massachusetts. Her son had benefited from the "Reading Recovery" program in the schools. The town was planning to cut the program.*

*The teachers planned to attend the meeting where the School Committee would make the decision about cutting the Reading Recovery program. But the teachers couldn't get on the agenda.*

*Cheri offered her advice to the teachers for how to advocate to save the program. Cheri told the teachers to speak directly to the School Committee members. If they wanted to affect the decision, it wouldn't be enough simply to be present in the room. Cheri told them to go up to the School Committee members, introduce themselves, and ask them to keep the Reading Recovery program. At a break in the meeting, the teachers walked up to the School Committee members, shook their hands, introduced themselves, and asked them to keep the program. The School Committee voted to keep the program.*

The personal approach kept the program. The results may not always be so successful, but your chances of success improve with a face-to-face meeting.

Social scientists recognize the power of personal communication in negotiations:

*Minorities received the highest level of positive attention and the greatest influence on the private opinions of members of the majority and on the final group decision when they communicated face-to-face.*

—Malcolm Gladwell, *The Tipping Point*

## A Positive Reaction: Another Kind of Surprise

Sometimes the reaction you receive in an action will surprise you.

## Story: "I love Italians!" or Don't Underestimate the Power of Your Presence

*In the early 1980s the leaders of Revere Fair Share were frustrated by the increasing costs of utility bills. There seemed to be no end in sight. They wanted to get a hearing in their own city, several miles outside of Boston, from the state agency that regulated the utilities, the Department of Public Utilities (the DPU, as it was commonly known). They had tried all the conventional channels of communication to request a local hearing, all to no avail. They were annoyed and feeling powerless.*

*The Chairman of the DPU was a man named Jon Bonsall. They had never met him, but he began to assume mythic proportions of power in their eyes. After several months of no response to all their entreaties, a few leaders—a carpenter, a retired saleswoman married to a retired postal worker, and a woman who was the mother of five grown children and the wife of a retired steelworker—and I decided to pay the DPU a visit. We figured we had little to lose.*

*We took the subway into downtown Boston and then rode the elevator up to the DPU offices in the high-rise State Office Building. When we got there we asked for Jon Bonsall. We had tried to get an appointment, we explained, but had been turned down. The receptionist asked who we were and what we wanted. We told her. She asked us to wait. In a little while, Jon Bonsall appeared. He was not, as we had assumed, ten feet tall. He was short and thin. He invited us into a small conference room.*

*We said we were from Revere. Then he fell all over himself telling us how much he liked Italians. (Revere was well known for being a largely Italian community, although the folks I had come with were Irish.) He went on about how much he loved Italians, how his wife was from Revere, and how he would be delighted to come out to Revere to hold a hearing on the gas increases. It was like "The Wizard of Oz": The supposedly all-powerful man behind the curtain was all-too-human and seemed almost afraid of our little party. We got a date for the hearing in Revere and went back home on the subway. Mission accomplished. Unless you act, you never know the power you have.*

## ▶ Putting It All Together— From Organizing to Action to Evaluation

## From the Ground Up— Building An Organization to Solve a Shared Problem

### Introduction: Back to the Basics

This case study brings together the basic steps of building an organization: the idea, telling your story, listening to others, forming a core group, developing goals, objectives, and a structure, mobilizing resources, moving to action, evaluating, reflecting, and re-assessing. These events took place in the late 1970s in Brattleboro, Vermont. I was working as an organizer for the Vermont Alliance.

### Story: Creating a Powerful Tenants Association

The tenants in Mountain Home Mobile Home Park had problems. They owned their trailers but rented the land on which the trailers stood. They expected the landlord to maintain the roads and utilities in the park, but rainwater swamped the dips in the roads. Some telephone wires hung so low that they hit pedestrians. The roads were rutted and poorly graded.

### The Idea

Dave lived in the park with his wife Beth.* He called our office and I went to visit them. Dave offered me coffee and something to eat. Then he explained to me that he was angry at the conditions in the park and that he cared about what was happening to others, especially the many

* Not their real names

elderly people who lived in the park. He was angry, but not only angry. He had a sense of humor and a sense of right and wrong. It seemed just plain wrong to him that he should be paying rent while the landlord was doing such a poor job of maintaining the park.

## Developing a Core Group

### Recognizing the Signs of a Leader

Dave had lived at Mountain Home a number of years and knew a lot of people. He was likeable and friendly. His house was orderly. I sensed he could keep track of things and do what he said he would do. He seemed honest and direct. He looked me in the eye when we spoke.

Dave brought some other tenants to his home. This told me that he was connected to people and that others would follow him. The ability to bring people together is often a test for any potential leader. The fact that his house was not a mess reassured me that his mind was likely not a mess.

The people he invited seemed reasonable. They wanted what was reasonable: They were willing to pay their rent for a decent place to live, but felt that the landlord had not lived up to his end of the bargain.

### The Long March Through the Kitchens

After this first meeting, Dave and I visited other people in the park. Many were concerned about the lack of maintenance. Before long we had formed the core group of the Mountain Home Tenants Association. We held meetings in the various trailers, trying to figure out what to do, and gathered information about what was wrong in various areas of the park.

### Numbers Mean Clout

We needed enough tenants to make the landlord listen. This took time. There were several hundred trailers in the park. A few tenants and I went door-to-door in the park, listening to other tenants, hearing their complaints, and encouraging them to join the association. We asked for $10 for membership. We drank coffee and Kool-Aid in many kitchens.

## Listen . . . To a Lot of People

We listened to many people. Some were too afraid to do anything. Some didn't think things were so bad that they had to take action. Some thought nothing could be done. "It has always been this way and I once spoke to the landlord and it didn't do any good," one said. Some left for Florida in the winter and were not very invested in fixing the problems.

By the time several dozen people had joined we had a sense that at least half the people were willing to try to do something to improve conditions.

## You Don't Need Everyone

You don't need everyone. With a supportive minority you can get a lot done. A substantial minority that agrees to pay dues to join and to put their names on the organization's membership list gives the group enough legitimacy. You will never get everyone to join, and not all members will take action. But an organized minority that has done its research, knows its rights, and is willing to negotiate for its beliefs can get a lot done. Even if only six people do the actual negotiating, the landlord knows that they represent others. The organization—along with their personal presence, their knowledge of the public health and building codes, and their willingness to take action—gives the group's representatives their power.

Action also helps in recruiting new people—especially the kind of people who like getting things done more than talking about getting things done. When you act to improve your living conditions, you are likely to get something, although you may not get everything that you wanted. You can let those who have not joined know what you won. This demonstrates to them the power of your organization and encourages them to join and participate.

## Getting Ready: Figure Out Exactly What You Want Before You Take It On The Road

After several months of going door-to-door, listening to tenants' problems, getting people to join, and meeting to discuss the specific improvements, the Mountain Home group felt ready to negotiate with the landlord. They spoke with his secretary many times and finally were able to set up a meeting in his office in the center of the park. Most tenants had been in the reception room only to hand their check to the secretary through a hole in a glass window.

The team included four tenants plus me, the organizer. The tenants' team included men and women from Mountain Home, people of different generations and in different living situations: Dave; a young, single woman; a middle-aged woman who was married; and an older, retired woman.

Everyone was nervous. What would the landlord do? Would he try to kick the leaders out of the park?

### Make the Goals and Objectives Clear

The Mountain Home tenants wanted the landlord to fix up the park, but vague demands (such as, "Fix up the park") don't help. The tenants and the landlord could easily differ on what "fix up" meant.

The tenants would also likely differ among themselves about what such a vague demand meant. In setting out what an organization wants, you must *combat all vagueness*. It may seem unnecessarily picky, especially when any improvement would be welcomed, *but vague goals breed future disagreements* among the group. There may be improvements, but not necessarily the *specific improvements that some wanted*.

Then, although you have the improvements, your organization may still fall apart. The improvements might help some people and not others. If you do not write down your specific requests with agonizing specificity you might not get the solution you need. If you know you need a culvert on the Hill Road, specify a steel twelve-inch culvert set at the low point of the road, encased with number three gravel. You have to be as specific as necessary if you are not going to argue with the result. If you ask for "a culvert" and get a six-inch culvert that allows the water to back up, you still have a problem. If you want the telephone wires raised, don't just say you want them "raised." Specify, "Raised to 18 feet and attached so that they will not fall down in an 80-mile-an-hour wind."

These solutions need to be in writing. Writing keeps a record and avoids misunderstandings. Putting your requests for solutions in writing forces you to take the time to see if that is the solution that everyone wants. In small groups people think they know what others mean. It is easy to be mistaken. Putting the solutions in writing avoids confusion, division, and potential harm to the organization.

You may need to research culverts, road specifications, utility requirements, and other details. Master the technical details. Otherwise you get a useless culvert or a falling phone line.

## Ultimate Goal: To Build the Organization

You make the requests so specific because you want to get exactly what you need, but also because you want to *build the organization*. If the improvements you want are not specific enough or if the improvements satisfy some members but antagonize others, the results can divide the group. So, you may win some improvements but divide your organization in the process.

This is no good. You need the organization not only to win the agreement, but also to monitor and follow up on the agreement. You want the organization to be around for a long time, to follow up and insure that the improvements are installed correctly. You need the organization for the long haul because you also are likely to face other problems in the future.

## Preparation for the Meeting

Before the meeting, we went over in detail what everyone would say. Who would start off? Who would say what? What would we do if the landlord said this or that? How would we respond? We sat on the couch in Dave and Beth's trailer and role-played the negotiation session. I played the landlord. We tried to think of everything that could possibly go wrong and planned what to do in each case.

### Like a School Play

Preparation is essential. Think of negotiations as if they were a school play. You need as much preparation and rehearsal time. Think of all the possible things that could go wrong and make contingency plans.

I knew that the landlord was not fond of me, calling me an "outside agitator," although it was his tenants who were upset and leading the group. (People in authority often invoke the devil of the "outside agitator." It is supposed to be bad for people without power or money to get outside help. People with power and money, however, routinely employ outside agitators. They are called consultants, lawyers, lobbyists, or advisors. They pay them well and don't see anything wrong when *they* get outside help.)

The landlord had seen me often in the park and had made nasty comments about me to tenants. I thought he might ask me to leave. He might threaten not to talk to them if I stayed in the room. It would be one way to divide us. The tenants had to decide how to handle that. We agreed that I would leave if the landlord requested it. Then we role-played how they would handle that and other requests.

## The Results

### The Negotiation Session

The day of the meeting with the landlord, we all gathered at Dave's trailer and walked down the hill and into the office. The secretary asked us if we had an appointment. We said we did. We were ushered into the landlord's office and sat down. Right away the landlord asked me to leave. We did what we had planned. I waited outside in the parking lot. Knowing that this was likely, I had arranged to have a friend meet me in the parking lot. She kept me laughing about being an outside agitator.

Inside, the negotiating team stuck together. They got the landlord to agree in writing to a number of specific improvements. They followed up later with the town's Health and Building Inspector to make sure that he was monitoring the trailer park's compliance with the codes and regulations. In the following years, they met with other trailer park tenant associations and organized a statewide mobile home tenants association.

### Half a Loaf is Better than No Loaf

The residents did not get everything they wanted, but some improvements are better than none. And they can always go back for more. Some people refuse to compromise in the name of "principle." But what principle? What is the principle of getting nothing when you can get something? If you are hungry, half a loaf is better than no loaf: At least with half a loaf, you won't starve to death. With an all-or-nothing attitude you may get nothing. How does that help you?

## *Reflection*

### Do With Others

The Mountain Home tenants were doing with others what they could not do alone: getting improvements in their trailer park. My role was to help them to think about how to negotiate with the landlord, to encourage them, to go with them to get their neighbors to join the association, to remind them of their legal rights, and to help them to see that if they worked together they could accomplish what they could not do alone. I was not going to do it for them. There was no guarantee they would succeed. The only guarantee I could give them was that if they did nothing they would get nothing.

### I Needed Help, Too

I also needed help. With my friend in the parking lot, someone who knew that I'd be worried about how the negotiation session would go without me, I did better than I would have done alone, waiting out the meeting and thinking about possible next steps for the association. If the Iron Rule of Organizing is, "Never do for someone else what they can do for themselves," I should add, "Don't be afraid to do with someone else what you can't do so well by yourself." Ask for help when you need it.

### Don't Forget the Ice Cream

People also need to have a good time in the organization. If it is all work, problems, and planning meetings, you will have a dull organization that few people will want to call their own. The core group used to go down to Page's Ice Cream at the bottom of the hill after our meetings, especially in the summer. Hanging out with ice cream was helpful. Meeting people and enjoying each other's company is part of the organizing process.

# CHAPTER 12

# Building Community

*Organizing is just a fancy term for building relationships.*

—Ernesto Cortes

In building a community organization, you want to develop a sense of community as well as achieve improvements in the world. These two goals are interdependent. People are more likely to show up when they feel a sense of belonging and community. Achieving common goals develops that sense of community.

How do you foster community? It starts with the *intention* to build a sense of community in addition to your organization's work out in the world.

## Story: Build the World You Want Right Now

This story illustrates how one organization helped its members, recognized their personal needs, and developed a sense of community, while addressing real problems out in the world.

*When I started working as a community organizer in the 1970s for an organization in Vermont whose primary goals included utility rate and tax reform, I had a young child. That made it easy for me to see how lack of child care prevented parents from participating in the organization. So we hired, out of the organization's funds, someone to take care of children brought to meetings. If a parent had a young child who needed care, but could not bring the child to the meeting, the organization paid for a babysitter at home.*

The organization was in the business of reforming state policies. It also was in the business of building a sense of caring and community among its members. Paying for child care helped the organization do its basic business.

# ▶ Organizations Are a Two-Way Street

The organization helps you. You help it. The organization meets you halfway. The organization helps us to help each other. Most people have something to offer the organization, but sometimes real-life concerns get in the way. In Vermont, we did not want to set up barriers that would keep parents from participating. The relationship between the organization and its members is a two-way street.

When a community organization helps an individual member address a problem with a hospital, government agency, utility, or other big institution, it is saying that it is not just up to individuals to get what is due them from the institution. In fact, it often is impossible for individuals to do so. Lone individuals do not have the power to force change from a large company or agency.

The community organization becomes a mediating organization between the individual and the institution. It tries to level the playing field. One individual against a government agency or utility company is not a fair fight.

## Group Responsibility for Individual Security

The value underlying the mediating organization is that there is group responsibility for individual security. The organization provides for people what they cannot provide for themselves by themselves alone. The existence of the organization is a statement about *group responsibility for individuals' problems.*

We do not live by bread alone. We also do not live by ourselves alone. I do not and cannot live—or certainly not well—without the relationships and support of others. The value that this expresses is: We have a responsibility to each other.

An organization's primary goal may be to improve the local schools, provide affordable housing, or protect the environment. But members also bring home-cooked casseroles for the family with a new baby. They drive a sick member to the doctor. People show up to carry boxes when a member moves to a new home. They celebrate at a birthday, wedding, new job, or graduation. They take up a collection for someone who is out of work who has to pay the landlord for the rent or pay the dentist for a broken tooth. They don't do this out of pity. The action comes from personal connection. Also, they know they might be in a similar position some day.

# ▶ Organizing and Mutual Assistance

## In Service to One Another

*Friends are people who know each other. They are free to give and receive help. In our time, professionalized servants are people who are limited by the unknowing friendlessness of their help. Friends, on the other hand, are people liberated by the possibilities of knowing how to help each other.*

—John McKnight, *The Careless Society*

Many unions and community groups started out practicing mutual responsibility. Some changed so that their members now pay dues to hire staff who service them. The members exchange their dues for service. Dues become the members' only contribution.

It is easy to see how an organization can change from organizing and mutual assistance to service, how it can stop developing new leaders or building a sense of community. It is what we have learned to expect. The media encourages us to consume. It is what we see all around us. Civic participation takes time. It also takes an *intention* to build a sense of community and mutual responsibility— putting the group's needs and others' needs on the same plane as our own.

There is little public support for civic engagement. The only advertising we see for participating in civic life involves the annual rite of voting, giving money to charities, or volunteering to "serve the needy." We do not see public service advertising encouraging us to attend City Council meetings, join the board of a local community organization, or run for public office.

How do you build a powerful organization that can negotiate for its members with those in authority and also nurture a community of mutual support? It starts with knowing that this is where we want to go, letting members know this, and then asking how we are doing on this goal. It continues with many little actions that let members know that we care about each other.

## Story: "Serving" and Building Community

*It is not in groups but in isolation that people are more apt to be homogenized.*

    —Robert Bellah, et al., *Habits of the Heart*

*For two years I served as chair of my congregation's Social Action Committee. We had a sub-committee responsible for helping people in the congregation when they needed help.*

*This was a suburban congregation. Most of its members were middle- or upper-income. The main complaint of the sub-committee's coordinator was that "no one ever called to ask for help." When people were sick they could order out for pizza or Chinese food, rather than call the congregation for someone to deliver a lasagna casserole. If they needed a ride to the doctor, they could call a cab, rather than bother someone from the congregation for a ride.*

## People Need to Be Needed

*Several years later our family needed help. A new baby and complications with the birth made life difficult. We could have gotten by with only help from our immediate family and by ordering out for food. But I remembered the complaint of the sub-committee's coordinator and made a special point of asking for help.*

*We got lots of help—from people we knew and from others whom we did not know. People cooked food and delivered it. They went shopping. We got to know some people better and discovered the culinary talents of others.*

*I asked for help not only because we needed it, but also because I thought that those helping needed it—in a different way. It is good to be needed. They wanted to be needed and useful. Too often we cannot discover how to be useful in the world. It feels good to help, and I wanted more people to feel good. It may sound funny, but asking for help not only helped us but also helped them—and it helped to build a sense of community in the congregation.*

## We Need Reminders of Our Connections

Every time someone in the organization plays a useful role because of his or her membership in the organization, the organization becomes stronger. The bonds of usefulness and friendship grow. We are reminded that even though we might be able to offer help now, we might need help later on. It reminds us of our connections to each other, of our interdependence. Such action builds community. In going to another's home—sometimes a home we have never seen—we strengthen the bonds between us. Too often we are under the illusion that we can get along without others, that we are fine just by ourselves. But we really need each other and are responsible for one another.

# ▶ Powerful Organizations Exercise Both Heart and Muscle

## What is Real Support?

How do you develop mutual support and a sense of community? One way is to ask. A question like, "What do you need to make this organization work for you?" will evoke a list of the real support that people need. If you take the time to ask and to listen to the answer to a simple question like this, you'll hear the little things that people need to make the organization work for them. For one person it might be some extra training in how to manage time. For another, a day off with the child he doesn't see very often. For someone else, a more flexible schedule to accommodate child care arrangements. For someone else, the trust and freedom to work on her own to complete a project.

## Balance

You need to balance individual and organizational needs. But people are likely to complete organizational tasks when they have the support within the organization for their own needs.

EXERCISE

## Fostering a Group that Meets Its Members' Needs

Gather your members (or leadership committee, or subset of members) in a group.

**First have each person answer this question individually:**

What needs is your organization not meeting that would make you a more productive or committed member?

_____

_____

_____

_____

**Then, turn to the group:**

Using large post-it notes, ask every member of the group to write down what his or her answer was to the above question. Collect the post-its and put them on the wall or on a large flip chart. Allow the group time to look at them so they can see what others want.

Now discuss what you have seen. Ask any clarifying questions. See if some people will make commitments to do what others want. See if the organization can make any changes to do what people want.

## Praise: A Simple Concept, But Often Overlooked

One of the most overlooked ways to support others is simply to praise them when they do a good job. Wally Roberts told me this story:

### Story: Real Thank You's Help

*"I've been working hard for the last couple of months to round up support for locating a new town office in an historic mill here in our village instead of way the hell out in nowhere on a dirt road, which is the choice of the Building Committee. I've been working with a group of people who've been very supportive. At various times they've praised me for different pieces of the work I have done—gathering signatures on a petition, speaking in public meetings, researching information and lining up support and grant money from other organizations, etc. I don't think many of us work to be praised or to be recognized. We usually do it because we believe in what we are doing. So when the praise comes, it's very sweet and it gives us a boost to continue. In that way it reinforces our commitment and determination to continue the work."*

## The Power of Community

To build community and mutual support, groups have to go beyond helping the individuals in the groups. They have to help all members to see themselves as part of a community that can help each other in many ways, and to use the power of the group to do this.

### Story: Discovering Our Overlapping Selves

*Nursing home workers in Greater Boston, mostly Haitian immigrants, are poorly paid, have few benefits, and often are forbidden from calling their homes during their shifts. Even for emergencies. The nursing homes, many now part of for-profit national chains, are often understaffed. The Greater Boston Interfaith Organization (GBIO) has begun a campaign to improve conditions for the workers. Many of the elderly patients they serve are the parents or grandparents of middle-class people who live in the suburbs. It is in the self-interest of both the Haitian workers and the middle-class families to have better staffed nursing homes and better paid nursing home workers. So GBIO brought together middle-class suburbanites and city dwellers, African Americans, Irish Catholics, Protestants, and Jews, to meet the nursing home workers (mostly Haitian). Then they brought GBIO member teams to meet with the nursing home supervisors and managers to tell them of their concerns and ask for better conditions for the workers. They have contacted the state Attorney General's office for legal sanction of their concerns.*

*They are starting to build a community of caring and concern based on the long-term mutual self-interest of varied groups of people with very different economic needs and backgrounds. At meetings, people from all backgrounds tell their stories. Haitian nursing home workers tell of not being able to see their children, of getting up at 5:00 a.m., of having to work a double shift, and of coming home, exhausted, at 11:00 p.m., only able to kiss the foreheads of their sleeping children. Suburban churchgoers tell of parents in nursing homes, hoping that they will be well cared for by the nursing home staff. Slowly, people are building a community of mutual support and caring, based not on sympathy, but on mutual self-interest and on understanding of each other's stories.*

A community is more than a group of people who exchange goods and services with an eye toward making an equal exchange. Building community into our organizations means more than the group providing support for individuals' needs. A community looks for ways that all can use their gifts. It raises everyone up. It is not just "tit" for you so that later, I will get "tat" for me. That kind of exchange is useful, but it lacks staying power. I will stay in such a group only as long as my needs are being met; I won't develop a sense of loyalty that makes me want to stay because I care about someone else's needs.

In fact, we need community because we never know what we will need. Most of us recognize that we cannot get by with just our own personal resources. Many of us want to live in a world where we help each other out of love and respect and feel part of something bigger than ourselves. That is the kind of community that powerful organizations can build.

## Community as a National Value

Just as the group has responsibility for each individual ("You are not in this alone"), community organizations can be models for the creation of a more caring nation and society. By helping individuals, community groups promote the values of community that we would like to see in state and federal policies. Community organizations can advocate for policies that ensure group (e.g., government) responsibility for things that the individual cannot provide for her/himself. Our government already takes care of the individual in many arenas: police and fire protection for individuals, water and sewer service for the public health of everyone, good public education for all children, health care for all, a respectful retirement plan through Social Security when people are too old or disabled to work, unemployment insurance if you lose your job, and paid time off of work when children are born or adopted so that families can be strong. As a society we provide public parks and other spaces where people can recreate and meet each other. We have sidewalks where people can walk safely. All of these are instances of the larger group taking responsibility for meeting the needs of its community of members.

This understanding of the value of community groups contrasts with the view often prevalent in popular discourse during the presidency of George W. Bush. The other view invokes an image of the "ownership society," where every person will "own" his or her own security. In contrast, powerful community organizations promote a vision of shared ownership of the common good and mutual responsibility for the welfare of all. This is the kind of community vision that organizers are pursuing as they nurture powerful, effective, and strong community groups.

# OUR FUTURE

*Shy people seldom learn.*

—Old saying

Now you have an organization. It is working. It has won some improvements in the lives of its members. It has developed a sense of community. Now what? Where does this take you?

It can take you lots of places. And you need not go it alone. Others who have gone before you have learned a few things. So take a look at the Bibliography and Resources at the back of this book to see what has been written and who is around who might be able to help you. There is a lot of help for you there. You only have to ask and be available to others when they ask.

This kind of help is like any action in organizing: The only guarantee I can give you is that if you don't ask, you won't get. That goes for money, for improvements in your neighborhood, your workplace, or any other system. It also goes for getting help around your particular situation or problem. So don't be shy about asking anyone, including me, for help.

The possibilities and promise of groups are beyond the vision of any one of us. That is why we form groups in the first place. If we could figure out how to change the world by ourselves, if we had the power to do it alone, we wouldn't need an organization. But we can't figure it out by ourselves. We are fortunate to have the power to create community organizations to help us get there collectively.

This section looks toward an unknown future. The basic approach to organizing I've outlined in this book—based on my past thirty years of experience plus the wisdom of many others who have gone before me or who have worked alongside me—won't change in these post-modern times, but some of the techniques and applications can be modified to fit today's (and tomorrow's) realities. What that will look like is anybody's guess. It is limited only by our own creativity. Together, we will be shaping this future as we go. One thing's for certain: The world needs powerful community organizations and the efforts of organizers now more than ever. With problems on a global scale, there's never been a more urgent need for the activism, leadership, and vision of powerful community organizations.

# Where Do We Go From Here?

## ▶ Looking Outward and Forward

No matter how talented you are, no matter how successful you have been in developing a vision, core group, structure, strategy, mission, goals, resources, and action, circumstances change. Forces beyond your control will affect your organization. As you continue to act, evaluate, and learn, you have to pay attention not only to all the complex internal dynamics that groups and people always bring, but also to the changes in the external political and economic environment.

### Beyond Your Doorstep

This may mean that you will have to organize on a much bigger scale than you had imagined. Federal and state policies may affect you when you try to improve the schools, public safety, or transportation in your city or town. If you want to build affordable housing, federal law may set up roadblocks. If you breathe the air in Pennsylvania, federal environmental regulations for a power plant in Indiana may affect you. If you pay an electric bill in California, federal regulatory policies made in Washington, D.C., or corporate greed in Houston may double your bill.

## The Free Market May Not Be "Free" For Your Group

The power of the free market also affects you. Modern corporations operate in a global market. They calculate the price of hiring a software engineer in India instead of Indiana and move operations to New Delhi. They calculate the cost of a factory worker in Mexico City instead of Milwaukee and move production to Mexico. If the job can be done cheaper elsewhere, it goes there. With high-speed Internet technology, satellite communication, and air travel, corporations can move where they find the cheapest labor, the best tax deal, and the least restrictive environmental regulations. No matter where you live in America, the global market affects you and your family.

The free market has marvelous power to produce efficiently and develop new products and processes. It has brought us wonderful products at prices we can afford. Just walk around any supermarket or electronics store and see for yourself.

The market also brings less attractive results. It allows tremendous inequalities of wealth, opportunity, and freedom. Some children are born into great wealth and opportunity. Many are not. The efficiencies of the market fail to factor in many of the market's effects on families and communities. The market also produces what economists call "externalities"—such as pollution and inequality. Such externalities may land on your head—in jobs lost, schools that are overcrowded, polluted air and water, and other problems that affect your family and neighborhood. For you, these effects are anything but "external."

## ▶ The Impact of Community Organizations

### Governments Protect You Because of the Community Organizing that Came Before You

*If you think the economy is working, ask someone who isn't.*

—Bumper sticker

Governments restrain the market. People have built organizations to force government to regulate monopolies and corporations so that the "externalities" don't hurt or kill people. They have forced government to establish unemployment insurance, minimum wages, and health, safety, and environmental rules that provide security for the majority who exercise little power in a market economy.

These improvements did not happen because those in authority decided to be nice to the less fortunate. They happened because people built organizations that developed enough power to force the changes. They pressed government for these protections and improvements for their families and communities.

### Think Globally—And Start Acting Locally

Today we face many of the same challenges, but the scope is international. This means that we are going to have to develop relationships with people and organizations across town, across the state, across the nation, and around the world. This will not be quick or easy. It certainly will not be cheap. The forms and structures are yet to be built.

This book focuses on the specific skills, methods, and complexities of building organizations. These remain important. All organizing starts with an idea and a vision. This is where we begin. It makes little sense to start with global issues, or even citywide concerns, when people's immediate needs are on their doorsteps. You need to re-open the library or bring back the reading teachers before tackling the global issues. The library or reading teachers may be all you can handle right now.

But, to solve some of the problems you face, at some point you are likely to need to hook up across town, across the state, and even across the border. Your town or city may want to keep the library open and add more reading teachers, but cutbacks in revenue from the state and federal governments may stop them. This means that you will need to think ahead—to imagine eventually having the power, the numbers of organized people and organized money, to get the results you want. It means you need to keep learning about the larger situation while you are dealing with the more immediate problems that you have the power to solve now.

## The Proof Is In the Pudding

Even in recent U.S. history, many changes in national policy came about because large numbers of people started organizing at the local level. The Civil Rights Movement, which led to changes in federal law, began with local bus boycotts and sit-ins against local department stores. These were local issues. The Black parents who shopped in the Nashville department stores could buy what they wanted but they could not sit down and take a rest with their children. People faced these problems every day. Courageous, organized action over many years in many places eventually led to changes in federal laws.

This was also the case in the development of unemployment insurance.

## Story: How "Crazy" Ideas Become the Norm

*In the 1930s, Rose Chernin, a Bronx housewife and community activist, went door-to-door in the apartment buildings in her neighborhood. She would knock on a door, and once the tenants were satisfied that she was not the landlord asking for rent, she would ask them if anyone in the family was out of work. There was always someone out of work. Then she would ask them to sign a petition asking their Congressman to sponsor a bill to pay people who were not working. "Jobs or money" was the demand.*

*Most people thought she was crazy, that such a demand was impossible. "You want the government to pay us for not working?" they asked, incredulous. "That is socialism. They will never do that."*

*But Rose Chernin persisted, as did thousands of others, forming Unemployment Councils of unemployed workers who forced the United States government to create unemployment insurance programs. Today, unemployment insurance is an accepted fact of economic life in the U.S. It did not happen by itself or from the kindness of benevolent politicians. It only came about from the patient, day-to-day and door-by-door work of thousands of organizers and neighborhood leaders like Rose Chernin.*

(From Kim Chernin's wonderful book, *In My Mother's House*.)

The efforts of mothers concerned about the impact on their children's health from corporate dumping of toxins led to "Right to Know" laws and the federal Superfund bill. The work of neighborhood organizers to stop predatory lending in low-income neighborhoods eventually led various small neighborhood organizations to band together to get the federal Community Reinvestment Act passed. This landmark national legislation made banks disclose their lending practices in the areas where they did business. These improvements came about when people realized that they needed changes in laws that were beyond the power of any one community organization, and a national coalition, organized by National Peoples' Action in Chicago, led the fight to Washington, D.C.

When the farmers in the Midwest in the late 1800s found themselves at the mercy of the railroads, they organized their local Grange Halls into a national organization to pressure the federal government to regulate the railroads. These regulations allowed them to get their produce to market at prices that would not bankrupt them. The railroads had already organized across state lines. The farmers had to do the same. When janitors cleaning a building in Boston owned by a company in Chicago wanted a fair wage, they needed to link up with janitors in New York and Los Angeles cleaning buildings owned by the same Chicago company.

## ▶ New Technologies, New Approaches, New Opportunities

### The Internet: The More Things Change, the More They Stay the Same

The Internet has changed how we shop, communicate, gather information, and even find dates and mates. It is changing some aspects of how we build and strengthen organizations, although the basic steps and skills are likely to remain unchanged.

Some Internet start-up companies thought we would do all our shopping on the Internet. Unfortunately for some investors, most people still want to squeeze melons before they buy them. People will still need to meet you eyeball-to-eyeball before they will trust you and invest themselves in your organization. The Internet may help you make contact with new people, it can provide information about any subject worldwide, but, to build a strong organization, at some point, you are going to have to sit down and have that cup of coffee.

As people's lives become less connected by neighborhoods, as people's daily schedules become more crowded and stressed, the Internet is likely to provide a place for people to "meet." People already are less likely to run into each other in the town common (if there even is such a place any more), as suburbs and strip malls cover the landscape and Americans spend so much time in their cars. The Internet provides opportunities to communicate and to organize around common interests for people who may live near each other but find it difficult to meet.

Even with so much virtual access, people's needs for affiliation and for solving common problems remain. The Internet provides new ways for people to get together around common interests—about everything from stamp collecting to electing candidates to public office. "Meeting" on the Internet might encourage people to then get out of their cars and houses and meet face-to-face. Once people who share common concerns about equality, about solving a shared problem, or about making a difference get in the same room, they will still need an organizer—even if they first met on the Internet. Someone has to run the meeting and make sure it does not drag on all night. Someone has to set organizational boundaries, collect dues, and help the group make decisions. People's need for a sense of community will remain—if not increase—as everyday opportunities for community diminish. No website or list-serv provides this.

The Internet allows a thousand websites to bloom. It allows people to gather and disseminate information from many sources. E-mail lists and electronic newsletters allow people to communicate quickly with thousands of people around the world. It does not mean that all messages are read and digested, but the potential is there. It is now much easier for two (or three, or four, or many more) to communicate with each other, nationally and internationally. The Internet allows back-and-forth communication with a much wider audience, maybe even a "community" of common purpose.

The Internet is used most effectively when there is a sense of an immediate need for broad-based communication. An upcoming Presidential election, a pending war, or another crisis that grabs the attention of many people are times when the Internet's potential is best mined. In the 2004 presidential election race, the Howard Dean for President Campaign made skillful use of the Internet. Using the website Meetup.com, it helped people connect over the Internet, donate money, and engage in a national electoral campaign.

However, this took more than the Internet. It took the skillful use of old-fashioned house meetings to galvanize most Dean supporters. As one close observer of the Dean campaign noted:

*The notion that the Dean campaign for the Democratic nomination is primarily an Internet-fueled phenomenon seems absurd when viewed from the living rooms of New Hampshire. Here it plays out like some sort of secular tent revival, winning over individual souls one at a time.*

—Hanna Rosin, *Washington Post*, December 9, 2003

## Electoral Campaigns Fade. Community Organizations Can Stay.

It is unlikely that such "meeting up" organized by the electoral campaign will continue once the electoral season concludes and the paid staffers leave. Other electoral campaigns have brought people together around a common purpose, the election of their candidate. After a winning campaign, some stay connected through employment by the candidate. Losers go their separate ways—perhaps connecting again around another candidate. Lacking a staffed effort to connect beyond Election Day, electoral campaigns rarely maintain an ongoing organization.

The Internet and e-mail overload are likely to increase the importance of face-to-face personal communication—not relegate it to the dustbin of history.

*We are about to enter the age of word of mouth, and . . . paradoxically . . . all the limitless access to information . . . is going to lead us to rely more and more on very primitive kinds of social contacts. We will have even more needs for information we can rely on from people we know and trust.*

—Malcolm Gladwell, *The Tipping Point*

If the Internet becomes a more efficient way to collect campaign donations or get people to meet up and feel involved during campaign season and possibly after, we will still need *organizations* more than individual candidates to solve our problems. Ongoing organizations were common years ago in many of our cities—where elected officials maintained control by vast networks ("machines") that ensured them continuous election. They still exist in some cities and counties. Their legacy and impact give us a glimpse of the potential for influence on civic life that committed, ongoing organizations could have.

## Community Organizations Can Hold Elected Officials Accountable

Today, however, elected officials are more likely to stay in office by access to money from large donors, enabling them to scare away potential opponents. Increased involvement in electoral campaigns will require more than new technology that offers a new means of communication. It also will require new organizations and probably a new kind of elected official.

This new type of public official will need to make a commitment to being *accountable to* and *listening to* her or his constituents (the voters), not only *representing* them. Elected leaders will need to solicit ideas, to educate, and to involve citizens actively. If public officials are going to be part of grassroots community organizations, they will have to be part of the larger effort to strengthen civic engagement at all levels. Candidates and public officials are going to have to maintain a strong, long-lasting commitment to developing leadership at the grassroots instead of building up their own power at the top. The legacy of this kind of public official will be seen in strong organizations that hold the power to make change, rather than in a disempowered electorate at the mercy of the decisions of a disconnected officialdom. This type of civic engagement—an elected official who collaborates with community groups to advocate for change—is the type of leadership we need in order to solve problems and change the world.

This might happen if community organizations see themselves as institutions in which candidates are recruited and held accountable, and if elected officials embrace this same view.

## Story: One Elected Official Accountable to a Grassroots Organization

The Connecticut Citizen Action Group (CCAG) and the Legislative Electoral Action Program (LEAP) did something like this in the 1980s. They actively recruited candidates for public office.

*One of these candidates, Doreen DelBianco, proudly declared at a public forum that she was "owned lock, stock, and barrel by CCAG." Most candidates would never make such a statement. It would mean they were bought by a special interest. But in this case the special interest was not a group of wealthy donors. It was a broad-based citizens' group that had helped a woman to develop leadership skills and had encouraged her to run for public office. CCAG and LEAP then held her accountable—and she welcomed that.*

## ▶ Coming Full Circle: It Takes an Organization to Raise a Village

Real democracy means more than voting once every year or two and then hoping that the people we elect do the job. If we believe the theory that those closest to the problems need to plan and implement solutions, then those closest to the problems need information, resources, and grassroots organizations where they have power. Government officials and experts can help tremendously by enacting good policies, but they can't solve all our problems from on high.

Solving the problems we face takes organizations. Organizations require organizers and leaders—people who understand the need for organizations, have the skills, patience, and commitment to build them, and exhibit the willingness to reflect upon their actions and learn from them.

Even with our American adoration of individual celebrities, we recognize that no matter how smart or rich we may become, there are many things an individual cannot accomplish alone. Most of us do not want to go it alone. We are looking for community. We are looking for meaning. We want to improve our lives and the lives of our families and friends. To do this we are going to have to build—and in many cases re-build—our community organizations.

# Your Turn

If you want to be healthier, or wealthier, or a smaller size, you can find whole sections of bookstores with advice on how to do this. If you want to learn how to raise your children, lower your stress, manage your time, make money in real estate, or deal with your mid-life crisis, there are shelves of books to guide you.

But if you want to help your community, not only yourself, it is much tougher to find the right information to guide you. There are some good books, but nowhere near the depth and breadth of choices you can find when you want "self-help."

This grassroots, bottom-up knowledge—the lessons of those closest to the problems—is not respected in many quarters. Especially, in my experience, when it comes to public policy. So, if those of us who value this knowledge want to spread it, we need to do it ourselves.

So far, we haven't done a very good job of this. People busy changing the world rarely take the time to write down all they have learned. (I know. It took me twelve years to write this book, and much of it was written while riding the subway to or from work or meetings or between 4:00 and 6:00 a.m.) Many times people who have made a difference in their world do not recognize how much they have learned or how valuable their stories and lessons are. But if you have solved a problem, built a group, built a sense of community—in your neighborhood, town, school, workplace, congregation, professional or community group, city, state, or county—you probably have learned some important lessons.

Much of the wisdom about community organizing is only available orally. Which brings me back to my grandmother. Through her stories, she taught me much of what I know about community organizing. Even today, her stories guide me in my work. However, this is a problem for newer generations of organizers because not enough of the Minnies of today are telling stories to their grandchildren, as they did a generation or two ago.

## Your Stories and Advice

*Wendy . . . was just slightly disappointed when he admitted that he came to the nursery window not to see her but to listen to stories. "You see, I don't know any stories. None of the lost boys knows any stories." "How perfectly awful," Wendy said.*

—J. M. Barrie, *Peter Pan*

This book started with a story, and then I proceeded to fill each of the chapters with stories. That is no coincidence. We remember stories that tell us who people are. Stories show what people do. Stories connect us to actions, not abstractions.

This book is an effort to start spreading our stories to a wider audience. My intention is to link the stories to learning, reflection, analysis, and more action. But this book is limited to *my* experience, *my* contacts, and what *I* have read. That is why we need you!

I propose that we, the people working at the grassroots to solve community problems and change the world, commit to sharing our stories. We can increase the likelihood of our success in making the world a better place by collecting and telling the many stories and lessons we have learned about how to build powerful organizations and make a difference.

To do this, we need a shared soapbox where we can stand (either virtually or literally) and exchange stories, so that the experience of many and the wisdom that has grown from the grassroots are accessible to many. We need a context—a place, a supportive environment, a habit, a comfortable pattern for fitting storytelling into our vocational or avocational lives—for swapping stories.

This is where I—no, *we*—need your help. Your community of fellow organizers, volunteers, coordinators, directors, family, and staff (including the readers of this book) wants your stories and the lessons you have learned. We need stories of successes and stories of failures. Stories that teach. Stories from all kinds of people from all over the world. Just as you need the perspectives and power of many people to build a powerful organization, the set of community organizing ideas and practices that we are developing here needs you.

## A New Storytellers' Commons

As for creating a context, there are three things you can do:

**1. Just start—in your own neighborhood, in your own back yard.** When you get together with your members, when you get together with the person or people whom you are developing as leaders, when you get together with other organizers . . . Tell stories! Help to create an oral tradition for the work of building powerful community organizations. Help to shape a habit and a culture of sharing stories as a part of community organizing work.

**2. Share and hear stories from around the country and around the world.** I have started a website, www.BuildingPowerfulCommunityOrganizations.com, where your stories and lessons will be posted. People who are looking for camaraderie, ideas, inspiration, or guidance for building powerful community organizations and solving community problems can turn there to find stories and suggestions about every step and all the details. It will be an interactive storehouse of stories and lessons, a guide for all sorts of people in all sorts of situations about how to make a difference in the world.

With your contributions of wisdom and stories, this website can become a dynamic, ongoing, interactive resource where visitors have the opportunity both to learn and to teach. The website can bring together the many lessons that are out there (right where you work!)—but that never have been written down—about building powerful groups to improve the world.

So send me your stories. They need not be long. In fact, short is beautiful. We will put them on the website, so that other organizers or people hoping to start or strengthen community organizations can turn to them for guidance. You can see the website at www.BuildingPowerfulCommunityOrganizations.com. It is one place to start.

**3. Get published in the next edition of this book.** I also will incorporate your stories into future editions of this book, making this collection that much richer by virtue of your input.

So, please write, call, shout, signal, or e-mail me to tell me what you find useful, useless, relevant, redundant, inspirational, puzzling, accurate, incorrect, surprising, or missing in this book. Let me know what you think should be changed or challenged. Send me your stories. Your feedback and reflections will make this community learning more useful. I'll incorporate your comments in the second edition, and I'll also post them on the website to spur further learning.

You can write to me or use the form in the back of this book.

Michael Jacoby Brown
Long Haul Press
10 Brattle Terrace
Arlington, MA 02474
U.S.A.
Telephone: 781-648-1508
E-mail:
Comments@BuildingPowerfulCommunityOrganizations.com
Or you can contact me through the website:
www.BuildingPowerfulCommunityOrganizations.com

I hope you will contribute to help all of us learn more about how to nurture powerful community groups that can solve problems and change the world.

# Community Organizing: A Very Annotated Bibliography

So many books, so little time. There is a lot you can read about creating groups that can solve problems and change the world. It is a complicated business and many people have had plenty to say in print about how to do it.

But where to start reading and when to stop? That is the question.

Sorry, there is no easy answer. In this Bibliography I will lay out some of my recommendations for what you can read that might help.

When I was a boy my mother would often recommend books for me to read. She was almost always right. I trusted her and so I trusted the books. There is no substitute for a personal guide you can trust. Reading opened for me a world that I could never experience first-hand. You still have that opportunity today: to read what you can never experience.

## No Substitute for Experience

But that leads me to the next important point. No book can substitute for experience. To learn how to change the world you have to go out there yourself and do it. Yes, it helps to read what others have done. Yes, it helps to read books that can provide guidance. But to learn you have to act. You have to mix it up in the real world, and use what you have learned and do the best you can. If reading becomes a substitute for action you have not learned much.

As with any subject that people care deeply about, there will be differences and sharp disagreements about strategy and effectiveness of various approaches. When the needs and problems are great, when progress seems slow, when the issues are complicated and the players are diverse, there will be lots of arguments over the best way to achieve similar ends.

So books can offer some guidance. The Internet also offers us expanded access to written knowledge and very specific information. Still, it is often hard to know what is worth reading and what is not. I try to sift through some of that here. Although, since I have not read everything and don't plan to (and can't), I am bound to leave out some very good sources. Hopefully, you, my readers, will enlighten me and I can add these resources in later editions of this book or on the website, www.BuildingPowerfulCommunityOrgani-zations.com.

## ▶ Recommended Reading

Alinsky, Saul. *Rules for Radicals: A Practical Primer for Realis-tic Radicals* and *Reveille for Radicals.* New York: Vintage Books, 1989 and 1991. These are the books that inspired a generation of community organizers. Full of no-nonsense advice and hard-hitting stories. I read these when I was sixteen and got hooked.

Andringa, Robert C., and Engstrom, Ted W. *Nonprofit Board Answer Book.* Washington, D.C.: BoardSource, 2002. The "non-profit" category includes everything from Harvard University to your local neighborhood group, so some of the information is hard to apply to specific situations. But this book contains a lot of helpful information about nonprofits in general.

Argyris, Chris, and Schon, Donald. *Organizational Learning.* Reading, MA: Addison-Wesley Publishing Company, 1978. Pretty dense academic language, but one of the best books you'll find about how to communicate in organizations and how to learn from action. A tough read, but worth the wade.

Bai, Matt. *The Multilevel Marketing of the President.* The *New York Times* Magazine, April 25, 2004. This article describes how the 2004 Republican campaign for President went right to the grassroots to enlist people to register and turn out voters. Most people in the business of politics seem to know that people bring people.

Bardoe, Cheryl. "Asset Management." *Neighborhood Works*, Jan.-Feb. 1996, p. 17. When you look for something, you are likely to find it. If you look for a community's needs and problems, surprise!—you will find them. If you look for its assets, those are what you will see. This article, like the work of John McKnight, looks at a community in terms of its strengths instead of its deficits.

Beckwith, Dave; with Stults, Karen; Williams, Charlene; and Williams, Roxanne. *Transforming Lives and Communities: Community Organizing for YOU!* Washington, DC: Center for Community Change, 2000. Voices of experience share their wisdom in this extremely practical curriculum guide to training community organizers. You can get this three-volume set of workbooks (about 75 pages each) through the Center for Community Change, 1000 Wisconsin Avenue, NW, Washington, D.C. 20007; 202-342-0519; www.communitychange.org.

Bellah, Robert, et. al. *Habits of the Heart: Individualism and Commitment in American Life.* Berkeley, CA: University of California Press, 1996. An in-depth exploration of the intersection of individualism and community in modern America. Based on detailed interviews with a cross section of Americans. This is not dry and detached academics. The work of committed people, it is a wonderful blend of psychology and politics.

Bobo, Kim; Kendall, Jackie; and Max, Steve. *Organizing for Social Change: Midwest Academy Manual for Activists*, 3rd edition. Santa Ana, CA: Seven Locks Press, 2001. A practical guide to direct action organizing as practiced by the Midwest Academy, a community organizing training institute in Chicago that has trained thousands of community organizers over the past 25 years.

Boyer, Richard O., and Morais, Herbert M. *Labor's Untold Story.* New York: United Electrical, Radio and Machine Workers of America, 1955. The story of a remarkable labor union. By policy, its president can never be paid more than the highest paid worker on the shop floor.

Branch, Taylor. *Parting the Waters: America in the King Years 1954-1963.* New York: Simon and Schuster, 1988. A history of Martin Luther King, Jr., and the early Civil Rights movement. Reads like a novel, but tells the story of the movement in detail, making clear that there was more planning, action, and risk-taking than "dreaming" in that movement. For those who romanticize the Civil Rights era, this book will help to de-romanticize the struggle for freedom. The Civil Rights movement was not only speeches and marches; this book highlights how much of it was planning and organizing.

Chambers, Edward T. *Roots for Radicals: Organizing for Power, Action, and Justice.* New York: Continuum, 2003. In this book, the director of the Industrial Areas Foundation reflects on the stories and lessons of his own experience and of the Industrial Areas Foundation, founded by his mentor, Saul Alinsky. This is a thoughtful work from a thoughtful man who has spent his lifetime organizing. The meaning behind the methods.

Chernin, Kim. *In My Mother's House.* New York: Harper, 1983. A biographical account of the author's mother, an American Communist activist whose grassroots activism in the 1930s and after led to unemployment insurance and other important improvements in millions of people's lives. An important piece of history, often overlooked by those who think that only famous people make history.

Doyle, Michael, and Straus, David. *How to Make Meetings Work.* New York: Jove Books, 1982. A terrific hands-on book that tells you everything you need to know about how to run meetings. Full of practical, nitty-gritty details, from flip charts to colored markers. The meeting maker's bible.

Eisenberg, Pablo. *Challenges for Nonprofits and Philanthropy: The Courage to Change.* Medford, MA: Tufts University Press, 2005. Eisenberg is among the most insightful critics of the world of philanthropy and how it uses and abuses its power in the world of social change. No armchair observer, Eisenberg was director of the Center for Community Change for many years. His columns also appear regularly in the *Chronicle of Philanthropy*.

Fellner, Kim. "Is Nothing Sacred?!" *The Ark* (the newsletter of the National Organizers Alliance), no. 10, January 1998, pp. 12-16. A good article about reflecting on strategy.

Flanagan, Joan. *The Grass Roots Fund Raising Book: How to Raise Money in Your Community*. Chicago: Contemporary Books, 1995. A basic book on what you need to know to raise money at the grassroots level.

Frankl, Victor E. *Man's Search for Meaning*. New York: Simon and Schuster, 1984. This is an autobiographical account of the author's survival in a Nazi death camp during World War II and a contemplation on the role of meaning in modern life from a psychological point of view. An indispensable read for anyone who thinks meaning is more important than money.

Freeman, Jo. "The Tyranny of Structurelessness." *Berkeley Journal of Sociology* 17 (1972-73): 151-165. A brilliant and timeless explanation for why there is no such thing as a "structureless group."

Freire, Paulo. *Pedagogy of the Oppressed*. New York: Continuum, 2004. A classic by the leader in popular education. Helpful for anyone trying to help adults learn through reflection and action.

Gecan, Michael. *Going Public: An Organizer's Guide to Citizen Action*. New York: Random House, 2002. A seasoned organizer writes about the Industrial Areas Foundation in New York, an important organization that has made a big difference in many people's lives. Great stories in an easy-to-read style.

Gladwell, Malcolm. *The Tipping Point*. New York: Little, Brown, 2002. Rich analysis, drawing on historical as well as current trends, of how to get your ideas to the point where they become popular, if not accepted, wisdom. Good insights about group psychology.

Greene, Melissa Kay. *Praying for Sheetrock: A Work of Non-Fiction*. New York: Ballantine Books, 1991. This book about a small Southern town during the Civil Rights movement reads like a novel, covering the complications of leadership, electoral politics, racism, and being human.

Heifetz, Ronald. *Leadership Without Easy Answers*. Cambridge, MA: The Belknap Press of Harvard University Press, 1994. Includes one of the best discussions I've seen about the difference between leadership and authority. Not written from a community perspective but good on how to lead groups in innovative ways.

Hertz, Judy. *Organizing for Change: Stories of Success*. Unpublished manuscript. March 2002. A good description of four organizing campaigns. Available from the COMM-ORG website, www.comm-org.wisc.edu.

Hoerr, John. *We Can't Eat Prestige: The Women Who Organized Harvard*. Philadelphia: Temple University Press, Labor and Social Change Series, 1997. This volume tells the story of how a determined group of women (and some men) organized a new kind of union at Harvard University. Easy to read, it flows like a novel.

The Hyams Foundation. "Joining Forces: Community Organizations and Labor Unions Form New Collaborations." A report, written by Lisa Ranghelli. Boston, March 2005. The Hyams Foundation just completed this study of its community organizing grantees that collaborate with organized labor. The report is available on their website, www.hyamsfoundation.org, or from The Hyams Foundation, 175 Federal St., 4th floor, Boston, MA 02110; 617-426-5600.

Kahn, Si. *Organizing: A Guide for Grassroots Leaders*. Washington, D.C.: NASW Press, 1991. An easy-to-read guide in a question-and-answer format, by a veteran organizer. Kahn is the director of Grassroots Leadership in Charlotte, N.C. A classic.

Klein, Kim. *Fundraising for Social Change*, 4th edition. San Francisco: Jossey-Bass, Chardon Press series, 2001. Lots of information and a good attitude toward the process of fundraising for grassroots groups. Just about everything you needed to know about fundraising but were afraid to ask.

Kotter, John P., and Cohen, Dan S. *The Heart of Change: Real Life Stories of How People Change Their Organizations*. Boston: Harvard Business School Press, 2002. Written for business managers who want to know how for-profit businesses can make change in their organizations, this book offers another take on the truth that people must feel the need in their hearts—not their heads—in order to really change. Much of the theory is the same as that behind the need for action and reflection in community or social change groups.

Kretzmann, John P., and. McKnight, John L. *Building Communities from the Inside Out: A Path Toward Finding and Mobilizing a Community's Assets.* Chicago: ACTA Publications, 1993. A good resource for anyone who wants to work in a community and see the glass as half full, not half empty. The authors turn the usual "needs assessment" process on its head, demonstrating how to view a community by its strengths instead of its problems.

Kuttner, Robert. "Philanthropy and Movements." *The American Prospect* 13:13, July 15, 2002. On Michael Jacoby Brown's required reading list for every foundation officer and everyone who solicits foundations for money.

Lappé, Frances Moore, and Du Bois, Paul Martin. *The Quickening of America.* San Francisco: Jossey-Bass, 1994. A well-written and well-thought-out guide to revitalizing democracy, with an orientation toward public life. You can order this book from the Center for Living Democracy, RR #1, Black Fox Road, Brattleboro, VT 05301.

Lewis, John, with D'Orso, Michael. *Walking with the Wind: A Memoir of the Movement.* New York: Simon and Schuster, 1998. A powerful story of one man who made a huge difference in the lives of millions of people. John Lewis, now a Congressman from Georgia, was a leader in the Civil Rights movement. His life and journey have been an inspiration to me and I am sure to many others.

Marrow, Alfred J. *The Practical Theorist: The Life and Work of Kurt Lewin.* New York: Basic Books, 1969. A wonderful biography of a man too few people know about. Lewin revolutionized the theory and practice of building groups. He is the father of virtually all the modern management theory practiced in business, although Lewin himself had wide interests and was very concerned about ethnic and racial justice.

McKnight, John. *The Careless Society.* New York: Basic Books, 1995. More good views from an important thinker.

MoveOn.org. *50 Ways to Love Your Country: How to Find Your Political Voice and Become a Catalyst for Change.* Maui: Inner Ocean Publishing, 2004. A practical book by MoveOn.org, an organization that uses the Internet to connect millions of people for political activism and political change.

Oshry, Barry. *Seeing Systems*. San Francisco: Berrett-Koehler, 1996. Oshry is the founder of Power and Systems, a terrific training program that simulates how power and people operate in real-life organizations. This book shows how things go "the way they usually go" and how you might be able to change them.

Osterman, Paul. *Gathering Power: The Future of Progressive Politics in America*. Boston: Beacon Press, 2002. This book describes the work of the Industrial Areas Foundation and argues that progressive politics needs to pay more attention to developing grassroots leadership than to broadcasting a better message through the media. It contains some meaty stories about organizing.

Pierce, Gregory F. Augustine, *Activism That Makes Sense: Congregations and Community Organization*. Chicago: ACTA Publications, 1984. A commonsensical, practical approach to organizing congregations. Good advice in a small package.

Putnam, Robert D. *Bowling Alone: The Collapse and Revival of American Community*. New York: Simon and Schuster, 2000. A big book by an academic, containing lots of data about the decline of what Putnam and other theorists call "social capital." A provocative, if over-generalized, review of how community life declined in the last part of the 20th century.

Putnam, Robert D., and. Feldstein, Lewis M. *Better Together: Restoring the American Community*. New York: Simon and Schuster, 2003. A collection of success stories of community groups across America.

Robinson, Andy. *Grassroots Grants: An Activist's Guide to Proposal Writing*. Berkeley, CA: Chardon Press, 1996. Specific guidance on writing proposals, with some good examples. If your group wants funding from foundations, you will need to learn how to write proposals.

Rosenfeld, Jona M., and Tardieu, Bruno. *Artisans of Democracy: How Ordinary People, Families in Extreme Poverty, and Social Institutions Become Allies to Overcome Social Exclusion*. Lanham, MD: University Press of America, 2000. A terrific book with insightful case studies about how the Fourth World Movement, an organization that works with very poor people, mounted effective campaigns around education, electricity cut-offs, and other issues. This excellent example of thoughtful organizing and reflection in action deserves a wide reading.

Rothstein, Richard. "What is an Organizer?" Unpublished, 1972. Available from the Midwest Academy, 28 East Jackson St. #605, Chicago, IL 60604; 312-427-2304; www.midwestacademy.org. A classic short article on what organizers *actually* do, not what people—including some organizers—often imagine that they do.

Ryan, Charlotte. *Prime Time Activism: Media Strategies for Grassroots Organizing*. Boston: South End Press, 1990. Written in the beginning of the 1990s, this book is still very helpful for community groups with an organizing orientation. Full of stories, Ryan's book presents an organizer's perspective on working with the media.

Salzman, Jason. *Making the News: A Guide for Activists and Nonprofits*. Boulder, CO: Westview Press, 2003. Easy to read, direct, full of practical advice for getting media attention. The author is a former Greenpeace organizer.

Schon, Donald A. *The Reflective Practitioner: How Professionals Think in Action*. New York: Basic Books, 1983. A great book for learning how to reflect on action and for understanding how your own "theories" might impede your effectiveness or that of your group. Schon's writing is key for anyone who does not want to keep making the same mistakes.

Sen, Rinku. *Stir It Up: Lessons in Community Organizing and Advocacy*. San Francisco: Jossey-Bass, Chardon Press series, 2003. Describes the work of twelve Ms. Foundation grantees. Offers important lessons on cutting-edge issues in community organizing and excellent case studies of current work in the field.

Shaw, Randy. *The Activist's Handbook: A Primer for the 1990s and Beyond*. Berkeley, CA: University of California Press, 1996. Based on the author's experience organizing in San Francisco, this handbook tells how to put together strategic community campaigns.

Slaughter, Jane (ed.). *A Troublemaker's Handbook 2: How to Fight Back Where You Work—And Win!* Detroit: Labor Notes Books, 2005. The best guide around for labor activists.

Staples, Lee D. *Roots to Power: A Manual for Grassroots Organizing.* 2nd edition. Westport, CT: Praeger, 2005. Full of practical information and detailed guidance.

Stoecker, Randy. "Cyberspace vs. Face to Face: Community Organizing in the New Millennium." Unpublished. A history and evaluation of the use of the Internet in community organizing. Available on-line at: http://www.vcn.bc.ca/citizens-handbook/ cyberorganize.html.

Trapp, Shel. *Dynamics of Organizing: Building Power by Developing the Human Spirit.* Self published: 2003. The story of Shel Trapp and National People's Action is a series of hard-hitting stories, up close and personal, that will make you think about how and why to go about the business of making the world a better place without wearing rose-colored glasses. It includes the history of the Community Reinvestment Act and how grassroots local action led to national legislation that has helped millions of people. This important book is hard to find; you can order it from the National Training and Information Center in Chicago, Illinois, by calling NTIC at 312-243-3035.

Wallack, Lawrence; Woodruff, Katie; Dorfman, Lori; and Diaz, Iris. *News for a Change: An Advocate's Guide to Working with the Media.* Thousand Oaks, CA: Sage Publications, 1999. Thoughtful and strategic, this book describes how media can be part of a campaign strategy.

Weisbord, Marvin. *Productive Workplaces: Organizing and Managing for Dignity, Meaning, and Community.* San Francisco: Jossey-Bass, 1987. Probably the best book I know for describing the history and practice of group and organizational behavior. Although written about businesses and workplaces, the material has much in common with other types of organizations, including community groups.

Yoon, Sam; Traynor, Bill; and Marks, Nancy (eds.). *Journal of Community Power Building: Reflections from Community Development Leaders and Practitioners, May 2004.* Eight instructive stories from people doing community development work about the specific challenges they face. Available from Massachusetts Association of Community Development Corporations through its website, www.macdc.org.

**Applied Research Center**
3781 Broadway
Oakland, CA 94611
Phone: 510-653-3415
Website: www.arc.org
This organization produces some excellent research and writing about organizing.

**BoardSource**
Suite 900
1828 L Street, NW
Washington, DC 20036-5104
Phone: 202-452-6262
E-mail: boardsource@boardsource.org
Website: www.boardsource.org
A wealth of published information about how to serve effectively as a member of a Board of Directors of a nonprofit organization. In general, their material is geared toward more established nonprofits, but it is very useful to look at if you are thinking of starting a nonprofit or joining a nonprofit Board, no matter the size.

**BuildingPowerfulCommunityOrganizations.com**
Website: www.BuildingPowerfulCommunityOrganizations.com
This is the website for this book. It is designed to serve as a useful resource where organizers can exchange ideas and get information.

**Center for Community Change**
1536 U Street, NW
Washington, D.C. 20009
Phone: 202-339-9300 or (toll-free) 877-777-1536
Email: info@communitychange.org
Website: www.communitychange.org
Headquartered in Washington, D.C., this organization holds conferences and distributes materials on organizing, providing consulting and training to community groups across the country. CCC also develops campaigns on a variety of topics.

**Center for Health, Environment and Justice**
150 S. Washington Street, Suite 300
P.O. Box 6806, Falls Church, VA 22040
Phone: 703-237-2249
E-mail: chej@chej.org
Website: www.chej.org
CHEJ provides groups with training and consultation, including technical assistance, with a special focus on working with those concerned about threats to health and the environment. The CHEJ's Executive Director, Lois Gibbs, says: *"For organizing help, the best thing is to call us. If you can't afford to call us, send us an e-mail or a postcard and we will call you. Organizing is organizing. If we can't help you, we will find someone who can. We have a huge network."*

**Center for Third World Organizing**
1218 East 21st Street
Oakland, CA 94606
Phone: 510-533-7583
Website: www.ctwo.org
Provides training in community organizing specifically for people of color.

***The Chronicle of Philanthropy***
Published by the *Chronicle of Higher Education*
Website: www.philanthropy.com
$72 per year
This biweekly news-magazine is targeted primarily to large-scale nonprofits, with information about grants, nonprofits, and national political changes that affect the nonprofit world.

**Direct Action Research and Training**
P.O. Box 370791
Miami, FL 33137-0791
Phone: 305-576-8020
Website: www.thedartcenter.org
Focus on congregations.

**Gamaliel Foundation**
203 N. Wabash Avenue, Suite 808
Chicago, IL 60601
Phone: 312-397-5015
Website: www.gamaliel.org
Focus on congregations.

**Grantmakers Concerned with Immigrants and Refugees**
Website: www.gcir.org
This group's website has some excellent materials and resources about leadership development and community organizing.

*Grassroots Fundraising Journal*
Kim Klein, Publisher
Stephanie Roth, Editor-in-chief
3781 Broadway
Oakland CA 94611
Phone: 888-458-8588 (for subscription orders)
Website: www.grassrootsfundraising.org
$32 per year for six issues

**Grassroots Leadership**
P.O. Box 36006
Charlotte, NC 28236
Phone: 704-332-3090
Website: www.grassrootsleadership.org
Provides community organizing training in the South.

**Industrial Areas Foundation**
220 W. Kinzie St., 5th floor
Chicago, IL 60610
Phone: 312-245-9211
Website: www.industrialareasfoundation.org
The IAF offers intensive national and regional trainings a couple of times each year in various locations. Mike Gecan, IAF organizer says: *"If you are interested in IAF training, contact the lead organizer of the group in your area to discuss dates, costs, and admission to the training."*

**InterValley Project**
Lead Organizer: Ken Galdston
1075 Washington Street
West Newton, MA 02465
Phone: 617-796-8836
E-mail: intervalleyp@aol.com
IVP is the regional organizing network of the Granite State Organizing Project, Kennebec Valley Organization Sponsoring Committee, Merrimack Valley Project, Naugatuck Valley Project, Pioneer Valley Project, and Rhode Island Organizing Project. These six New England organizations are patterned after the model pioneered by the Naugatuck Valley Project, which com-

bines citizen action organizing and democratic economic development—worker-owned companies, cooperative housing and community land trusts—in regional organizations of congregations, labor union locals, and tenant, community, and small business groups.

### Jewish Organizing Initiative
99 Chauncy St., Suite 600
Boston, MA 02111
Phone: 617-350-9994
Website: www.Jewishorganizing.org
Provides community organizing training and fellowship program to young Jewish adults.

### The Midwest Academy
28 East Jackson St. #605
Chicago, IL 60604
Phone: 312-427 2304
Website: www.midwestacademy.org
The Midwest Academy runs trainings in various parts of the country on direct action organizing. Their website has an excellent guide on holding accountability sessions with public officials.

### National Environmental Justice Resource Center
Clark Atlanta University
223 James P. Brawley Dr.
Atlanta, GA 30314
Phone: 404-880-6911
Website: www.ejrc.cau.edu/

### National Organizers Alliance
715 G. Street, SE
Washington, DC 20003
Phone: 202-543-6603
Website: www.noacentral.org
A national clearinghouse for community and labor organizers, dedicated to improving the lives and learning of those working in this field. Offers a portable pension plan for organizers.

### The Neighborhood Funders Group
Website: www.nfg.org
This website offers some good resources, including "The Community Organizing Toolbox: A Funder's Guide to Community Organizing."

### The On-line Conference on Community Organizing and Development

Website: www.comm-org.wisc.edu

"COMM-ORG," as this website is called, offers articles and many other resources for community organizers. Moderated and edited by University of Wisconsin professor Randy Stoecker, COMM-ORG also operates a list-serv with regular news of jobs and queries about topics in community organizing.

### Organizing Apprenticeship Project

2525 E. Franklin Ave., Suite 301

Minneapolis, MN 55406

Phone: 612-746-4224

Website: www.oaproject.org

OAP provides training and internships in community organizing in Minnesota.

### People's (formerly Pacific) Institute for Community Organizing

171 Santa Rosa Ave.

Oakland, CA 94910

Phone: 510-655-2801

Website: www.picocalifornia.org

Focuses primarily on congregations.

### Power and Systems, Inc.

P.O. Box 990288

Prudential Station

Boston, MA 02199-0288

Phone: 800-241-0598 or 617-437-1640

Website: www.powerandsystems.com

E-mail: info@powerandsystems.com

Terrific training about how power works in real organizations for "tops, middles, bottoms, and customers." Although the primary audience has been business leaders, Power and Systems and its founders, Karen and Barry Oshry, have a strong commitment to nonprofits and social change.

### Southern Empowerment Project

343 Ellis Avenue

Maryville, TN 37804

Phone: 865-984-6500

Website: www.southernempowerment.org

Provides training in community organizing for people throughout the South.

**United for a Fair Economy**
41 Winter Street
Boston, MA 02111
Phone: 617-423-2148
Website: www.ufenet.org
Offers training on economic issues in our society and about the growing divide in the U.S. between rich and poor.

**Western States Center**
P.O. Box 40305
Portland, OR 97204
Phone: 508-228-8866
Website: www.westernstatescenter.org
Holds an annual training conference.

# How to Get Tax-Exempt Status

Many organizations start off informally. The organization is us, whoever is in the room. Little thought is given to money or to long-term funding. But if you want your organization to be around for any length of time, you will want to incorporate in your state and also become a tax-exempt organization in accordance with the regulations of the federal Internal Revenue Service. Tax-exempt status allows donors to take a tax deduction on their donations to your organization. Anyone who is going to make a substantial donation will want and expect this. For foundation funding and many federal grants, you are not even eligible to apply without this designation.

If you want to accept tax-deductible donations right away, or you have a potential donor who wants to give you a substantial donation right now and wants the tax deduction, you may want to start off by arranging for a "fiscal agent" (another tax-exempt organization) to act as a conduit for your contribution. Fiscal agents will take a percentage of all funds that they manage, normally five to ten percent, in exchange for their fiscal management services. If your fiscal agent wants to take any more than this, find another fiscal agent or start the process of getting your own tax-exempt status.

Getting tax-exempt status—called "501(c)(3) status" in reference to the section of the tax code that authorizes this status—takes time. It requires a lawyer with experience in this specific area of tax law. Many lawyers will do this for free. They call this *"pro bono"*—a Latin term meaning "for good"— which is short for *"pro bono publico,"* or "for the public good." So ask if they will do the work for you *pro bono.* (This sounds cooler than asking, "Can you do this for free?")

The federal government grants the privilege of tax-exempt status to organizations that it deems to be working for the public good. It draws a strict (but complicated) line between working for the public good and being involved in partisan politics. Specifically, the federal government does not want tax-exempt organizations to be involved in directly influencing government decisions. Such activity would be considered a violation of 501(c)(3) status. However, the precise definition of what constitutes political influence is an area of intense political debate and controversy. The arena of non-profit organizations, tax law, and regulations about electoral politics and public policy is vast, ever-changing, and beyond the scope of this book.

What I can tell you, in brief, is that working to get specific candidates elected to public office is the real no-no. You want to be especially careful not to endorse or do anything to support any specific candidates. 501(c)(3) organizations are not permitted to engage in that kind of activity if they want to keep their tax-exempt status.

The rules for "educating" the public or your members (often two different categories according to IRS rules) about public policy, legislation, or electoral-related matters are complex and, again, change often. There is some leeway here, but you should get a lawyer to advise you on exactly what activities are permissible under the tax law and what proportion of your overall activities can be devoted to such efforts.

Spending your organization's money to influence legislation or to lobby *may* present problems. Consult a lawyer specializing in this area if you intend to spend a lot of your time and money influencing legislation. IRS regulations generally allow some tax-exempt money to be spent on activities that seek to influence public policy or legislation, but these regulations are very complex and frequently change!

If you are opposing policies of a current administration, remember that they have the power to make your life miserable with tax audits and requests for your accounting records. If you think you might be a target because of the nature of your work, be very careful to consult a lawyer experienced in this specialized area of the law.

## Story: Tax Regulations Can Be Used As a Political Tool

*In the 1980s, during President Reagan's administration, the Internal Revenue Service promulgated new regulations about how much of a tax-exempt organization's funds could be spent on influencing legislation. The IRS launched grueling audits of the books of various progressive organizations that were using some of their money to influence legislation. The same organizations were trying to keep within the law by setting up 501(c)(4) organizations that could receive other money to do more lobbying. I worked for the Jobs with Peace campaign at the time. I remember spending hours filling in forms to account for how I spent every hour of every day. All the bookkeeping and extra accounting was defensive action we had to take to avoid losing our tax-exempt status. It also took precious hours away from our real work every single day.*

Getting your 501(c)(3) status will take you at least six months—and that's if you are lucky. The timing depends on the Internal Revenue Service and how busy it is, as well as on how skillfully your application is written. You may get a reply asking for more information. Hiring a competent lawyer makes all the difference in how many times you may have to amend your application. It is best to be careful the first time.

When you have been granted your tax-exempt status you will receive a "letter of determination" from the IRS. You'll see your IRS number at the top of the letter. Keep the original letter safe and make lots of copies to use. Every foundation that you ask for money will want a copy. Some individual donors will, too.

Congratulations! You are now a grown-up organization. You have just become eligible to accept tax-deductible contributions. This is a big deal. This is also a good time to celebrate. Every organization needs to party.

# INDEX

# ABOUT THE AUTHOR

Michael Jacoby Brown has worked as a community organizer for over 30 years. He has recruited and trained hundreds of volunteers and professional community organizers, conducted dozens of workshops, worked as a staff organizer for several community organizations, and started some organizations himself. He has worked with unions, fighting for better wages and working conditions for fire fighters, garbage collectors, and public school teachers. He also has worked as a community activist, fighting for fair utility rates, fair taxes, better schools, and many other issues.

He started out in community organizing as a volunteer, while working as a teacher and construction worker. In 1978 he got his first job as a paid community organizer, for the Vermont Alliance. Since then, Brown has organized mobile home tenants, low-income renters, and low- and middle-income people around a wide range of issues. He has knocked on thousands of doors, sat in thousands of kitchens, and consumed gallons of coffee and Kool-Aid. He has organized hundreds of community meetings in dozens of church basements and storefronts to build organizations with volunteers from a wide range of ethnic and racial backgrounds.

Brown has worked with and for dozens of health, political, labor, and religious organizations, including the Vermont Alliance, Massachusetts Fair Share, the Jobs with Peace Campaign, and B'nai B'rith. He mostly had fun and learned a lot throughout it all. He also has made thousands of mistakes, sometimes over and over again, until he finally learned not to make those same mistakes. One motive for writing this book is a desire to help others avoid the same mistakes he made.

In addition to decades of on-the-job training, Brown also has studied organizational development and behavior. He holds a B.A. from Columbia University and an M.P.A. from the Kennedy School of Government at Harvard University. In his work and in his writing, he has tried to bridge the academic world of theory and the daily reality of practice at the community level.

Brown also has served as an elected official (in Rutland County, Vermont) and as the founder and editor of the *Rutland Voice*, a community newspaper. In 1998 he founded the Jewish Organizing Initiative, where he has raised and leveraged several million dollars to train dozens of young people as community organizers. He lives in Boston, Massachusetts, is married, and has two children.

# Adding Your Stories

## Your Turn, Your Stories, Your Lessons Learned

*"The destiny of the world is determined less by the battles that are lost and won than by the stories it loves and believes in."*

—Harold Goddard, *The Meaning of Shakespeare*

If you have a story that teaches a lesson that you think would be useful to others, we want it to add it to future editions of *Building Powerful Community Organizations* and to our website, www.BuildingPowerfulCommunity Organizations.com.

Many important lessons in building groups that can solve problems and change the world are never shared widely. As a result, many efforts are not as effective as they could be. We want to change that. You may have an important story or lesson learned that could be helpful to others. It may be a tale of success or failure. (We often learn more from our mistakes than from our successes.) It's a big and diverse world. To be effective we need many stories from all communities. If you have a story or idea you think we should add, please let me know. Please fill out the form on the next page and send it in. You also can e-mail me your stories at Comments@BuildingPowerfulCommunityOrganizations.com or log on to the website and submit the story electronically. Again, that's www.BuildingPowerfulCommunityOrganizations.com.

# Adding Your Stories

Name:*_____

Address:_____

City:_____ State:_____ Zip:_____

Home Phone:_____ Work Phone:_____

Cell phone:_____ Fax:_____

E-mail address:_____

Website (if you have one):_____

## Category of my story or lesson learned:

❏ The idea arrives or the problem finds you
❏ Crafting a vision
❏ Telling your story
❏ Listening to others
❏ Putting your idea into writing
❏ Developing a sponsoring committee
❏ Bringing together a core group
❏ Drafting a mission, goals, and objectives

❏ Developing a structure
❏ Recruiting people
❏ Developing leaders
❏ Raising money
❏ Using and understanding strategy
❏ Action
❏ Evaluation
❏ Reflection
❏ Other _____

## Story:

❏ Attached.

## Lesson Learned:

❏ Attached.

*Please attach a separate page with your story and lessons learned.*

## Permissions: *(check one)*

❏ I give permission to use my name and story in future editions of *Building Powerful Community Organizations* and to place this story with my name on the website.

❏ I give permission to use this story in future editions of *Building Powerful Community Organizations* and to place this story on the website, but I do not want my name used.

_____          _____

Signature                                Date

*\*All personal information will be kept confidential*

# Time for Your Feedback

## What do you think of the book?

What was helpful? _____

_____

What should be changed? _____

_____

What should be added? _____

_____

I disagree with _____

_____

Other: _____

_____

I would like more information about:  ❑ Speaking/Seminars  ❑ Consulting

**Possible topics include:**

❑ Recruiting
❑ Fundraising
❑ Starting a new organization
❑ Planning a campaign
❑ Lessons learned for building powerful community organizations
❑ How to use this book and its exercises to build powerful community organizations

❑ Making your organization more of a community
❑ Finding your stories, listening to your stories
❑ Planning a campaign that is rooted in your community's needs
❑ For middle class activists who want to help
❑ And others

**Please send me your thoughts. You can use this form, or just write me in your own words:**

Michael Brown, Long Haul Press, 10 Brattle Terrace Arlington, MA 02474

Or e-mail me at Comments@BuildingPowerfulCommunityOrganizations.com

The form is on www.BuildingPowerfulCommunityOrganizations.com website as well, so you also can fill it out there.

Thanks,

*Michael Jacoby Brown*

# Quick Book Order Form

**Phone orders:** 781-648-1508

**Or mail your order to:** Long Haul Press
10 Brattle Terrace
Arlington, MA 02474

**Or order on-line, via our website:**
www.BuildingPowerfulCommunityOrganizations.com

❏ **Please add me to your mailing list:**

Name:_____

Address:_____

City:_____ State:_____ Zip:_____

Telephone:_____

E-mail address:_____

❏ **I would like to order more books:**

**Price:** $19.95 per book.

**Bulk orders:**   10 – 19 books: $17.00 each     20 or more: $15.00 each

**Shipping:** $5 shipping for first book. $2 for each additional book.

**Number of books ordered:** _____   **Total amount enclosed: $**_____

**Shipping Address:**

Name:_____

Address:_____

City:_____ State:_____ Zip:_____

Telephone:_____

E-mail address:_____

**Payment:**  ❏  **Check (enclosed)**
     ❏  **Credit Card**
     ❏  **Visa**   ❏  **MasterCard**   ❏  **AMEX**   ❏  **Discover**

**Card Number:**_____

_____     _____

**Name on card**  (please print)                       **Exp. Date**

**Billing address on card, if different from shipping address above:**

Name:_____

Address:_____

City:_____ State:_____ Zip:_____